FRINGES OF
EMPIRE

Peoples, Places, and Spaces
in Colonial India

FRINGES OF
EMPIRE

edited by
Sameetah Agha and Elizabeth Kolsky

OXFORD
UNIVERSITY PRESS

OXFORD
UNIVERSITY PRESS

YMCA Library Building, Jai Singh Road, New Delhi 110 001

Oxford University Press is a department of the University of Oxford. It furthers the
University's objective of excellence in research, scholarship, and education
by publishing worldwide in

Oxford New York
Auckland Cape Town Dar es Salaam Hong Kong Karachi Kuala Lumpur
Madrid Melbourne Mexico City Nairobi New Delhi Shanghai Taipei Toronto

With offices in
Argentina Austria Brazil Chile Czech Republic France Greece Guatemala
Hungary Italy Japan Poland Portugal Singapore South Korea Switzerland
Thailand Turkey Ukraine Vietnam

Oxford is a registered trademark of Oxford University Press
in the UK and in certain other countries

Published in India
by Oxford University Press, New Delhi

ISBN-13: 978-0-19-806031-4
ISBN-10: 0-19-806031-9

Typeset in Minion Pro 10.5/12.6
by Eleven Arts, Keshav Puram, Delhi 110 035
Printed in India at Star Printobind, Delhi 110 020
Published by Oxford University Press
YMCA Library Building, Jai Singh Road, New Delhi 110 001

Contents

Foreword

'Beyond the Fringe'[1]

Nicholas B. Dirks

When J.R. Seeley delivered his famous Cambridge lectures on the expansion of England in the 1870s,[2] he chided historians of England for neglecting the extent to which their history in fact took place outside England. He further suggested that the embarrassment stemming from the loss of the Americas, and the haphazard nature of the conquest of India, together seemed to have consigned the history of imperial England to a secondary status. And he was concerned that this neglect would imperil the future, especially given the likelihood that any real disruption of England's imperial position would speed the process whereby two new imperial powers would steadily supplant England on the world stage. He had in mind the United States and Russia, both of which had been successfully converting imperial expansion into national destiny on massive and contiguous land masses that more than rivalled the territorial extent and accumulated wealth of England's own, dispersed, and vulnerable imperial holdings.

Seeley was right to note both the significance of England's empire for its modern history, and to predict its likely eclipse by the other two rising giants. But as astute a historian as he was, he trafficked in many imperial assumptions that made the rise of academic imperial history continuous with imperial self-representation and policy. Seeley's history assumed a coherent imperial state and a compliant colonial society. Lecturing at the height of Britain's imperial self-confidence, in the wake of the quelling of the 'Sepoy Mutiny' of 1857 and the assumption of direct rule, and at a time when Britain was set to markedly expand its imperial presence across vast new areas of the globe, he neither attended to the complex fissures of colonial rule nor to the growing discontent about this rule. Indian voices were entirely absent, but so too were the stories of the many bit players of empire, who, whether Indian or European, gave form to a far larger historical tableau than either formal imperialism, even in its declining years, or official nationalism, once it finally flowered, could fully accommodate within their respective historical imaginations.

In the decades immediately after Seeley's lectures, the early expressions of nationalism through elite societies and nascent political expression gave way first to revolutionary anti-colonial violence and then to the rise of a mass movement. Britain's national sense of self and global centrality suffered near fatal blows in the Great War, but the war had the not-altogether ironic effect of making Britain even more dependent upon and committed to the continuation of the empire. Nationalist sentiment was greeted first with contempt and neglect. But soon the colonial state directed its full bureaucratic and political machinery to maintain the status quo, deflecting claims about national unity and representation by cultivating religious, ethnic, regional, and political differences; commencing a reform process that was accompanied by new repressive measures; and undermined by a relentless unwillingness to give up any real political power or economic control. Only when Britain was both exhausted and bankrupted by the Second World War did independence become an irrevocable outcome, though too late to render unnecessary the disruption and violence of the Quit India movement and the formation of the Indian National Army, not to mention to stem the tide of partition and a long legacy of communal conflict and political instability for South Asia. Nevertheless, Britain held on to the view that power was transferred,[3] voluntarily relinquished rather than seized, that the empire had been not just benevolent, but, for the most part at least, accepted as legitimate by majority of the Indian people.

Imperial history was therefore positioned to continue to tell tales of empire that minimized the struggle and the violence, naturalized many of imperialism's most pronounced social, cultural, and economic effects, while asserting that empire's fundamental weakness and vulnerability vindicated professions of progress and assertions of acceptance. Nationalist history, released from reserve and censorship along with independence, told a very different tale. Focusing on the freedom struggle—teleological history to be sure—nationalist historiography refused outright to accept the legitimacy of anything other than self-rule. Nationalist history was as fundamental to the new Indian, and Pakistani, nation states as imperial history had been to the imperial state, and it was on the right side of history: independence from British India prefaced first Suez and then the full scale decolonization of other Asian and African colonies. But as necessary as it was for nationalist history to emerge in South Asia as it had in Europe, it did, for many years at least, put imperial history in a state of suspension. And even when it engaged the questions of imperial history head on, it neither focused on the contradictions of social, cultural, economic, and political life under empire, nor on the complex character of empire both for Britain and for India. It assumed a Manichean world view, and despite important Marxist economic history that made clear the material interests that were served by empire, it was fundamentally uninterested in empire as a political form or for that matter a social history.

Meanwhile imperial history became more measured, changing its tone to accommodate the new verdict on empire, but it never lost its popularity, not to mention its popular audience. As an academic field, however, it was reinvented several times, not just by nationalist Marxist historians but also by academics working primarily in American universities. Bernard Cohn trained his anthropological sensibilities on the British empire and engaged in extraordinarily influential studies of imperial rituals, grammars, ethnographies, and histories.[4] Edward Said produced a paradigm changing critique in his landmark work, *Orientalism*,[5] arguing not just about the power of western scholarship but also about the power of empire in reconstituting the fundamental relationship between the West and the East. While anthropologists and literary critics played a dominant role in the new field of post-colonial studies, new generations of historians, trained in area studies rather than European history and influenced more by Cohn and Said than by Seeley and Spear,[6] installed new curricular protocols and little by little gained acceptance as the professional arbiters of a new and important historical field, a field now totally divorced from imperial history.[7] Empire became more of a historical foil than a serious subject for new kinds of historical attention, at least before the Iraq war made clear how much a model the British empire continued to be for policymakers in the US. In Britain, where imperial history had never really receded, C.A. Bayly, who had established himself as one of the most innovative new historians of India, played a critical role in changing approaches to empire in his work on the military fiscal state, the importance of information for the imperial state,[8] and his capacity to command the respect and readership of British historians as well as South Asianists. Bayly built on the work of several excellent imperial historians, most importantly Peter Marshall and K.T. Chaudhuri, and provided new models for engaging the history of South Asia with its imperial context as well.

In the end, however, it was perhaps even more important that British historians themselves came to recognize the truth of Seeley's observation that Britain's own history could not be detached from the larger history of empire that provided the basis for a rebirth of imperial history. Linda Colley[9] might have reacted sharply to Said's proposals (echoing Fanon) that empire was constitutive of Europe, but she began to write increasingly about the British overseas, stimulating much important new work by others as well. In the last decade, and not unrelated to the increasingly comparative and even global character of much new European history, Seeley would have felt that at last his fellow historians of England had accepted his advice and broken down the distinction between metropolitan and imperial history. Empire, of course, has become a hot subject again, and the clear historical view that stretched from the Suez to Vietnam seems once again to have been muddied by the global reactions to 9/11, the debate over Iraq, not to mention the economic rise of China and India.

The problem with some of the new imperial history is that it looks too much like older genres—still committed to rescuing the history of empire from nationalist critique, still writing the history of empire without colonized players and perspectives, still arguing that the critical and agentive roles of the colonized confer legitimacy on empire as a political form, still not coming to terms with what it means to recognize the subaltern character of empire for colonizers as well as the colonized.[10] And there is a residual defensiveness among many writing the history of empire, a reticence to accept that empire was a deeply troubled and troubling historical regime of domination that was mired in scandal, inequality, and racial as well as cultural arrogance. This is where the present volume provides such a refreshing and innovative example of new kinds of history that blur the borders not just between metropolitan and colonial history, but between many other genres of historical writing as well, that accepts the problematic character of imperial history while working creatively to complicate, humanize, and extend it. As Elizabeth Kolsky makes clear in her introduction to this superb volume, the present essays have learned from many different strands of imperial historiography, taking on board the violence and exploitation of colonial rule, while also recognizing that some of the starker tales of history played themselves out in multiple and contradictory ways within the larger tensions of empire,[11] tensions that were not only about race and ethnicity, but also class and gender, ambition and careers, as well as differential access to power and knowledge. And where better to follow the tensions and contradictions than on the fringes of empire?

Philip J. Stern begins by demonstrating the falsity of one of Seeley's major claims, that India was conquered in a 'fit of absence of mind'. The East India Company, far from being only interested in trade and commerce, was organized far more like a state than previous imperial history had suggested, and deliberately sought to establish itself as a political power in the subcontinent from at least the late seventeenth century. Marina Carter extends Stern's insight about the tense political relationship between the Company and the Crown by focusing on the role of pirates, who played on the fluidity of political and economic power and often contributed to the aims of Company rule.

If the sea was one kind of permeable political border in the early annals of imperialism, so too were the formal land boundaries of British rule. Alex McKay uses the canonic work of Frederick Jackson Turner on the American frontier to demonstrate the constitutive nature of efforts to extend the sphere of British control on the Tibetan border. Sameetah Agha takes us to the other side of the northern frontier of India, traversing the site of the great game rather than the silk route, demonstrating as well the importance of boundary regions and groups. It is sometimes difficult to understand the reasons for British fear of Russia, except perhaps for their recognition of Seeley's truth that a direct and contiguous empire was inevitably bound to win over a colonial system dependent on long sea voyages. And Mridu Rai examines the peculiar colonial politics of Kashmir, how the British installed Hindu rulers and encouraged them, much as they did other princely rulers across the subcontinent but never with such enduring and dangerous political legacies,[12] to transpose political power into ritual authority and religious orthodoxy. In all three cases, imperial concerns about the borderlands of empire have exacerbated the instability of post-colonial politics in India and Pakistan, mixing communal and ethnic conflict into the already dangerous stew of boundary politics.

Borders were not the only sites of colonial efforts to control the hybrid menace of mixed identities. Satadru Sen focuses on the penal colony of the Andamans and the case of a Muslim prisoner convicted of treason after the 'Sepoy Mutiny' of 1857; Sen shows how this convict trespassed religious boundaries and transformed the space of the prison to create a different kind of hybrid colonial history, though one that crashed against the imperial order once again upon his release. Clare Anderson tells the fascinating story of an African convict who challenged imperial notions of order and brings to historical light the significance of the colonial penal colony. And James H. Mills recounts the role of insane asylums, which not only became weapons for intra-familial discord but also reflected colonial ambivalence about the colonized subject and the murky boundary between sanity and alterity.

There were contentious and shifting boundaries between colonizing subjects too, as Douglas M. Peers makes clear in his engaging account of the Mhow court martial case, where military discipline, class relations, and sexual identities played out the larger tensions of empire in dramatic fashion. And if this notorious case made clear the significance of imperial theatres for metropolitan audiences in late nineteenth century Britain, Lisa Mitchell demonstrates that literary audiences within India itself were also undergoing a period of sustained transformation during the same period. In Britain, stories of empire became darker in the late nineteenth century. There were no longer any Edmund Burkes to hold forth in parliament about imperial abuses, and so the scandals of empire either concerned Indian culture or violence within the colonizing community (where the tensions of empire became fraught in some of the precise ways disclosed by Peers). But in India, the dramas of imperial life became increasingly heterogeneous and layered thanks also to the rise of new reading publics, political groups, civic spaces, and literary forms. Mitchell's nuanced reading of the changing nature of Telugu literary production could be transposed onto other cultural and social narratives that would begin to tell another genre of the fringe stories of empire, increasingly focused now on the colonized rather than the colonizing subjects of empire. But that story of empire would continue to move us beyond the fringe, to those productive engagements with the lesser known characters and places of India's extraordinary imperial history.

NOTES AND REFERENCES

1. For another invocation of the idea of fringe in empire studies, see Bernard S. Cohn and Nicholas B. Dirks, 1988, 'Beyond the Fringe: The Nation State, Colonialism, and the Technologies of Power', *Journal of Historical Sociology*, 1 (2), pp. 224–9.

2. J.R. Seeley, 1971 [1883], *The Expansion of England*, Chicago: University of Chicago Press.

3. The great compilation of British documents about the final stages of decolonization was entitled *The Transfer of Power*.

4. See Bernard S. Cohn, 1996, *Colonialism and Its Forms of Knowledge*, Princeton: Princeton University Press.

5. Edward Said, 1978, *Orientalism*, New York: Random House.

6. That is, the historian Percival Spear. See, for example, Spear's classic, 1965, *History of India*, vol. 2, New York: Penguin Press.

7. There were, of course, critical exceptions. The leading historian of British empire in the US, Thomas Metcalf, was also influenced by the preoccupations of area studies, social history, and other new forms of interdisciplinary history. See Metcalf, 1994, *Ideologies of the Raj*, Cambridge: Cambridge University Press.

8. See C.A. Bayly, 1989, *The Imperial Meridian: The British Empire and the World 1780-1830*, London: Longman, and C.A. Bayly, 1998, 'The British Military-Fiscal State and Indigenous Resistance: India, 1750-1820', in Patrick Tuck (ed.), 1998, *The East India Company: 1600-1858*, vol. 5, London: Routledge, pp. 198-234.

9. Linda Colley, 1993, 'The Imperial Embrace', *Yale Review*, 81(4) (October), pp. 92-8; see also Linda Colley, 2004, *Captives: Britain, Empire, and the World: 1600-1850*, New York: Random House.

10. See, for example, the relatively recent five volume work, *The Oxford History of the British Empire*, Oxford: Oxford University Press, 2000.

11. See Frederick Cooper and Ann Stoler (eds), 1997, *Tensions of Empire: Colonial Cultures in a Bourgeois World*, Berkeley: University of California Press.

12. See, for example, Nicholas B. Dirks, 1987, *The Hollow Crown: Ethnohistory of an Indian Kingdom*, Cambridge: Cambridge University Press.

Acknowledgements

This book grew out of a panel on 'Fringes of Empire' presented at the 32nd Annual Conference on South Asia in Madison. In listening to each other's papers, and from the many conversations that ensued, it became clear to us that we were onto something with this notion of the imperial fringe. Even though our topics and interests spanned widely across space and time, we found that we were all grappling with a set of similar concerns surrounding marginal people and places in imperial history—what we have conceptualized as 'fringes'.

The editors would like to thank their co-panelists in Madison, Jim Mills and Satadru Sen, for their encouragement and involvement in the initial planning of the volume. We would also like to thank the contributors for persevering with us throughout the long publication process. This book would not have been possible without the editorial support and guidance of the editorial team at Oxford University Press, to whom we are much obliged.

Sameetah Agha: I would like to thank my colleagues in the Department of Social Science and Cultural Studies and in the School of Liberal Arts and Sciences at Pratt, especially Gloriana Russell for springing to my technological rescue many a time; Dean Toni Oliviero; Sophia Babb; and Chantel Foretich (who no longer works at Pratt). I want to thank Steven who, in bringing me Scotland and Celtic FC, opened up the 'fringes' of the metropole thus changing my perspective on empire forever. I want to thank David for his unwavering commitment and support. My family is behind everything I do. I want to thank Daddy, Apa, and especially Lala, who as always, helped me put it all together, and Cailean for being my constant source of joy.

Elizabeth Kolsky: I would like to thank my colleagues in the History Department at Villanova University for their ongoing support of my research agenda and Villanova University for its financial support. As nothing good is possible without the love and support of friends and family, my deep gratitude and appreciation extend to all, and especially to my beloved and adorable domestic cabal: Isaiah, Vivienne, and Prunty.

Introduction

Elizabeth Kolsky

'In Moulmein, in lower Burma, I was hated by large numbers of people—the only time in my life that I have been important enough for this to happen to me.' So begins George Orwell's semi-autobiographical essay, 'Shooting an Elephant', written in 1936, a decade after Orwell concluded his service in the imperial police. The march of Orwell's narrative is driven by the tumultuous events of one day in the life of a British colonial officer stationed far away on the northeastern frontier of British power. The narrator, in equal parts repulsed by the colonized Burmese and by the imperatives of British colonialism, is summoned to subdue an elephant that has killed a coolie in the local bazaar. As the elephant wanders innocuously in the grass, thousands of Burmese gather to watch. The narrator finds himself in an imperial dilemma: he has to shoot the elephant but he does not want to: 'A sahib has got to act like a sahib; he has got to appear resolute, to know his own mind and do definite things'.[1]

By 1914, the British empire comprised 80 territorial units, ranging from self-governing dominions to informal and formal colonies, consisting of 11 million square miles of territory, and 400 million subjects in Africa, Asia, Australia, and the Americas who recognized Britain as their sovereign. These numbers grew after the First World War when Britain gained control of former German and Ottoman territories in Africa and the Middle East.[2] Contrary to J.R. Seeley's famous quip over a century ago that British imperial expansion occurred in 'a fit of absence of mind', it is clear, as Orwell points out, that the sahib had to act definitely in order to conquer and control such a vast and sprawling dominion.[3] He may not have been all-knowing, ill-intentioned, or unambiguous, but the colonizer simply could not afford to be absent-minded. And yet, despite the rich literature on the history of the British empire, it remains difficult to understand how so few Britons subdued so many people as far away from the British Isles as the port town of Moulmein in lower Burma.

The historical essays in this volume revisit this question of how the British empire in India was built and sustained by taking as their central subject the people, places, and moments at the imperial margins. The literature of empire has brilliantly foregrounded the imagined lives and uncertain futures of figures on the blurred boundaries of the empire. Authors from Joseph Conrad to E.M. Forster to Orwell himself, all former agents of empire, used literature to envision how colonial power was both exceedingly brutal and transparently vulnerable at its unstable fringes. Colonial historians, by contrast, have paid less attention to the impact that people and places at the margins of empire had on life and policymaking at the centre.

In recent years, there has been an enormous resurgence of scholarly and public interest in the history of empires and empire-building, and especially in the relationship between Britain and its empire. The present legacies and practices of colonialism rightfully demand ongoing investigations into the colonial past. As a journalist noted in a recent profile of Douglas Feith, former United States President George W. Bush's neo-conservative Undersecretary for Defence, his massive personal library houses over 5,000 books, a collection weighted disproportionately towards histories of the British empire.[4] This is a sobering reminder of the fact that how we think about and write about the history of Britain's empire remains a matter of present political import.

This collection takes up the 'fringe' as theoretical site, geographical location, and social position. The relationship between the London metropole and the colony is itself conventionally described in terms of a centre and a periphery. However, an oppositional framework that cleanly divides the metropolitan core from the colonial margin does not provide adequate space to explain or understand what happened on the fringes *within* the colonial world, on the fringes of the margin itself. That is, while the colonies were themselves fringes when viewed in relationship to the imperial centre, they also had their own centres of power and peripheral, hard-to-control margins. By restoring less visible, if not forgotten, characters such as the European poor, Indian lunatics, pirates, soldiers, convicts, linguists, and frontiersmen to the history of colonial India, this volume positions these intra-colonial fringes as sites for reframing the larger imperial picture.

The underlying theme that unites the diverse essays presented here is how people and places at the margins of the British empire had the greatest freedom for initiative and innovation, but it was there that the colonial state also faced the greatest challenges to its control and authority. Colonial anxiety about policing internal and external boundaries, as well as the movement and behaviour of individuals, expressed itself in cultural, legal, and political initiatives aimed at preventing subjects from subverting imperial authority. In exploring these themes from a variety of regional and temporal perspectives, this volume asks that we consider the fringe of empire as a powerful and productive space with complex and contradictory opportunities and outcomes.

THEORIZING THE IMPERIAL FRINGE

In a fascinating essay on Victorian fashion, cultural critic Elaine Freedgood suggests that the extensive use of trim, edge decoration, and fringe in nineteenth century Britain reflected contemporary anxieties about borders and boundaries. The fringe, initially utilized as a practical method to stop the fabric from fraying, offered imperial Britons a literal and symbolic form of 'border control' during the age of empire when the nation's political, economic, and cultural limits were porous and expanding. The colonies themselves, as Freedgood notes, were conceived in nineteenth century histories as 'a kind of fringe on the fabric of the metropole', a soft edge that was both feminine and evocative of the 'Oriental'.[5]

As a geographical term, the fringe primarily figures in British histories of empire-building in the British Isles. At the northwestern edge of the European continent, the internal colonies of Ireland, Scotland, and Wales were referred to as the 'Celtic Fringe'.[6] The advance of the English Pale over and onto the Celtic Fringe was an early manifestation of cultural imperialism, as the English attempted to stamp out the purportedly backward and peripheral Celtic cultures, languages, and traditions which they defined as different from and inferior to their own.[7] England's difficulty in conquering what in hindsight was a proximate periphery—proximate when compared to the far-flung territories England would control in later centuries—was partially caused by this unsuccessful attempt to foist upon non-English Britons a common British identity based on a strong and distinct sense of Englishness.

In the nineteenth century, ideas about Celtic, and especially Irish, difference and inferiority were defined in racial terms. Literally and figuratively represented in English political culture as 'black', the Irish were portrayed in cartoons and illustrations of the day as members of a lower evolutionary species, 'white chimpanzees'[8] linked in polygenetic terms to the 'Africanoid', the lowest form of man in Victorian race science.[9] L. Perry Curtis argues that 'peasant Paddy' was transformed into an 'ape-man or simianized Caliban' when increasingly radical and politicized Irishmen were assigned by the English 'to a place closer to the apes than the angels'.[10] A cartoon from *Punch*, published in October 1891, depicts 'anarchy' as an ape-like Irishman barbarically threatening Anglo-Saxon law and order. 'Separate and subject', the Irish were ideologically positioned for colonial domination rather than equal citizenship.[11] The 'science' underlining this notion of Celtic otherness, if there ever was any, was recently debunked by a major genetic study of Britain's population that revealed that the majority of Britons are Celts with shared genetic connections to populations from Spain.[12]

The growth of English nationalism offers a productive framework for understanding the expansion of Britain's empire, and the tension seen in the early phase of imperial expansion between a unified imperial identity and an insistence on colonial difference would become a defining feature of Britain's imperial history.[13] As the Irish case demonstrates, ideas about colonial difference were simultaneously spatial and racial: colonized 'others' (them, not us, a race apart) were from out there (not here, home, in the nation). Ideologies of colonial difference, whether cast in racial, national, cultural, or civilizational terms, had a clear and obvious political function: to deny so-called backward people the right to self-government and to make room for Britons to do the job of, what Rudyard Kipling called, 'the white man's burden'.[14] Not only did colonialism require ideas about the difference of colonized others to sustain itself, it also offered different laws and codes of conduct to colonizers abroad.[15]

For many years, the assumption in British imperial history was that empire was enacted out there on the colonial periphery rather than at home in the metropole where it supposedly had little impact. Then along came Frantz Fanon who provocatively proposed that Europe's home was created by the world outside: 'Europe is literally the creation of the Third World'.[16] Fanon's remarks reminded readers that just as the colonial masters remade the laws, governments, economies, and minds of the colonized, so too did colonization have a profound effect on the colonizing countries. In recent years, British historians representing the 'new imperial history' have sought to restore the history of Britain's empire to the history of the British nation by placing metropole and colony, home and empire in a unitary field of analysis.[17] Eschewing their predecessors' focus on states, institutions, and metropolitan concerns, the new imperial historians place questions about culture, race, identity, and 'theorizing difference' at the centre of their studies.[18]

The new imperial history grew out of and along side the emergence of the interdisciplinary field of colonial/post-colonial studies. Launched by the publication of Edward Said's seminal text, *Orientalism*, colonial/post-colonial scholars have demonstrated that ordinary people in Europe not only consumed the actual fruits of empire like sugar, tea, tobacco, and cotton, but they also consumed the culture of empire in forms high-brow (such as novels and opera) and low-brow (such as newspapers, advertising, and the various world fairs, like the Wembley British Empire Exhibition which was viewed by over half of the British population in 1924).[19] Said decisively debunked both the idea that European home culture was unaffected by European imperialism abroad and the old imperial history's framing of empire as a project of political, economic, and military domination.[20] Colonialism, we have learned, was also a project of cultural control and the production of colonial knowledge was a means of dominating, restructuring, and exerting power over the colonies. Said's notion that the 'Orient' was Europe's imaginary other offered a cultural reading of Fanon in reverse: the people, resources, and markets of the colonized world made Europe even as Europe produced an imaginary Orient as an object of knowledge that could be managed, classified, and controlled. In a subsequent study, *Culture and Imperialism*, Said demonstrated that representations of people and places on the colonized periphery were a ubiquitous, if shadowy, presence in the culture and literature of the imperial core.[21] The cultural consequences of European efforts to know, understand, and control their colonies have since been explored and debated at great length.[22]

Scholarship emerging from the Saidian tradition sought to break down the binary opposition that sharply distinguished the metropolitan centre, 'the place from which power flowed',[23] from the colonial periphery, conventionally seen as a passive object of colonial interventions.[24] We have been encouraged to read the histories of Britain and the colonies at once and contrapuntally in a 'cross-current', so as to recognize both their interdependence and mutual constitution.[25] Britain did not only change the world by expanding its empire, Britain itself was changed along the way. This back and forth reading also allows us to recognize that the colony was not a passive laboratory for modern metropolitan actions and experiments. Structures of colonial dominance, like all structures of dominance, were shaped, recognized, and understood in different ways by those who were subject to them.

The nuanced approach to colonial power also pushed scholarship on colonial culture and society in new directions. Eschewing a binary model of colonial social relations, over a decade ago, Ann Stoler and Frederick Cooper persuasively argued that the empire was never a Manichean world divided neatly in two.[26] Colonial rule not only impacted colonial society differentially, it also highlighted the differences within, bringing to the fore questions of race, class, and gender that could never be defined or contained by impermeable or stable boundaries.

But let us return to Freedgood's theory about the imperial fringe. Freedgood suggests that the Victorian use of the fringe softened anxieties about porous national borders by invoking the feminine and the newly colonized 'Oriental'. The salience of the imperial margin has recently been invoked by William Dalrymple and Maya Jasonoff, both of whom support the notion that the fringe softened the hard edges of empire by emphasizing the cultural accommodations and the personal intimacies that blurred the boundaries between East and West on the spatial and temporal fringes of the eighteenth century British empire.[27] Although the language of the imperial fringe is predominantly associated with the internal colonies in the British Isles, it is worth noting that the dominant metaphor used to describe India's relationship was also a wearable one, though not something fabric: namely, the jewel in the Crown. The tendency in British history is to see the 'question of India' as one of marginal interest to nineteenth century Britons. However, recent work on the culture of colonialism suggests that India was both out there on the global margins of the empire and also right here, a constant presence in the classic Victorian novels of Austen, Dickens, and Thackeray.[28] In a sense, situated majestically in the centre of the Queen's crown itself, India could be no closer to home.

After 1876, when Queen Victoria crowned herself Empress of India, what was formerly known as 'British India' was now called 'The Indian

Empire'. This term signals the unique place India holds in the history of the British empire, as it implies that India was practically an empire unto itself. The relationship between Britain and its colonies is generally defined in spatial terms that connect the metropolitan centre or core to the colonial periphery. The vastness and importance of the Indian empire made Britain's crown jewel a periphery and a centre at once.

In 1953, the publication of Ronald Robinson and Jack Gallagher's article, 'The Imperialism of Free Trade', dramatically transformed how scholars studied and understood the relationship between the British metropolitan centre and the colonial periphery.[29] Turning on its head the conventional paradigm that interpreted empire as a project propelled by metropolitan forces, Robinson and Gallagher positioned the colonial periphery as the central force behind Britain's massive imperial expansion in the nineteenth century. Emphasizing the critical role played by the 'subimperialists', men on the fringes of British empire, their thesis posited a two-tier imperial system, an informal empire built wherever possible and a formal empire of direct rule established only when necessary. Robinson and Gallagher's work on informal empire and subimperialism was enormously influential but predominantly impacted studies of colonial Africa and Latin America.[30]

The most productive debate about the relationship between metropolitan centres and colonial peripheries is found in the literature on the economics of empire. Since the publication of Adam Smith's *The Wealth of Nations* in 1776, political economists have questioned the costs and benefits associated with the holding of overseas colonies.[31] At the turn of the twentieth century, J.A. Hobson and V. Lenin argued that European imperial expansion was fuelled by economic motives as capitalists and industrialists in the colonizing nations looked at the colonies as new markets for the sale of goods and the investment of surplus capital. A slightly different way to analyse the growth of modern global capitalism was subsequently proposed by Immanuel Wallerstein who theorized that the economic development of individual nations was determined by their place in the world system, ranging from the core to the periphery to the semi-periphery to the external.[32]

Differing in content and argument, all of these accounts of the economics of empire presented the imperial relationship in vividly spatial terms—the core metropolitan towns were literally fed by the peripheral colonial countries, which provided both food stuff and raw materials for European manufacturing and industry.[33]

This interdependent economic relationship had drastic and lasting consequences for those living in the colonies who saw their individual life chances and the development of their national economies decline. At the turn of the twentieth century, Indian economic historian R.C. Dutt argued that colonialism had created an economic gulf between the British metropole and the Indian colony caused by the annual 'drain of wealth' that led to progress and prosperity in the former and poverty and distress in the latter.[34] Looking at the fate of Africa, Guyanese Marxist historian Walter Rodney passionately proposed that European colonialism was a 'one-armed bandit' that took all and offered nothing to the colonies. In *How Europe Underdeveloped Africa*, Rodney argued that colonial capitalism was monopolistic, destructive, and self-serving: 'It is fairly obvious that capitalists do not set out to create other capitalists, who would be rivals. On the contrary, the tendency of capitalism in Europe from the very beginning was one of competition, elimination, and monopoly.'[35]

But where does this leave us in terms of understanding the imperial fringe in South Asia?

It is clear that we know more about the Indian subcontinent in the nineteenth century than in the seventeenth. We know more about the imperial centres of Calcutta and Delhi than the distant lands in Kashmir, Tibet, and the Northwestern Frontier. We have learned a lot about colonial knowledge producers like Sir William Jones and Colin Mackenzie but less about their Indian translators and surveyors. We have a growing literature on the business history of the East India Company and the transactions of traders but we know close to nothing about the power plays of pirates. We have read volumes on the trials of high level colonial administrators like Warren Hastings while we know close to nothing about the daily trials of ordinary soldiers and sailors.

The essays in this collection borrow from the contributions offered by imperial historians, post-colonial theorists, and historians of modern India reviewed earlier and seek to fill these gaps. To focus on the fringes within the colonial world is to disrupt the polarity that conventionally divides studies of the imperial centre from studies of the peripheral colony. In contrast to the conventional time frames, territorial expanses, and imperial personages who have dominated the story of Britain's conquest of India, this volume emphasizes the importance of different times, places, and people in the empire. Viewed in its entirety, this volume proposes that in order to understand the empire one has to look at its fringes, at less privileged and less visible people, places, and time periods.

CHAPTER OVERVIEW

The volume is divided into two thematic parts. Part One presents work that explores the fluid nature of the empire's temporal and geographical borders and boundaries. Part Two offers essays featuring unfamiliar people and places, insiders and outsiders.

Nineteenth century British historians defined India's past in Eurocentric terms that placed South Asia within European historical frameworks, thereby legitimizing the authority of British rule.[36] The transition to British colonialism was neatly equated by historian-administrators like James Mill and Henry Maine with the transition to modernity. In these early colonial histories, the British functioned as the inevitable agents of historical progress and the guardians of Indian antiquity.[37] Although subsequent generations of historians have questioned the sharp line dividing the pre-modern and modern periods, few have paused to rethink the divide between the pre-colonial and colonial periods. As Philip J. Stern points out in his essay, we continue to view the Mughal and British periods in exclusive rather than overlapping terms. Because little attention is paid to the rise of the seventeenth century Company state, Robert Clive's defeat of Siraj-ud-Daulah in the Battle of Plassey in 1757 appears, as Stern puts it, 'as if it came from nowhere'. The much neglected seventeenth century, in Stern's appraisal, provides a crucial key to understanding the emergence of Company Raj a century later. Stern's important contribution reconstructs the conventional spatial and temporal margins that define the making of the British empire in India. There were not traders first and sovereigns later; from its inception, the East India Company exhibited the attributes of an early modern polity.

Marina Carter's essay takes a view from the sea that also pushes us to reflect upon time, territoriality, and the early colonial state. Carter argues that whereas 'outlaws of the sea', as pirates were called, are sometimes seen as marginal figures who obstructed state development, they actually played diverse and sometimes productive roles in forming a critical mass of people who participated in the European competition for control of key territories. Stern's and Carter's essays both challenge us to question the sharp breaks and boundaries that have traditionally divided the political and economic ambitions of pirates, traders, and sovereigns. Instead of seeing marauding pirates and rapacious traders as marginal, illegitimate characters standing menacingly outside imperial order and sovereignty, we are asked to reflect on their role in aiding colonial state formation.

The historical literature on British colonial expansion in India has not only stuck to a time-honoured temporal narrative, but it has also offered a standard spatial vision of conquest. The conventional narrative about British territorial expansion begins with Bengal, moves south to Mysore and the Deccan, across Maratha territory, through the Punjab, and culminates, more or less, in 1842, with Charles Napier's famous quip about the conquest of Sindh, 'Peccavi'. But what about the notoriously unstable borders to the Northwest and the Northeast, the disastrous forays into Afghanistan, and the military clashes with the peoples of Assam and Burma? Whereas the literature on frontiers and borderlands in other world areas has received significant attention, the far-flung physical margins of colonial India remain in the historical shadows. As Alex McKay, Sameetah Agha, and Mridu Rai demonstrate in their contributions, the processes by which British colonial borders in India were ideologically defined and militarily secured involved inconsistencies, contradictions, and varying geo-political strategies.

McKay's essay on the applicability of Frederick Jackson Turner's American frontier thesis to the Indo-Tibetan border brings the mythological aura surrounding Tibetan history into a comparative colonial framework. Turner's 'Frontier Thesis' has had a major influence on the study of the history of the American west. In contrast, the role of the frontier in colonial India has been largely ignored. In the nineteenth century, as the Russian and Chinese empires closed in on the Raj, British imperialists such as Lord Curzon became increasingly preoccupied with frontier theory and the ways in which the frontier transformed the character of Britons who served there. Placing the Indo-Tibetan colonial encounter within the framework of Turner's frontier theory, McKay shows that there were layered zones of authority in an undefined Himalayan zone where boundaries were constantly in a flux.

Moving from the Northeast to the volatile Northwest Frontier, Sameetah Agha's essay examines contradictions in the policy of imperial defence as it played out in the late nineteenth century. Due to a real or imagined Russian threat to the British empire in India, British statesmen became obsessed with safeguarding their most prized colonial possession: India. The policy of enlisting and allying with 200,000 independent Pukhtun tribesmen from outside British India's administrative frontier was seen as the best way to prepare for the possibility of an invasion by Russia. Challenging colonial and current historiography on the subject, Agha elucidates the complex connections between the colonial military apparatus and the colonial state at a moment of political crisis, foregrounding the gap between what was said and what was done.

Mridu Rai's essay on the princely state of Kashmir links the process of colonial state formation and legitimation to the growing emphasis on religious difference. The religious identity of the Dogras as Hindus qualified them for colonial support as the British viewed the Dogras as a political counterpoint to Sikh and Muslim dominance in neighbouring regions. Rai argues that the colonial state invented and employed religious and ethnic difference in order to legitimate power.

Satadru Sen's essay focuses on the penal colony of the Andaman Islands, which was by definition a fringe both in terms of its territorial relationship to the Indian mainland and its social composition of transported criminals, native tribals, and what the British colonizers called a diverse zoo of people. Sen argues that the penal colony functioned as a transformative space that allowed for those dislocated from home to radically reimagine themselves and their communities. Convict society on the fringes developed along lines that were partially autonomous of both British expectations and what was permissible at home on the Indian mainland. Unpredictable experiments in religious, familial, and political identification affected the transported convict's sense of his place in the mainland centre as well as in the newly formed society on the margin.

Clare Anderson's essay takes the case of a convict of African descent in India to examine the racial dynamics that characterized the overseas penal settlements where non-Europeans and Eurasians were sent during the nineteenth century. In examining the complex processes of identity formation in the Indian Ocean region, Anderson argues that these fringe characters challenge us to think about the social, racial, and geographical boundaries of empire as fluid and shifting across time and space.

James H. Mills also takes up the question of the social fringe by examining colonial attempts to control the movement and behaviour of itinerant wanderers on the margins of the Indian social order. In his essay on Indian vagrants in nineteenth century lunatic asylums, Mills explores both colonial efforts to manage and police the mobile and dangerous elements of the Indian population, as well as local efforts by Indian families to use British institutions to rid themselves of difficult and mentally ill family members. Mills argues that the incarceration of itinerant Indians in insane asylums reflects colonial anxieties about preserving public order and state control.

Douglas M. Peers shows how a seemingly inconsequential court martial in the cantonment of Mhow in central India escalated into a major imperial scandal whose reverberations were felt globally precisely because it touched upon gender, class, and the operation and discipline of the Indian Army. Peers's essay plays with the relationship between centre and periphery both by examining a central state institution (the Army) at a distant geographical margin (in Mhow), and by comparing reactions to the trial in England (metropole) and in India (colony). By examining how court martials played out in these two arenas and how their meanings changed over time, Peers argues that a more nuanced perspective can be gained into the complex interplay between rank and gender in colonial society.

The production of knowledge about India and Indians both enabled the state to govern its subjects and altered local identities and transformed social relationships in Indian society. However, British dominance, as Ranajit Guha instructs, did not necessarily engender hegemony and recent work on colonial knowledge has emphasized the dialectical nature of its production and the role of Indian subjects in the making of colonial modes of knowing and ruling.[38] Mitchell's essay contributes to the growing scholarship on the processes of colonial knowledge production and the path of its impact. Mitchell examines the processes by which south Indians assimilated colonial forms of rule into existing categories of understanding, while at the same time finding themselves increasingly incorporated within a world governed by colonial power. Engaging with the broader debate about the impact of British colonialism on Indian society, Mitchell's essay pushes us to ask to what extent did the British fundamentally alter subcontinental structures of state, political economy, culture, and society, and how much was colonial power advanced by adapting to pre-existing networks and relying on local collaborators and indigenous networks? Less interested in colonial representations of native others, Mitchell asks this question from the perspective of those subject to the new administration and seeks to understand how new forms of knowledge were experienced locally.

NOTES AND REFERENCES

1. Originally published in 1936, George Orwell's 'Shooting an Elephant' can be found online: http://www.online-literature.com/orwell/887, last accessed on 5 March 2009.
2. For a concise history of the British empire, see Philippa Levine, 2007, *The British Empire: Sunrise to Sunset*, London: Pearson Longman.
3. J.R. Seeley, 1883, *The Expansion of England: Two Courses of Lectures*, London: Macmillan, p. 10.

Introduction 13

4. Jeffrey Goldberg, 2005, 'Letter from Washington: A Little Learning', *The New Yorker*, 9 May.
5. Elaine Freedgood, 2002, 'Fringe', *Victorian Literature and Culture*, vol. 30, p. 260.
6. Michael Hechter, 1975, *Internal Colonialism: The Celtic Fringe in British National Development, 1536–1966*, Berkeley: University of California Press.
7. Laura O'Connor, 2006, *Haunted English: The Celtic Fringe, the British Empire, and De-Anglicization*, Baltimore: The Johns Hopkins University Press.
8. Quoted in L. Perry Curtis, 1968, *Anglo-Saxons and Celts: A Study of Anti-Irish Prejudice in Victorian England*, New York: New York University Press, p. 84.
9. Robert Knox, 1850, *The Races of Men*, Philadelphia: Lea and Blanchard.
10. L. Perry Curtis, 1971, *Apes and Angels: The Irishman in Victorian Caricature*, London: David and Charles.
11. David Fitzpatrick, 1999, 'Ireland and the Empire', in Andrew Porter (ed.), *The Oxford History of the British Empire: The Nineteenth Century*, vol. III, Oxford: Oxford University Press, pp. 495–521.
12. Ian Johnston, 2006, 'We're Nearly All Celts Under the Skin', *The Scotsman*, 21 September. For a masterful debunking of Victorian race science, see Stephen J. Gould, 1996, *The Mismeasure of Man*, New York: W.W. Norton.
13. On the 'rule of colonial difference', see Partha Chatterjee, 1993, *The Nation and its Fragments: Colonial and Postcolonial Histories*, Princeton: Princeton University Press.
14. Rudyard Kipling, 1899, 'The White Man's Burden', http://www.fordham.edu/halsall/mod/Kipling.htm., last accessed on 5 March 2009.
15. On how colonial difference affected the behaviour and actions of the colonizers, see Elizabeth Kolsky, 2009, *Colonial Justice in India: White Violence and the Rule of Law*, Cambridge: Cambridge University Press and Kate Darian-Smith, Patricia Grimshaw, and Stuart Macintyre (eds), 2007, *Britishness Abroad: Transnational Movements and Imperial Cultures*, Melbourne: Melbourne University Press.
16. Frantz Fanon, 1967, *The Wretched of the Earth*, New York: Grove Press, p. 102.
17. An overview of the new imperial history can be gleaned from recently edited collections, including Frederick Cooper and Ann Laura Stoler (eds), 1995, *Tensions of Empire: Colonial Cultures in a Bourgeois World*, Berkeley: University of California Press; Sarah Stockwell (ed.), 2008, *The British Empire: Themes and Perspectives*, London: Blackwell; and Kathleen Wilson (ed.), 2004, *A New Imperial History: Culture, Identity and Modernity in Britain and the Empire, 1660–1840*, Cambridge: Cambridge University Press.
18. Catherine Hall, 2000, 'Introduction', in Catherine Hall (ed.), *Cultures of Empire: A Reader. Colonizers in Britain and the Empire in the Nineteenth and Twentieth Centuries*, Manchester: Manchester University Press, p. 16.
19. Edward Said, 1978, *Orientalism*, New York: Vintage. On material forms of colonial consumption, see James Walvin, 1997, *Fruits of Empire: Exotic Produce and British Taste, 1660–1800*, London: Macmillan. On ideological forms of colonial consumption, see John MacKenzie, 1984, *Propaganda and Empire: The Manipulation of British Public Opinion, 1880–1960*, Manchester:

Manchester University Press; and Anne McClintock, 1995, *Imperial Leather: Race, Gender, and Sexuality in the Colonial Contest*, New York: Routledge.
20. Bernard Cohn, 1996, *Colonialism and Its Forms of Knowledge: The British in India*, Princeton: Princeton University Press; Nicholas B. Dirks, 1992, *Culture and Colonialism*, Ann Arbor: University of Michigan Press; C.A. Bayly, 1988, *Indian Society and the Making of the British Empire*, Cambridge: Cambridge University Press.
21. Edward Said, 1993, *Culture and Imperialism*, New York: Knopf.
22. Authors who emphasize the harsh impact of colonial cultural interventions include Cohn, *Colonialism and Its Forms of Knowledge* and Nicholas B. Dirks, 2001, *Castes of Mind: Colonialism and the Making of Modern India*, Princeton: Princeton University Press. For a different perspective on the production and consequences of colonial knowledge, see C.A. Bayly, 1996, *Empire and Information: Intelligence Gathering and Social Communication in India, 1780–1870*, Cambridge: Cambridge University Press; and Eugene Irschick, 1994, *Dialogue and History: Constructing South India, 1795–1895*, Berkeley: University of California Press.
23. Catherine Hall, 2008, 'Culture and Identity in Imperial Britain', in Stockwell (ed.), *The British Empire*, p. 199.
24. In this regard, see Cooper and Stoler (eds), *Tensions of Empire*.
25. Gauri Viswanathan, 1998, *Outside the Fold: Conversion, Modernity and Belief*, Princeton: Princeton University Press.
26. Frederick Cooper and Ann Laura Stoler (eds), 1995, 'Introduction', in Cooper and Stoler (eds), *Tensions of Empire*, pp. 1–58.
27. William Dalrymple, 2002, *White Mughals: Love and Betrayal in Eighteenth-century India*, London: HarperCollins and Maya Jasanoff, 2006, *Edge of Empire: Lives, Culture and Conquest in the East, 1750–1850*, New York: Vintage Books.
28. See, for example, Catherine Hall and Sonya O. Rose (eds), 2006, *At Home with the Empire: Metropolitan Culture and the Imperial World*, Cambridge: Cambridge University Press.
29. Jack Gallagher and Ronald Robinson, 1953, 'The Imperialism of Free Trade', *Economic History Review*, 6 (1), pp. 1–15.
30. Jack Gallagher and Ronald Robinson, 1961, *Africa and the Victorians: The Official Mind of Imperialism*, London: Macmillan.
31. See A.R. Dilley, 2008, 'The Economics of Empire', in Stockwell (ed.), *The British Empire*, pp. 101–29.
32. Immanuel Wallerstein, 1974, *The Modern World System: Capitalist Agriculture and the Origins of the European World Economy in the Sixteenth Century*, New York: Academic Press.
33. See B.R. Tomlinson, 'Economics and Empire: The Periphery and the Imperial Economy', in Porter (ed.), *The Oxford History of the British Empire*, vol. III, pp. 53–74.
34. R.C. Dutt, 1904, *The Economic History of India: India in the Victorian Age*, London: Keagan, Paul, Trench, Trubner & Co. Dutt drew on the work and

phraseology of Dadabhai Naoroji, 1901, *Poverty and Un-British Rule*, London: S. Sonnenschein.

35. Walter Rodney, 1981 [1973], *How Europe Underdeveloped Africa*, 2nd edn, Washington, DC: Howard University Press, p. 206.
36. Dipesh Chakrabarty, 2000, *Provincializing Europe: Postcolonial Thought and Historical Difference*, Princeton: Princeton University Press.
37. Thomas Metcalf, 1997, *Ideologies of the Raj*, Cambridge: Cambridge University Press.
38. Ranajit Guha, 1998, *Dominance Without Hegemony: History and Power in Colonial India*, Cambridge, MA: Harvard University Press.

PART I

BORDERS AND BOUNDARIES

From the Fringes of History
Tracing the Roots of the English East India Company-state

Philip J. Stern

'Tis probable the Mogull can not continue long, when ever he goes off y^e Stage great confusions & intestine broiles will in all apperance inevitably ensue in his Empire, & when ever this happens we will with all fidelity consider your directions & act in compliance therewith according to the best of our understandings for your intrest.[1]

Through the last decades of the seventeenth century, officials of the East India Company continued to warn of 'the unsettlednesse of the Mogull in his Throne, which in all probability hee cannot long hold'.[2] By 1699, the Company's governing Court of Committees in London (later, Directors) urged the council in Calcutta to reinforce their fledgling Fort William, in anticipation of the 'Civill Wars...likely to ensue'. A couple of years later, the governor of Madras was similarly instructed to keep careful diplomacy with local officials rather than the Mughal court, 'as is very probable the Mogols Kingdom should be Cantell'd out into severall Sovereignties' after his death.[3]

While their timing was, of course, premature, Company officials' read of the political situation in South Asia was fairly prophetic. Though long seen as precipitating a decline in the Mughal Empire, Aurangzeb's death in 1707 indeed laid bare a patchwork of 'severall Sovereignties', a network of fragmented and layered forms of regional political power that had only partly been masked and managed by the practices of Mughal state and sovereignty. As Sanjay Subrahmanyam and Muzaffar

Alam have suggested, the Mughal empire never was, 'an all-powerful Leviathan', the vision of it as such being more 'an idealized vision of the British Empire in India, projected backwards into the late sixteenth century'.[4] As such, eighteenth century India was characterized by the emergence of localized polities from within, beneath, and aside the Mughal regime—the so-called 'successor states', increasingly politically and financially independent of the Mughal centre, but nonetheless strikingly reliant on the symbols and appurtenances of its rule. Timurid political culture and even the authority of the emperor himself became crucial for political stability, from Mughal feudatories like the nawab of Bengal, the nizam of Hyderabad, and various nawabs of the Karnatic, to its enemies and competitors, such as the Maratha, Rajput, and Mysore regimes.[5]

Thus, it seems safe to say that a colonial-era, Gibbonesque vision of an eighteenth century Mughal 'decline and fall'[6] has been replaced with a 'mixed scenario of shadow and light': an era of 'decentralization', which may have been marked by a feebler reach of the Mughal centre, but which by no means precipitated the collapse of the institutions or structures of South Asian state and society.[7] But what exactly has this meant for the other great development of eighteenth century South Asian history, namely, the coming of British territorial power, first in eastern and then in southern and western India? The clear rejection of an image of eighteenth century Mughal 'decline' has helped challenge the now somewhat passé, but not entirely extinguished, notion that the British expansion in India was necessitated by a 'power vacuum' left in Aurangzeb's wake.[8] The vibrancy of the eighteenth century in South Asian studies has of late also imploded a self-confident Eurocentric narrative about its trajectories and meanings.[9]

At the same time, it seems to have produced its own historiographical vacuum about precisely how we should regard the coming of the English East India Company as a political power in India. At times vitriolic debate over 'continuity' and 'change' has given rise to a historiographical conflict that remains as much about approach as it is about interpretation.[10] On the one hand, we are presented with enduring socio-economic structures—such as fiscal institutions and information networks—that emphasize the crucial utility of Indian 'agents' or 'collaborators' in facilitating early Company rule.[11] On the other side, a focus on the political maintains quite clearly the significant break represented by British forms of law, sovereignty, and the dominant power of the modern colonial regime—distinct from both South Asian forms as well as the 'metropolitan bourgeois state that had sired it'.[12]

That is to say, from the perspective of the commercial and the social, the eighteenth century in India has come to seem more 'evolution' than 'revolution', which also renders the political dislocations of colonialism, as P.J. Marshall has argued, more products of the 1820s rather than the 1760s.[13] At the same time, it is hard to escape a vision of British colonialism that does not, at some point, occasion a sea change in Indian politics, even if it is one that grew 'more secure and more ambitious' over the course of the nineteenth century.[14]

In both these cases, though, there seems to be unlikely common ground to be found in the central assumption that the rise of East India Company power itself was somewhat of a mid-eighteenth century novelty, which only came into its own over the course of the late eighteenth and nineteenth centuries. Both arguments also resist the suggestion that the Company was 'simply another "Indian state",' but rather debate the extent to which this Company *drew* upon indigenous forms or imported European ones in constituting its political power and authority.[15]

Despite ably dismantling all of the other historiographical truisms that have underpinned our discussions of eighteenth century India, the sense remains quite broadly in the literature that the East India Company-state emerged somehow from the fringes to become a state and empire in the eighteenth century, and against a backdrop of some form of manipulation of markets in Bengal—whether the Company's or the private ambitions of its servants.[16] It is somewhat of a cliché to observe that before then and especially off the coastal regions, European companies—particularly the English—were little noticed and derisively regarded by Mughal officials as mere *koolah-pushan*, hat-wearers, and *feranghi*, foreigners. The disjuncture is often noted, for example, with the example of Sir Thomas Roe, whose embassy to the Mughal Emperor Jahangir in the 1610s is not mentioned once in Jahangir's memoirs, the *Tuzuk-i-Jahangiri*.[17] Moreover, in an understandable correction to generations of scholarship fuelled by Eurocentric assumptions derived from colonial archives, the impact of the European companies in the 'longue durée' of the wider Indian Ocean world before the eighteenth century continues to be a matter of ambivalence and debate.[18]

If the companies seem to have existed on the geographical and political fringes of the Mughal empire, they are also often regarded as operating on an alien 'frontier' of Europe, as Holden Furber put it, 'characterized in the East as in the West by an omnipresence of danger, an untrammelled scramble for wealth quickly acquired and often as quickly lost, an opportunity to build a new career in a new land after failure in the old, combined with a freedom to shift from one occupation to another and to associate with other Europeans of differing social and national origins'.[19] In commerce, the Company's early history has been rendered either exceptional or irrelevant to later events, and when important, as a form of 'pre-modern' multinational corporation rather than a political body with connections to its later history.[20]

These expectations of the East India Company's place in seventeenth and early eighteenth century Asia have both fuelled and been fuelled by the sense that the Company's territorial acquisitions, and thus the Company-state that followed, were novel, dangerous, and somewhat unnatural. This perspective was only reinforced by contemporary reactions in Britain, which decried the idea of a merchant sovereign as, in Adam Smith's words, 'strange absurdity'.[21] Waves of parliamentary intervention from 1767 to 1813 effectively annexed the Company, fiscally and politically, to the British state under the banner of 'reform'.[22] Thus, the acquisition of territory, in the form of the *diwani* (revenue collector in Bengal) of 1765 and subsequent expansion in eastern and southern India, ultimately seems to have transformed the Company from one fringe to another: from Furber's seventeenth century commercial frontier to what Sudipta Sen has called a 'colonial frontier' of the Hanoverian state.[23]

In both phases of its historiographical career—the 'trader' and the 'sovereign'—the East India Company tends to be regarded as being on the 'fringe': an inscrutable, exceptional, and ultimately abnormal intervention into both the trading world of Asia and the world of modern states and empires. The mid-eighteenth century thus becomes a distinct rupture in the Company's own nature and the nature of British contact with South Asia: a 'Plassey revolution', without long-term causes rooted in the internal troubles of Bengal—though there is of course a debate as to the role of the Company itself in creating those troubles in the first place.[24]

This essay insists upon an alternative approach to understanding the East India Company's rise to power in eighteenth century India; it attempts to find common ground between these discourses of continuity and change by dislocating our discussion of the Company's roots from *commerce* to *politics*, but a politics that was not novel but rather endemic to the early modern Eurasian world. It contends that we need to see the early East India Company not as a merchant, but as a form of body politic which existed in a world defined by composite, fragmented, and hybrid forms of state and sovereignty.[25] As a political body, the seventeenth century Company experimented with any number of forms that would become critical as it grew as a *territorial* power in the mid-eighteenth century. Moreover, as a corporate polity, it was in both form and function particularly well-suited to thrive amidst the 'layered and shared sovereignty' that characterized pre-colonial India.[26] Calling on both British and Mughal forms for its legitimacy, and pursuing a very fragmented and layered form of empire itself, the Company was neither clearly a successor state nor a novelty in South Asian politics; it was rather something quite clearly in-between, a global form of layered polity, whose early modern practices translated into and informed its early transformation into a territorial power. Thus, the Company-state that emerged in the eighteenth century appeared at the heart, rather than the fringes, of both its own history as well as that of early modern South Asia.

FROM THE FRINGES OF EMPIRE

The English East India Company was, from its first chartering in 1600, in form like other corporations for trade and plantation in the Atlantic, not to mention a host of municipal governments, universities, and corporate groups on the British Isles—by nature a political organization, with the obligation to govern itself and to govern those subject to its command. From 1607, the Company had the expectation of 'perpetual succession' which in 1657 was matched with a permanent joint stock, thus marrying an expectation of political with fiscal immortality. Though, of course, initially a corporation for conducting Eurasian commerce, by the second half of the seventeenth century, the Company's operations led it to make claims to governance both over sea lanes as well as over incipient city-colonies in India and the South Atlantic, each obtained on rather different jurisprudential foundations. By the dawn of the eighteenth century, these included: Madras from 1639, held initially on grants from the local powers in south India; Bombay, transferred from the Portuguese to the English Crown in 1661 and then from the Crown to the Company in 1668; and St Helena, granted on charters from the Protector Richard Cromwell in 1658 and then again by King Charles II in 1673. In the 1690s, the Company experienced a growth spurt, pursuing fortified settlements in south India (Cuddalore and Anjengo), Sumatra

(Bengkulu), and, of course, Bengal, where the Company obtained from the nawab the zamindari of three villages, which would form the foundations for the city of Calcutta.[27]

Thus, Company charters endowed it, not unlike its Atlantic counterparts, with a range of political capacities—to appoint its own leadership, to make and execute law, to erect fortifications, mint money, and to make war and conduct diplomacy. At the same time, from its first factory at Surat, the Company collected similar rights, prerogatives, and autonomies by virtue of its agreements, grants, and *farmans*, or grants of immunities, from Asian powers as well. This, combined with its own institutional behaviour, I have argued elsewhere, created for it a sort of 'structural autonomy' in which the Company was simultaneously subject to many different forms of sovereignty and independent of them all.[28]

Founded upon these political constitutions and behaviours, the pre-Plassey Company in its city-colonies experimented with various forms of governance that had striking parallels with their later manifestations. While these engagements with governance took any number of forms, by the late 1680s, the governing Court of Committees had outlined three prevailing objectives for the exercising of 'sovereign power' delegated from the English Crown and empowered by Company officials: raising revenue from inhabitants, coining money, and by 'punishing all Neglects & abuses there', that is, administering justice in India.[29]

By the second half of the seventeenth century, revenue for the Company leadership was the key not to underwriting the Eurasian trade, but to maintaining self-sustaining and defensible settlements in Asia. Their model, clearly, was the Dutch, who the committees consistently argued had been remarkably successful in 'making places conquered or fortified to pay the charge of their future preservation as well as the first Cost of the Settlement'.[30] Bombay, Madras, St Helena, and other settlements collected land taxes, customs, excise taxes, licensing and registration fees on publicans, fishermen, and shopkeepers, and murage duties to pay for the erection of city walls and fortresses—all of which was intended not to be recycled into the Eurasian commerce but rather into defence, infrastructure, and civic improvement. In 1687, the Company even incorporated the city of Madras—complete with aldermen, burgesses, and maces and silver oars—in part to facilitate the collection of taxes, or, in their words, to 'enduce all the Inhabitants to contribute cheerfully to some publick workes'.[31]

This revenue regime gave birth to a form of military fiscalism that would seem somewhat familiar to its late eighteenth century descendants, if perhaps more defensive than offensive. In 1692, the Court of Committees reminded Madras that it was only local revenue that 'enables [the Dutch] to secure by great expences and Forts their soveraigne state in India, Enlarge their Dominion as well as their Trade, and to be alwaies in a condition to revenge any affronts that are offered them... It's nothing but Revenue can maintain great and chargeable fortifications and Garrisons or secure them when we have them'.[32] Revenue, in turn, gave a right to governance—both de facto, in a place like Madras, and somewhat literally, as in the zamindari over Calcutta.

The zamindari in Calcutta also represented another feature of the nature of early Company authority: its ability to take on positions of titular authority under the Mughal Empire. Contemporaries took the diwani of 1765 to be an anomaly and an innovation, but indeed accumulating rights, privileges, and autonomies under Mughal authority was a consistent form of Company behaviour and policy through the seventeenth century. As early as the 1690s, the Company's president at Surat, Samuel Annesley, imagined proposing the Company as a *faujdar*, or Mughal tributary police and military force, for the 'salt water'—as a way of both aggrandizing the Company's authority and sating Mughal demands for protection from European and American pirates in the Indian Ocean.[33] The 1717 farman from the emperor Farukhsiyar, most remembered for the rights to customs-free trading it conferred on the Company in Bengal, also positioned the Company within the Mughal political hierarchy, and very clearly facilitated its widening power in Bengal in the years before Plassey and diwani. Some even came to call it the 'Magna Carta of the Company in India'.[34] In 1759, in recognition of its growing power in the western Indian littoral, Bombay assumed the military and political office of *qiladar*, or governor of the fort, at Surat. But even this was not an eighteenth century innovation, as Company officials with similar ambitions can be found as early as the 1660s, when seeking such a post was suggested by Bombay's governor, Sir George Oxenden, not very long after the island's acquisition.[35]

Thus, in practice, there was precedence for something like the diwani, dating back almost a century and rooted in the very same principles—to bolster not simply commercial but political ambitions in coastal India. As an institution, the Company was well placed to participate in the kinds of layered and divided sovereignty that characterized both European and Asian polities, something no more evident than in the second pillar to the Company's late seventeenth century political strategy: coinage. More than mere fiscal instruments, coins, for example were, as the committees insisted to Bombay in 1686, 'so necessary an appendix to all Sovereign Governments'.[36] 'Till your Mint is goeing', they were told on another occasion, 'you are lame of one foot, and not an intire Soveraign State'.[37]

Coins also represented the multivalent nature of the Company's authority. At different moments in the late seventeenth century, Bombay minted rupees in both English and Persian, including perhaps most famously the 1693 'William and Mary rupee', a silver coin with Persian characters, bearing the names of the joint English monarchs, but which was so controversial at the Mughal court that officials threatened an invasion of Bombay.[38] Most often, though, local coinages featured not the names of English sovereigns but local iconographies. The 1696 Fort St David pagoda (a coin and a unit of currency current at Madras), for example, featured an image of a Hindu deity on the obverse, surrounded by an outline of the Company's balemark and the word 'Tevnapatnam'.[39] After 1692, and until 1707, the Madras mint coined pagodas (gold) and rupees (silver) in Aurangzeb's name, though its 1689 *fanam*, another coin minted at Madras, as described by the French traveller Jean-Baptiste Tavernier, continued to bear the image of Vishnu or Hanuman on the obverse. The rupee, however, bore a Persian inscription, with 'Shah Aurangzeb 'Alamgir' inscribed on the reverse, and the location of the mint ('Chinapatan') impressed.[40]

Bombay also minted its 'tinny' or *budgrook*, a low-value tin coin meant not for the Company's trade, but for local circulation—'Beneficiall to the Inhabitants and poorer Sort of this Island buying Provisions and other Things'[41]—which was similarly inscribed with the balemark and the year of issue on the back. However, its copperoons (Bombay's version of the copper pice, or *paise*) were from 1672 until well into the eighteenth century struck on the obverse with the crest of the Company's arms, with the encircling inscription 'HON:SOC:ANG:IND:ORI' (Latin abbreviations for The Honourable English East India Company) and on the reverse was marked 'MON:BOMBAY:ANGLIC: REGIM' (Money of the English Government of Bombay), with the encircling inscription '*a deo pax and incrementum*' (from God comes peace and expansion). The 1672 'Angelina', the island's version of a silver rupee, was struck similarly. However, in 1676, the Angelina was given a simpler design, stripped even of the commercial iconography of the balemark: the new coin had only the Company's arms on the obverse (no encirclement), and 'pax deo' on the reverse, surrounded by the words '*moneta bombaiensis*'. The council at Surat noted that they 'like well of the new stamp with Pax X

Deo on one side and the Company's armes on the other side, but not with the Company's mark'.[42]

Fort St George also began issuing pagodas as early as the mid-1640s, with rights ceded under the terms of successive agreements with neighbouring powers: the Raja of Chandragiri, Sri Ranga Rayulu III, the sultan of Golconda, and later, the Mughal *subahdar*, or provincial governor.[43] The original grant, as translated by the Company, allowed, 'The priviledges of mintage, without paying any Dewes or dutyes whatsoever, more than the ordinary wages or hire unto those that shall Quoyne the moneys'.[44] The Company also spent a great deal of time and money attempting to procure authority from the sultan of Golconda, and later the Mughal emperor, for such coins to pass current in the surrounding country. However, the expense of that policy and the frequent change of neighbouring governments led the Company to abandon the practice and seek authority from Charles II instead. As the committees informed Madras,

We have often writt you to procure a Phirmaund for Coyning of Rupees, fanams and pice at the Fort, and thereby some additionall Revenue might accrue to us by our Mint, but since his present Majesty Our gracious Sovereign hath been pleased by his Royall Charter to grant us that liberty of Coyning, We would have you by vertue of that power from our own King to coyne those Species of mony, and to proclaime them to be Currant money in Madrass, and all places where this Company have dominion, and the exercise of Sovereign power in India, under and by authority of our most indulgent Sovereign.[45]

But even the committees, if assertive, were not comfortable with having only one source or the other. As Bombay was told soon after,

neither would We have it [coining] putt off any longer, upon a pretence that such a Phirmaund cannot be obtain'd from the Mogull, because We have a power in our last Charter from his present Majesty to coyn all sorts of foreign Coynes, currant in India, which power We are resolved to assert and maintain against all contradiction so far at least as our Own Dominion extends, and for the future to make it one Article, with any Princes We agree with in India, that our Coynes shall be currant, in their respective dominions.[46]

In the end, the best authority for the Company was achieved by a confluence of all three pillars: local, Crown, and Company. Note, for example, the Court's reminder to Bombay in 1689 about minting money on the island itself:

We hope likewise you do not omit to coin small money for the use of the Island, and that in all you do calculate to make some reasonable profit to the Company as all governments in the world do, which may lawfully exercise that Royall Prerogative of Coinage which is granted us by his Majesties Charter, as well as by the Mogulls Phirmaund and Husball Hookum.[47]

In 1692, Madras reached another agreement with Muhammad Kam Bakhsh, the subahdar, for coining with Mughal iconography in the name of Alamgir (Aurangzeb) for use in Bengal; he even provided the iron stamps to strike them. From then, the practice of minting coins in the name of the Mughal emperor in British India continued unabated until 1835.[48]

But, more than any representation of authority, it was of course the execution of justice which Company governors in both London and Asia continually observed was crucial to any reasonable and long-lasting settlement. Laws in these cities were an odd mixture of local and English customs and equity but, ultimately, it was Company orders that were, as St Helena was instructed in the 1680s and again in 1709, to be 'as good Law as Magna Charta is to England'.[49] Though rough going at first, as with all early days of colonial plantations, the Company nonetheless aspired to maintain regular justice through judicature and admiralty courts, prisons, and even, at Bombay, a sort of small claims court meant to serve the 'poorer sorts'. Laws and court fees were to be made public, while governing councils and courts dealt with issues ranging from capital crimes, like murder and rape, to probate, property disputes, the prices of staples and essentials, famine and poor relief, the regulation and taxation of taverns and liquor, and, at times most importantly, the regulation of piety, morality, and sexual misconduct, like adultery and fornication.

The basis for Company law came again from a number of sources—English charters, local leases and grants, and, of course, the de facto sovereignty that followed from the Company's own behaviour, including the farming of revenue. The attention to law, in turn, was not simply a concern with maintaining order, but a means of encouraging inhabitants' civic and moral health—literally, from the odd obsession the Bombay council exhibited in 1705 with curtailing inhabitants' use of fish as fertilizer (which had evidently become a 'Pestilential Greivance' and a 'Nautious Corrupting the Ayre') to their more general and pervasive concerns with the protection, preservation, and promotion of Protestantism. Good laws were also a principle of sound political economy: it was, the committees insisted, 'the free Enjoyment of Liberty and Property that makes our Territoryes worth courting'.[50] Thus, laws that kept people and their property safe and, in some way tended towards the improvement of both, was as London put it to Madras in 1686, 'that great Justice we would have you impartially exercise toward all Inhabitants, being such foundations as must in time induce a great & famous superstructure'.[51]

FROM FRINGE TO FRONTIER? INTO THE EIGHTEENTH CENTURY

Though the assumption of responsibility over a rural peasantry and large amounts of territory would raise new issues of governance, the later eighteenth century Company-state's later manifestations can be no more severed from its forbears than that regime can be completely distinguished from the transformations of British India into the 'Crown Raj' after 1858. The institutions and ideologies that emerged as 'British India' in the eighteenth century were not that far removed from their recent history. While vestiges of the early modern legacy of fragmented sovereignty can be seen in policies such as the sustained relationships with subordinated 'princely states' through the entirety of British rule in India,[52] a serious consideration of the direct connections of these nineteenth century political strategies with the seventeenth century remains to be written.[53] And the list could go on. As P.J. Marshall has noted, the famed Indian Civil Service found its roots in the early Company's concept of 'covenanted' servants: that is, those particularly responsible for the Company's 'public' affairs in India.[54] Despite historians' assumptions to the contrary, the 'secret committee' for political and martial affairs, which would become an important organ guiding Company expansion in the later eighteenth century, had roots in the late seventeenth century as well,[55] as did the sorts of relationships in London and the provinces that became the backbone of the Company's domestic commercial and political power.[56] The caste—and community-based systems of rule that would come to characterize colonial policy had analogues as far back as the population management strategies of Gerald Aungier in early Bombay and Elihu Yale in Madras.[57] If as C.A. Bayly has argued, the Company came to rely on 'native informants' and 'brahminical spies' in the late eighteenth century,[58] this too was something that can be found in occasional seventeenth century-political practices. Social and military policies based in the enumeration, codification, and balancing of caste—even the idea of a British Indian census—also have their own seventeenth century examples in Bombay, Madras, and elsewhere. This is not to argue by any means that there was a direct lineage from the incorporation of Madras to the Indian Council Acts or ideologies of separate electorates, nor is it to draw a straight line from Elihu Yale to

Morley, Minto, Risley, or Ilbert (though the latter did have a sense of his legal forebears).[59] It is merely to suggest that at least some of these connections are worthy of further enquiry and should at least not be dismissed offhand.

This somewhat incomplete and anecdotal laundry list aside, there were even more fundamental and important connections between the Company's early history and its later manifestations as a territorial power. Perhaps most crucially, all of the types of revenue that arose from diwani—rent from land, particular revenue farming privileges, rights to fines and forfeitures, and rights to customs[60]—were asserted and extracted on a more local scale by the early Company in its city-colonies. Of course, the Presidencies themselves, the backbone of the expansion of the British in India, obviously had seventeenth century genealogies. Even the very incorporation of these towns—the example of Madras in 1687 was later followed by Calcutta and Bombay[61]—and particularly the use of the Mayor's Court, set the form of Company justice in its cities, as well as the object of critique for state intervention in the creation of the Supreme Court of Calcutta in the 1773 'Regulating' Act, a fact recognized by many eighteenth century Company and Crown lawyers but somewhat lost on the historiography, which tend to date the origin of these corporate cities from their royal chartering in 1726.[62]

The ways in which these three Presidencies related was also a product of the particular politics of the early eighteenth century. For most of the later seventeenth century, the Company was governed somewhat centrally through a 'General' (to some extent a forerunner of the 'Governor General'), rooted in one of the cities, usually Bombay. In 1698, the committees, however, recognized that the political landscape was changing. Noting that 'it can't be amiss to communicate to each others your Designs, Endeavours and Applications, and give your mutual advice as you have opportunity', given the imminent possibility of a breakdown in centralized Mughal authority, they insisted that 'in all Emergencyes let each of the three Places go on with their own particular Addresses', that is, their own relatively independent diplomacy and policy.[63] Again, the semi-autonomous Presidency system that guided early Company territorial expansion—and also informed the 'reform' of Company administration in the 1773 Regulating Act, which created a governor general at Calcutta—was rooted in seventeenth century foundations, themselves a combination of European importation and reactions to political circumstances in South Asia. Continuing conflicts with Asian powers in the late seventeenth century, including wars with both the

Mughal Empire and Siam and ongoing troubles for Company officials in western India as a result of Anglo-American piracy in the Indian Ocean, had set the Company's ambitions on a footing that could not help but condition its later behaviour: as the Company's general noted in 1702, 'nothing but force will Secure your estates, rights & priviledges & our lives & liberties from the violence of the Moores'.[64]

The seventeenth century Company, while by no means highly militarized, did of course rest its defence and authority in garrisoned soldiery and an armed fleet meant to dominate, as much as possible, the sea lanes. Comparisons can certainly be made between its fortified settlements and the sort of 'garrison government' that Stephen Saunders Webb has argued created a sort of 'imperial ethos' in the American colonies.[65] At the same time, though undergoing significant transformations over time, it is impossible to separate this early modern development from the highly militarized East India Company 'garrison state' that scholars have argued emerged in the late eighteenth century and beyond.[66]

On the seas, the maritime power that would underwrite Company territorial expansion in western India, particularly the naval force found in the Bombay Marine, had clear institutional roots in the late seventeenth century, especially in attempts to suppress piracy in the 1690s and beyond. Under the banner of piracy extirpation, the first royal men of war entered the Indian Ocean, at the Company's behest, only further underwriting British maritime strength in the western Indian littoral.[67] Moreover, as the attempts to suppress the Anglo-American piracy of the 1690s—and famous figures like Henry Avery and Captain Kidd—largely succeeded by the 1720s,[68] the political and legal regime was easily refocused on the Company's two biggest remaining maritime rivals: the Marathas and the Qawasim, or the 'Muscat Arabs'. Though generally treated as two distinct phases in the Company's history of piracy suppression, it is impossible not to see the two efforts as continuous and as deeply related to the establishment of Company power in Asia. In 1699, the first British royal ships appeared in western India, with particular instructions to pursue pirates. Others followed, but by 1721, another Royal Navy squadron—much like the pirate-hunting fleet that had first carried the Norris embassy to India—was fitted out for the first time with the explicit purpose of suppressing both Anglo-American pirates in Asia as well as Indian 'pirates'.[69] Under this continuing mandate, the Company engaged in pitched battles with the Maratha tributary 'navy' led by Kanhoji Angre, against whom Bombay had been ordering offensives since 1703 for 'injurious & Pyratical Actions on ye Inhabitants of this Island'.[70] To the Company, he was simply the most powerfull of 'Sevajees' pirates,[71] of course a matter of terminology,[72] and Kanhoji and his successor Tulaji became the Company's main targets in the western India littoral. Tulaji eventually broke with the Marathas and in an ironic turn, fell victim to a joint Maratha–East India Company offensive, including a sepoy detachment headed by none other than Robert Clive.[73]

The defeat of Angre was a fundamental turn in the establishment of a British legal regime over the Indian Ocean and Arabian sea and the hegemony of British naval power on the Indian coast. More immediately, it gave the Company the power to enforce up and down the coast yet another seventeenth century facet of its polity building: the pass system.[74] By the end of the century, as coastal India was mostly subdued, the Company turned its attention to the infamous 'Muscat Arab' pirates, who had also presented a political problem in the 1690s, along what was quickly dubbed the 'Pirate Coast'.[75] By the early nineteenth century, the 'Pirate Coast' had become the 'Trucial Coast'; in declaring the 'cessation of plunder and piracy by land and sea on the part of the Arabs', the East India Company transformed the Arabian peninsula into an informal empire. Again, this all had late seventeenth century roots.

On the other side of India, the moves made at Fort St George towards the end of the seventeenth century also were deeply related to the Company's later eighteenth century expansion. In 1702, the faujdar of the Karnatic, Daud Khan, laid siege to Madras for three months; the Company's successful repulsion of the attack, in the words of John Richards, 'sealed the autonomy of what had become a city-state'.[76] Calcutta's ability to supplant the nawab as the regional power in Bengal also depended upon (though was by no means determined by) its ability to sustain itself against perceived Mughal *strength* in the midst of Aurangzeb's progress through the Deccan. Indeed, the impulses behind the wars the Company fought in Bengal and Bombay in the 1680s were remarkably similar to those in Bengal a half-century later. As Philip Lawson has noted, 'the essential motive behind Child's strategy was identical to that which brought success to Robert Clive's territorial wars in the 1750s; the only difference between the two campaigns lay in execution and the resources available', although both remain for him 'state imperialism by proxy'.[77] Bruce Lenman, has made the same observation, that 'it may be argued that the Childs and James II never aimed at direct rule in Bengal, but then neither did Clive in 1757. What was at stake both times was military and commercial ascendancy. There is no reason to believe that victory for the Childs would have had results any different from those which followed Clive's triumph: subversion of indigenous institutions leading to direct rule'.[78]

If the Company's martial regime in the eighteenth century was built upon its earlier manifestions, albeit as a work-in-progress, so too were the tensions between the Company's own military power and that of the British state, including the disjuncture between their diplomatic policies and interests. Though the Company is often seen as a simple extension of 'British' overseas interests, its leadership consistently defended its institutional and jurisdictional autonomy from outside interference. In 1687, for example, Company Governor Josiah Child had argued to James II that officials in India should never be commissioned solely by the Crown, as 'it would be prejudiciall to our service by their arrogancy. As such, Company officials 'must be always in some measure Subject to the Controul of our President & Council'.[79] By the middle of the eighteenth century it seemed Company leadership still had much the same attitude. Though ultimately becoming deeply involved in both the War of the Austrian Succession and the Seven Years' War, the Company had initially sought with the French Company to establish a neutrality to all lands and waters from the Cape of Good Hope to 20 miles east of the Canton River; there were also proposals to declare St Helena neutral, as well as all east India shipping on both sides.[80] When this failed, the Company continued with more local approaches; at one point Calcutta alone proposed a 'Simple Neutrality with the French within the Ganges, by Sea and Land'.[81] Moreover, during the war, the royal authority in India continued to cause Company officials a great deal of trouble. In 1757, George Pigot, the Governor of Madras, wrote to the Company's Secret Committee to warn them that if war should break out, conflict between the Company's leadership and the newly arrived Royal fleet, led by Admiral Watson, and the infantry regiment he brought with him, under the command of one Colonel John Aldercron, was inevitable. The story was one that almost mimicked these rare encounters in the seventeenth century: upon his arrival, Aldercron published a declaration proclaiming his rank over the Company's forces, claiming himself 'accountable...to none but his Majesty'. Pigot countered by preferring Company troops and officers. As he wrote,

This Step I apprehend has been represented home as derogatory to the Honour of his Majestys Troops, but I flatter myself your Honours knowing our Motives, will perceive the necessity of it...those Gentlemen [the Royal officers] have such high

Notions of the Superiority which they imagine His Majestys Commission gives them over your Servants that I am very apprehensive We should be under a necessity of making such Concessions (if we expect their Service) as would not be consistent with your Interest...I look upon the Powers and Prerogatives claimed by Colonel Adlereron, to bee incompatible with the Nature of your Governments, and contrary to your Interest.[82]

He proceeded to recommend that the Company figure out a way to have the field officers recalled and, if possible, have the soldiers incorporated into the Company's military even in peacetime, 'for as I apprehend it would be still necessary, to keep a respectable Force on Foot at your Several Settlements in India'.[83]

FRINGE OR FOCUS: SOME CONCLUSIONS

The basis for the eighteenth century Company-state and empire is found in the long-term development of the Company's institutions, ideologies, and its very organization. The committees in London and officials in Asia were resolute that they should build a commercial and political system with a firm footing for English dominion. It was a responsibility not only to stockholders but to posterity; it was also a charge to govern people, English and otherwise, subject to Company rule at sea and on land. Company doctrine and policy established the institutional and ideological foundations for a system that valued foremost political expansion and the protection of sovereign power. That Company leaders did not immediately achieve their grandiose designs cannot be the point worth stressing. They planned as much for posterity as for the present and generally revealed sensitivity to the fact that such ambitious plans for creating civil and colonial society took time. As George Oxenden remarked in Bombay's first days as an English colony, 'story tells us, Rome was not built in a day'.[84]

The late seventeenth century Company was indeed attempting to build a sort of Rome—or at least a form of polity—which, though by no means predetermined or unchanged by eighteenth century events, certainly made them possible and conditioned their trajectory. In some cases, the seventeenth century institutional and legal precedents fed the structures that informed eighteenth century expansion. At the same time, those early modern institutions and behaviours, like the Mayor's Court, became the very object of critique and 'reform' that underpinned parliamentary intervention into the Company's affairs. Despite inevitable contingencies and disjuntures, such an observation makes it increasingly difficult to continue to keep the seventeenth century

Company on the fringes, either of European overseas activity or of the historiography of the development of British Empire in India. For a long time before its acquisition of territorial power in Bengal and its military expansion in southern and western India, the Company had made vigilant and consistent arguments about the nature of its jurisdiction, rooted in the European law of nations but always recognizing Asia as a specific and unique concern. Its leaders and lawyers were preoccupied with principles of just and effective *governance* founded upon ideologies of civic responsibility and political economy, and informed by a responsibility to govern not only over trade but over people. In return, Company leaders expected political obedience and deference to hierarchy, and attempted to foster such values through typically early modern civic republican institutions such as the militia and office holding. It was also a polity, contrary to the assumptions historians make about what companies—especially the East India Company— 'do', deeply concerned on a number of levels with the protection of Protestantism and even its expansion.

Still, our thinking about overseas commercial expansion, amongst other aspects of early modern politics, is overburdened by prolepsis and by the need to see clear political hierarchies, with the national state at its apex. Diversions from that hierarchy are defined as outliers, anomalies, or rogue elements. In an eighteenth century South Asia marked by diffuse and fragmented sovereignty, the political system the Company had established in the seventeenth century could thrive; indeed, it was an eventuality which Company leaders had consciously evaluated and for which they had prepared. However, in Europe, its fate was to be entirely different. It was an age in which fragmented sovereignty was increasingly unacceptable and even unthinkable. As the British multiple monarchy itself gave way, first in 1707 to the Anglo-Scottish union and again in 1801 with the incorporation of Ireland, early modern politics only seemed like chaos. As Alexander Murphy has argued, 'the growing ability of state rulers in western and central Europe to exert control over their realms was the principal political-geographic story of the seventeenth and early eighteenth centuries'.[85]

It was against the backdrop of this larger, more world-historical process of state formation—rather than the 'reform' of a commercial company run amuck—that the East India Company conquered parts of India *and* the British state and Empire conquered the East India Company. Beginning with enquiries into the Company's affairs in the 1690s, and certainly accelerating after Plassey and the diwani, it took the British state over a century to erode the Company's corporate independence. Not until the 1813 charter renewal did the British state truly succeed in demoting the Company's sovereignty in India itself. And even this was a process that was not in fact even technically completed until 1858, when British India was annexed to the Crown's dominions. By that point, the Company was but a shell of its former self and had become an anachronism; its abolition and reconstitution as a 'supervisory council' to the Government of India, Henry Maine noted, was 'a re-baptism of the East India Company...[that] might perhaps mitigate the gross ignorance which is plainly attributable in part to the retention of a historical nomenclature'.[86]

Eventually, however, the sort of modern national sovereignty that swallowed up the East India Company was imposed on the Indian empire itself. As early as the eighteenth century, the writing was on the wall. In 1767, English legal opinion had come to hold that the Company had no right to tax anyone at its settlements that were not their servants, without their own or Parliament's consent.[87] In 1798, the Company's conquest of Ceylon from the Dutch was deemed to be a Crown, not a Company possession, by virtue of its acquisition in war from a European power.[88] By 1800, the Company flew only the Union Flag at its settlements, no longer the Company's flag or the St George Cross.[89] In 1824, the Company finally lost a battle with the Admiralty that had started as early as 1674; the Court of Directors noted in their minutes that they had been forbidden from wearing any but the red ensign, that is the merchant colours, not the Company jack and ensign.[90] In 1835, St Helena was taken away from the Company and made a Crown colony. In the same year, the first Company coin to bear an *image* of a British monarch (the 'William IV' rupee, designed by James Prinsep) was struck, as well as the last Company coin minted in Persian in the name of a Mughal emperor. English also replaced Persian as the official language of government.[91] This move away from fragmented and overlapping forms of authority came most notably under the administration of Governor General Dalhousie (1848–56), in particular in the Company's efforts to annex a number of surviving subsidiary successor states, most notably with the annexation of Awadh in 1856. The rebellion of 1857 can be seen, in part, as a consequence of the stresses placed not just on the military and the peasantry, but on the very form of state governance that was rapidly being introduced. Moreover, with the abolition of the East India Company in 1858 and the imposition of direct Crown rule upon India, Britain effected a fundamental shift in the nature of state and colonial sovereignty. With the Imperial *durbar* and the proclamation of Victoria as Empress of India in 1877, Britain 'imported the notion of unitary sovereignty from post-Enlightenment Europe into colonial India to replace pre-colonial India's view of layered and shared sovereignty'.[92]

Thus, what Edmund Burke and others in late eighteenth century Britain found so mystifying—a body that could be subject to both the 'dual sovereignty' of the Mughal and the British Crowns, while also seeming to defend its own autonomy and act according its own objectives—was not a novelty, but rather increasingly an anachronism. The Company had not been a body of 'mere traders, ignorant of general politics' having to deal with an 'empire which had strangely become subject to them'.[93] Indeed, it had been a form of sovereign—in the very incomplete, overlapping, and fragmented way typical of early modern corporate politics—all along. Yet, by the dawn of the modern period, such composite forms of sovereignty were increasingly unthinkable, as all the 'competitors' to the early modern state—from enclaved states and even the Catholic Church to the crew of non-state agents that had dominated, or at least complicated, early modern international politics, such as pirates, privateers, and mercenaries—lost their political viability in the face of national, territorial, and unitary forms of sovereignty.[94] Seen in this light, it seems possible to imagine that it was a political process and our modern historiographical assumptions about companies and states that managed to look back on the birth of British India and see an anomaly. That is to say, the East India Company-state that contemporaries saw—and historians have seen since—as emerging from the fringes in the mid-eighteenth century may have actually been there, hiding in plain sight, all along.

NOTES AND REFERENCES

1. Bombay Council to East India Company Court of Committees, London (herinafter EIC), 16 April 1698, India Office Records, Oriental and India Office Collections, British Library, London (herinafter IOR), E/3/54 f. 9.
2. Surat Consultations, 10 March 1682/3, IOR G/36/5 f. 19.
3. EIC to Bengal, 20 December 1699, IOR E/3/93 f. 255; EIC to Nathaniel Higginson, 28 January 1697–8, IOR E/3/93 f. 20.
4. Muzaffar Alam and Sanjay Subrahmanyam, 1998, 'Introduction', in Muzaffar Alam and Sanjay Subrahmanyam (eds), *The Mughal State 1526–1750*, New Delhi: Oxford University Press, p. 70.
5. See, amongst many others, Muzaffar Alam, 1986, *The Crisis of Empire in Mughal North India: Awadh and the Punjab 1704–48*, New York: Oxford University Press; Richard Barnett, 1980, *North India Between Empires: Awadh, the Mughals, and the British 1720–1801*, Berkeley: University of California; Kate

Brittlebank, 1997, *Tipu Sultan's Search for Legitimacy: Islam and Kingship in a Hindu Domain*, New Delhi: Oxford University Press; Bernard S. Cohn, 1962, 'Political Systems in Eighteenth Century India: The Banaras Region', *Journal of the American Oriental Society*, vol. 82, pp. 312–19; Stewart Gordon, 1998, 'Legitimacy and Loyalty in Some Successor States of the Eighteenth Century', in John Richards (ed.), *Kingship and Authority in South Asia*, New Delhi: Oxford University Press, pp. 286–303; Stewart Gordon and John Richards, 1994, 'Kinship and Pargana in Eighteenth-Century Khandesh', in Stewart Gordon (ed.), *Marathas, Marauders, and State Formation in Eighteenth-Century India*, New Delhi: Oxford University Press, pp. 371–97; Norbert Peabody, 2002, *Hindu Kingship and Polity in Precolonial India*, Cambridge: Cambridge University Press; Andre Wink, 1986, *Land and Sovereignty in India: Agrarian Society and Politics under the Eighteenth-Century Maratha Svarajya*, Cambridge: Cambridge University Press.

6. For a typical and influential nineteenth century articulation of this interpretation, see W.W. Hunter, 1886, *The Indian Empire: Its People, History, and Products*, London: Trubner & Co., reprinted, 2005, New Delhi: Asian Educational Services, p. 312.

7. Sugata Bose and Ayesha Jalal, 2004, *Modern South Asia: History, Culture, Political Economy*, 2nd edn, New York: Routledge, p. 38.

8. For example, Peter Marshall, 1998, 'Western Arms in Maritime Asia in the Early Phases of Expansion', in Patrick Tuck (ed.), *Warfare, Expansion and Resistance*, London and New York: Routledge, p. 140.

9. See Robert Travers, 2007, 'The Eighteenth Century in Indian History', *Eighteenth-Century Studies*, 40 (3), pp. 492–508. For two excellent and emblematic anthologies, see P.J. Marshall (ed.), 2003, *The Eighteenth Century in Indian History: Evolution or Revolution?* New Delhi: Oxford University Press; and Seema Alavi (ed.), 2002, *The Eighteenth Century in India*, New Delhi: Oxford University Press.

10. Travers, 'The Eighteenth Century in Indian History', pp. 493–5.

11. See, for example, C.A. Bayly, 1996, *Indian Society and the Making of the British Empire*, Cambridge: Cambridge University Press and C.A. Bayly, 1996, *Empire and Information: Intelligence Gathering and Social Communication in India, 1780–1870*, Cambridge: Cambridge University Press.

12. Ranajit Guha, 1997, *Dominance Without Hegemony: History and Power in Colonial India*, Cambridge, MA: Harvard University Press, p. xii.

13. P.J. Marshall, 2003, 'Introduction', in Marshall (ed.), *The Eighteenth Century in Indian History* New Delhi: Oxford University Press, p. 34.

14. Nicholas B. Dirks, 2001, *Castes of Mind: Colonialism and the Making of Modern India*, Princeton: Princeton University Press, p. 311.

15. Seema Alavi, 2002, 'Introduction', in Alavi (ed.), *The Eighteenth Century in India*, p. 36.

16. Kumkum Chatterjee, 1996, *Merchants, Politics and Society in Early Modern India: Bihar, 1733–1820*, New York: Brill; Sudipta Sen, 1998, *Empire of Free Trade: The East India Company and the Making of the Colonial Marketplace*, Philadelphia: University of Pennsylvania. For arguments on the links between

private trade and the coming of empire, see I. Bruce Watson, 1980, *Foundation for Empire: English Private Trade in India 1659–1760*, New Delhi: Vikas; P.J. Marshall, 1976, *East Indian Fortunes: The British in Bengal in the Eighteenth Century*, Oxford: Clarendon Press.

17. William Pinch, 1999, 'Same Difference in India and Europe', *History and Theory*, 38 (3), p. 403.

18. Kenneth McPherson, 1998, *The Indian Ocean: A History of People and the Sea*, Oxford: Oxford University Press, p. 5, as reprinted in Sanjay Subrahmanyam (ed.), 2004, *Maritime India*, New Delhi: Oxford University Press. Compare with, Niels Steensgaard, 1975, *The Asian Trade Revolution of the Seventeenth Century*, Chicago: University of Chicago.

19. Holden Furber, 1976, *Rival Empires of Trade in the Orient, 1600–1800*, Minneapolis: University of Minnesota, p. 336, as reprinted in Subrahmanyam (ed.), 2004, *Maritime India*, New Delhi: Oxford University Press.

20. K.N. Chaudhuri, 1981, 'The English East India Company in the 17th and 18th Centuries: A Pre-Modern Multinational Organization', in Leonard Blussé and Femme Gaastra (eds), *Companies and Trade*, The Hague: Leiden University Press. See also K.N. Chaudhuri, 1965, *The English East India Company: The Study of an Early Joint-Stock Company, 1600–1640*, London: F. Cass; Ann M. Carlos and Stephen Nicholas, 1988, 'Giants of an Earlier Capitalism: The Chartered Companies as Modern Multinationals', *Business History Review*, vol. 62, pp. 398–419; Nick Robins, 2006, *The Corporation that Changed the World: How the East India Company Shaped the Modern Multinational*, London: Pluto Press.

21. Adam Smith, 1776, *An Inquiry into the Nature and Causes of the Wealth of Nations*, London, vol. 2, bk. 4, p. 479.

22. See, amongst others, H.V. Bowen, 1991, *Revenue and Reform: The Indian Problem in British Politics 1757–1773*, Cambridge: Cambridge University Press.

23. Sudipta Sen, 2002, *Distant Sovereignty: National Imperialism and the Origins of British India*, New York: Routledge, p. 6.

24. Robert Travers, 2007, *Ideology and Empire in Eighteenth-Century India: The British in Bengal 1757–1793*, Cambridge: Cambridge University Press, p. 4, n.13.

25. For fuller articulations of this argument, see Philip J. Stern, 2008, ' "A Politie of Civill & Military Power": Political Thought and the Late Seventeenth-Century Foundations of the East India Company-State', *Journal of British Studies*, vol. 47 (April), pp. 253–83; Philip J. Stern, 2007, 'Politics and Ideology in the Early East India Company-State: The Case of St Helena, 1673–1709', *The Journal of Imperial and Commonwealth History*, 35 (1), pp. 1–23.

26. Sugata Bose, 2006, *A Hundred Horizons: The Indian Ocean in the Age of Global Empire*, Cambridge, MA: Harvard University Press, p. 70.

27. Stern, 'Politie of Civill & Military Power', p. 264.

28. Ibid, p. 267.

29. EIC to Bombay, 28 September 1687, IOR E/3/91 f. 196.

30. EIC to FSG, 20 July 1683, IOR E/3/90 f. 87.

31. EIC to FSG, 22 January 1691/2, IOR E/3/92 f. 172–3.

32. EIC to FSG, 22 January 1691/2, IOR E/3/92 f. 171.
33. Surat to John Gayer, 30 October 1695, IOR G/3/22 f. 13; Stern, 'Politie of Civill & Military Power', p. 254.
34. John Keay, 2000, *India: A History*, London: Harper Collins, p. 375.
35. Lakshmi Subramanian, 1998, 'Power and the Weave: Weavers, Merchants and Rulers in Eighteenth-Century Surat', in Rudrangshu Mukherjee and Lakshmi Subramanian (eds), *Politics and Trade in the Indian Ocean World: Essays in Honour of Ashin Das Gupta*, New Delhi: Oxford University Press, pp. 411–47; G.Z. Refai, 1977, 'Sir George Oxinden and Bombay, 1662–1669', *The English Historical Review*, vol. 92 , p. 575.
36. EIC to Bombay, 14 July 1686, IOR E/3/91 f. 79.
37. EIC to Bombay, 3 August 1687, IOR E/3/91 f. 161.
38. 1692 'William & Mary' silver rupee, British Museum, Coin Department, 1986–9–31–1; F. Pridmore, 1975, *The Coins of the British Commonwealth of Nations to the End of the Reign of George VI 1952: Part 4 India, Volume 1 East India Company Presidency Series c1642–1835*, London: Spink & Son, p. 108.
39. Fort St David Consultations, 5 March 1695/6, in *Records of Fort St. George: Fort St. David Consultations, 1696* (1935, Madras: Madras Record Office), p. 27.
40. Pridmore, *Coins*, pp. 58–9, 65; R. Kemal, 1957, 'The Evolution of British Sovereignty in India', *The Indian Year Book of International Affairs*, vol. 6, p. 147.
41. Bombay Consultations, 24 April 1705, IOR P/341/2, p. 175.
42. Surat to Bombay, 23 March 1675/6, in George W. Forrest (ed.), 1887, *Selections from the Letters, Despatches, and Other State Papers Preserved in the Bombay Secretariat*, 2 vols, Bombay: Government Central Press, pp. 83–5; Pridmore, *Coins*, pp. 148, 156–7, 166.
43. John S. Deyell and R.E. Frykenberg, 1982, 'Sovereignty and the "SIKKA" under Company Raj: Minting Prerogative and Imperial Legitimacy in India', *The Indian Economic and Social History Review*, 19 (1), p. 13.
44. Pridmore, *Coins*, p. 4.
45. EIC to FSG, 9 June 1686, IOR E/3/91 f. 70; EIC to FSG, 7 January 1686/7, IOR E/3/91 f. 122.
46. EIC to Bombay, 13 May 1687, IOR E/3/91 f. 149.
47. EIC to Bombay, 18 February 1688/9, IOR E/3/92 f. 11. Emphasis added.
48. Deyell and Frykenberg, 'Sovereignty and the "SIKKA"', pp. 13–15.
49. Court of Committees to St Helena, 3 August 1687, IOR E/3/91 f. 181. Extract of Court of Committees to St Helena, 5 May 1708, British Library, Manuscripts Department, Add. MS 20240 f. 3.
50. Court of Committees to FSG, 26 January 1697/8, IOR E/3/93 f. 16.
51. Court of Committees to FSG, 14 January 1685/6, IOR E/3/91 f. 17.
52. Edward Keene, 2002, *Beyond the Anarchical Society: Grotius, Colonialism and Order in World Politics*, Cambridge: Cambridge University Press, pp. 76–92.
53. A close, but brief, attempt at this is C.A. Bayly, 1994, 'The British Military-Fiscal State and Indigenous Resistance: India 1750–1820', in Lawrence Stone (ed.), *An Imperial State at War: Britain from 1689 to 1815*, London and New York: Routledge, pp. 322–54.

54. Marshall, *East Indian Fortunes*, p. 9; Henry Davison Love, 1913, *Vestiges of Old Madras 1640–1800, Traced from the East India Company's Records Preserved at Fort St George and the India Office, and from Other Sources*, 3 vols, London: John Murray reprinted 1968, New York: AMS Press, vol. I, pp. 390–400.
55. C.H. Philips, 1940, 'The Secret Committee of the East India Company', *Bulletin of the School of Oriental Studies*, 10 (2), pp. 299–315; H. Philips, 1940, 'II. The Secret Committee of the East India Company, 1784–1858', *Bulletin of the School of Oriental Studies*, 10 (3), pp. 699–716.
56. See Jame Thomas, 1999, *The East India Company and the Provinces in the Eighteenth Century, Volume I: Portsmouth and the East India Company 1700–1815*, Lewiston, NY, Queenston, Ontario, and Lampeter, Wales: Edwin Mellon Press, chapter 2.
57. Frank Conlon, 1985, 'Functions of Ethnicity in a Colonial Port City: British Initiatives and Policies in Early Bombay', in Dilip K. Basu (ed.), *The Rise and Growth of the Colonial Port Cities in Asia*, Berkeley: Center for South and Southeast Asia Studies, University of California, pp. 52, 67–8; Furber, *Rival Empires*, p. 93.
58. C.A. Bayly, 1993, 'Knowing the Country: Empire and Information in India', *Modern Asian Studies*, vol. 27, pp. 6–7; Bayly, *Empire and Information*.
59. Sir Courtenay Ilbert, 1915, *The Government of India Being a Digest of the Statute Law Relating Thereto, With Historical Introduction and Explanatory Matter*, 3rd edn, Oxford: Clarendon Press, pp. 1–26.
60. Bowen, *Revenue and Reform*, p. 9.
61. Sir Charles Fawcett, 1979, *The First Century of British Justice in India*, Oxford: Clarendon Press, reprinted 1979, Aalen: Scientia Verlag, p. 57. The committees had even contemplated the incorporation of Bombay as early as 1688 (EIC to Bombay, 6 January 1687/8, IOR E/3/91 f. 249).
62. H.J. Leue, 1992, 'Legal Expansion in the Age of the Companies: Aspects of the Administration of Justice in the English and Dutch Settlements of Maritime Asia, c. 1600–1750', in W.J. Mommsen and J.A. de Moor (eds), *European Expansion and Law: The Encounter of European and Indigenous Law in Nineteenth and Twentieth-Century Africa and Asia*, Oxford and New York: Berg, pp. 132–3. Cf. Tarit Kumar Mukherji, 1999, 'Aldermen and Attorneys: Mayor's Court, Calcutta', in A.J.R. Russell-Wood (ed.), *Local Government in European Overseas Empires, 1450–1800*, Aldershot: Ashgate, pp. 501–16.
63. EIC to Nathaniel Higginson, 28 January 1697/8, IOR E/3/93 f. 20.
64. Surat to EIC, 10 October 1702, E/3/70 no. 8630.
65. Stephen Saunders Webb, 1979, *Governors-General: The English Army and the Definition of the Empire, 1529–1681*, Chapel Hill: University of North Carolina Press, p. 5; Stephen Saunders Webb, 1977, 'Army and Empire: English Garrison Government in Britain and America, 1569–1763', *William and Mary Quarterly*, vol. 34, pp. 1–31.
66. Douglas Peers, 1995, *Between Mars and Mammon: Colonial Armies and the Garrison State in India, 1819–1835*, London: I.B. Tauris.
67. In January 1702, both East India Companies obtained from the king a homeward convoy from the Cape and St Helena of six 50 gun ships of war. East Indiamen

received nine separate commissions to seize pirates between 1709 and 1716, and by 1715, it Court of Directors had resolved that all outward bound ships carry commissions for seizing pirates. The practice was still going on in the middle of the century: between 1748 and 1755, the Company requested 21 commissions for seizing pirates. Within a couple of years of both the accession of George I and George II, the Company sought to have the commissions for trying pirates at Madras and Bombay renewed, and under each monarch, the Piracy Statute of 1699 was revised and updated, notably to make the law treat accessories to piracy as equal to pirates themselves. Privy Council Register, 8 January 1701/02, PRO PC 2/78 f. 295; PRO CO/77/16 f. 158–62; Minutes of the Court of Directors, 28 October 1715, B/53 f. 471; IOR H/93 f. 1, 2, 4, 5, 9, 81, 141, 199, 219, 288, 289; See Minutes of the Court of Directors, 18 December 1717, 8 and 15 January 1717/8, IOR B/54 f. 528, 548, 554; Warrant for a Bill to try Pirates in Madras, 8 March 1731/2, BL Add. MS 36130 f. 37–41 (Warrant for Bengal on f. 43–8 and for Bombay on f. 49–53); 11/12 William III c.7 (1698–9); 4 Geo I c.2/c.11 s.7 (1717–18); 8 Geo I c.24 (1721–2); 18 Geo II c.30 (1744–5). On the accessories omission, see Privy Council Register, 16 May 1700, PRO PC 2/78 f. 28–9.

68. Arne Bialuschewski, 2001, 'The Golden Age of Piracy, 1695–1725: A Reassessment', in Luc François and Ann Katherine Isaacs (eds), *The Sea in European History*, Pisa: Edizioni Plus, Università di Pisa, p. 234; Robert C. Ritchie, 1986, *Pirates: Myths and Realities*, Minneapolis: James Ford Bell Library, pp. 18–19.

69 . John Keay, 1992, *The Honourable Company: A History of the English East India Company*, London: Harper Collins, pp. 259–62.

70. Bombay Consultations, 18 September 1703, IOR G/3/5 bk v, f. 10.

71. See Bombay to EIC, 6 January 1699/1700, IOR G/3/17 f. 2.

72. Patricia Risso, 2001, 'Cross-Cultural Perceptions of Piracy: Maritime Violence in the Western Indian Ocean and Persian Gulf Region during a Long Eighteenth Century', *Journal of World History*, vol. 12, p. 293. For a more traditional interpretation, see Keay, *Honourable Company*, pp. 255–70. Keay's notion that Kanhoji was more legitimate than a pirate, however, rests upon his troublesome, absolute claim that although 'the Marathas were not...pirates...[although] Native pirates certainly existed'. Keay, *Honourable Company*, p. 255.

73. Richard Bourchier to Robert Orme, 11 July 1763, EurMSS/Orme/India.III, f.774; Keay, *Honourable Company*, pp. 265–9; Anonymous, 1795, *The Arabian Pirate, or Authentic History and Fighting Adventures of Tulagee Angria*, Newcastle: G. Angus.

74. Risso, 'Cross-Cultural Perceptions of Piracy', p. 309; Ashin Das Gupta, 1987, 'India and the Indian Ocean in the Eighteenth Century', in Uma Das Gupta (ed.), *The World of the Indian Ocean Merchant 1500–1800: The Collected Essays of Ashin Das Gupta*, Oxford: Oxford University Press, p. 200.

75. Muhammad Al-Qasimi, 1986, *The Myth of Arab Piracy in the Gulf*, London, Sydney and Dover, NH: Croom Helm; Risso, 'Cross-Cultural Perceptions of Piracy', pp. 308–16.

76. John Richards, 1975, 'European City-States on the Coromandel Coast', in P.M. Joshi (ed.), *Studies in the Foreign Relations of India*, Hyderabad: Andhra Pradesh State Archives, p. 516.

77. Philip Lawson, 1993, *The East India Company: A History*, London and New York: Longman, pp. 50–1.

78. Bruce Lenman, 1987, 'The East India Company and the Emperor Aurangzeb', *History Today*, 37(2), p. 29.

79. EIC to Elihu Yale, 12 December 1687, IOR E/3/91 f. 231.

80. See Etrait des Articles du Projet de Neutralité, nd (May 1753), IOR H/93 f. 110–11; EIC Secret Committee to the Earl of Holdernesse, 18 July 1754, IOR H/93 f. 113–16; 'The Copy referred to in the before going letter', nd, IOR H/93 f. 116–20; Earl of Albermarle to Earl of Holdernesse (marked seceret), 23 January 1754, BL Add. MS 32848 f. 101–3; Earl of Holdernesse to Earl of Albermarle, 24 January 1754, BL Add. MS 32848 f. 114–20.

81. Fort William to Charles Watson, 14 January 1757, IOR H/94 f. 364.

82. Extract of a letter from George Pigot, 2 March 1756, IOR H/94 f. 77–80.

83. Ibid. Keay, *Honourable Company*, p. 340.

84. Oxenden to William Rider, 30 December 1665, BL Add. MS 40707 f. 8 quoted by Refai, 'George Oxinden', p. 578.

85. Alexander Murphy, 1996, 'The Sovereign State as Political-Territorial Ideal: Historical and Contemporary Considerations', in Thomas Biersteker and Cynthia Weber (eds), *State Sovereignty as Social Construct*, New York: Cambridge University Press, p. 93.

86. Quoted by Timothy L. Alborn, 1998, *Conceiving Companies: Joint-Stock Politics in Victorian England*, London and New York: Routledge, p. 49.

87. Opinion of Sayer on Recall of Military Officers and Residents in India also assessing Inhabitants of Calcutta, 12 October 1767, Emphasis IOR L/L/6/1 f. 145–7.

88. Opinion of G. Rous on government at Ceylon, 25 January 1798, IOR L/L/6/1 f. 611–12.

89. This was raised as an issue as the Union flag underwent revision in anticipation of the Union with Ireland in 1801. See John Meheux to William Ramsay, 12 November 1800, IOR H/67 f. 140; Ramsay to Meheux, 12 November 1800, IOR H/67 f. 141; Meheux to Ramsay, 13 November 1800, IOR H/67 f. 153.

90. Sir Charles Fawcett, 1937, 'The Striped Flag of the East India Company and its Connexion with the American "Stars and Stripes"', *The Mariner's Mirror*, vol. 23, pp. 449–76.

91. The Company's coinage with Mughal iconography in fact ceased much later than in other Mughal successor states. Jonathan Williams, Joe Cribb, and Elizabeth Errington, 1997, *Money: A History*, New York: St Martin's Press, pp. 108–10; John S. Deyell, and R.E. Frykenberg, 1982, 'Sovereignty and the "Sikka" under the Raj: Minting Prerogative and Imperial Legitimacy in India', *The Indian Economic and Social History Review*, XIX (1), pp. 15–17; Brittlebank, *Tipu Sultan's Search for Legitimacy*, p. 65ff.

92. Bose and Jalal, *Modern South Asia*, p. 103.

93. Thomas Babington Macaulay, 1884, 'Lord Clive', (1840) in *Critical and Historical Essays contributed to 'The Edinburgh Review'*, London: Longmans, Green and Co., p. 526.

94. See, amongst others, Hendrik Spruyt, 1994, *The Sovereign State and its Competitors: An Analysis of Systems Change*, Princeton: Princeton University Press; Janice Thomson, 1994, *Mercenaries, Pirates, and Sovereigns: State-Building and Extraterritorial Violence in Early Modern Europe*, Princeton: Princeton University Press, pp. 7–42; Charles Tilly, 1975, 'Reflections on the History of European State-Making', in Charles Tilly (ed.), *The Formation of National States in Western Europe*, Princeton: Princeton University Press, pp. 21–5; Graeme Gill, 2003, *The Nature and Development of the Modern State*, Houndmills: Palgrave Macmillan, pp. 73–114.

Pirates and Settlers

Economic Interactions on the Margins of Empire

Pirates are one group in a range of characters inhabiting the fringes of empire whose activities are generally seen as antithetical to and obstructive of colonial state development. In practice, the role of pirates was more complex than this stereotypical appraisal suggests. At a time when European powers were vying for control of key territories in India, and had yet to establish fortified colonies along the Indian Ocean trade routes, the activities of pirates, while initially a source of harassment and irritation to settler communities, were often also harnessed to further the development of embryonic colonial states. This essay provides an overview of the activities of the European pirates who invaded the Indian Ocean in the late seventeenth and early eighteenth centuries, and describes their pirate haunts on the southwest islands, and the interactions which took place between pirate visitors and settlers on these sparsely populated outposts and watering holes of the Dutch and French en route to and from the Indies. The essay reveals the various roles of this group of marginal men who, taking advantage of the vulnerability of frontier societies, were able to move rapidly from the status of outlaws to positions of respectability and responsibility in their adopted territories when they chose to do so.

PIRACY: THE EVOLUTION AND DEFINITION OF SEA BANDITRY

Frenchmen from Normandy and Brittany were among the first of the northern maritime nations to plunder Spanish argosies returning from the New World. They were known as corsairs. Increasingly, such individuals sailed under royal commission and legal protection. They carried 'letters of marque', authorizing them to capture vessels belonging to hostile nations and became known as privateers. However, the encouragement of privateering at times of war could spell trouble in periods of peace, when men who had become accustomed to the thrills and profits of privateering might be tempted into plunder for its own sake. Thus it was that scores of disaffected soldiers and sailors, or ill-treated indentured servants, became renegades, settling on deserted islands and secluded coasts. Buccaneering in the Caribbean is conventionally dated from about 1640, when bands of rovers from the recently settled British and French islands in the outer Antilles established themselves in locations along Spanish trade routes where they could obtain supplies in between hijackings. The term buccaneer evolved after their method of smoking or 'boucaner' the hogs and cattle which they sold to passing ships.[1]

The distinction between authorized privateers and the outlaws of the sea who were called pirates frequently depended on one's perspective. English privateers, even as distinguished a man as Francis Drake, would have been considered pirates by the Spanish and vice versa. Notorious pirates often started their careers as privateers and attempted to disguise their piracy by claiming only to capture foreign ships. Piracy became a particular problem after 1603, when 50 years of Anglo-Spanish fighting ended, and again after 1713 when the Peace of Utrecht was signed and 40,000 Royal Navy sailors were discharged. Commenting on the cycle of lawlessness which followed, Starkey describes its 'epicentre' as being the Caribbean, with 'tremors' felt as far away as West Africa and the Indian Ocean, with up to 5,000 men engaged in freebooting, a wave marked by 'an anarchic, anti-authoritarian strain'.[2]

PIRACY IN THE CARIBBEAN

Once Spanish, Portuguese, and Italian navigators had charted routes to the New World in the second half of the fifteenth century, trade in exotic products and slaves became highly profitable. Over the course of the sixteenth century, the Spanish carried home the equivalent of three times the total European stock of gold and silver. And where treasure ships sailed, pirates and privateers inevitably followed.

By the seventeenth century, Spanish domination was being challenged in the New World as English, French, and Dutch settlers also established themselves in the Caribbean, from where they could launch raids against the rich port towns of the Spanish Main. Thus these embryonic colonies spawned the buccaneers—frequently men who had escaped from religious persecution at home, and forced labour on ships and plantations overseas—to become the feared flibustiers or freebooters of the West Indies.

The attitude of local governors to the presence and activities of privateers was ambivalent. They could provide a welcome source of defence to counteract the raids and threats of hostile nations. At the same time, encouragement of privateers often simply served to escalate attacks and counter-attacks which troubled sea-borne trade in the region, while raising an army of plunderers could prove doubly counter-productive when some of their number turned to piracy, and began to attack their own side. In practice, Caribbean officials vacillated between reeling in pirates with pardons or pursuing them relentlessly with the aid of naval squadrons.

The numerous isles and islets of the Caribbean thus provided refuges and safe havens for the flotsam and jetsam of humanity—runaway sailors and apprentices, adventurers, and exiles—who washed up on its shores. Small uninhabited islands with secluded coves made ideal hideouts for pirates who would lie in wait for passing merchant ships and stop to refit, careen their ships, and take on water between voyages of plunder. Pirate safe havens were essentially sheltered natural harbours, preferably well fortified with cannon, where warehouses and taverns were established for the trading of booty and the spending of loot, where carpenters were on hand to repair ships, and medical help available to the casualties of boarding parties and pitched battles on the high seas.

The northern coast of Hispaniola (present day Haiti and St Domingue), was occupied by buccaneers from the early seventeenth century. Following the takeover of Jamaica by the English many buccaneers were encouraged to bring their prizes to Port Royal, which rapidly developed into the Caribbean's premier safe haven for free booters. Port Royal's nemesis came on 7 June 1692 when part of the city collapsed into the sea as the result of a massive earthquake. The island of New Providence in the Bahamas (modern day Nassau), achieved notoriety in the early eighteenth century as a base for pirates.[3]

Royal Navy cruisers found it difficult to flush out the pirates from their New Providence lair, and accordingly it was left to a consortium of London merchants to take the Bahamas in hand. Leasing the islands from the Crown, they sent out an experienced sea captain and former privateer, Woodes Rogers, to take charge of the island, and declare war on the pirates. Meanwhile, the British government was also waving a flag of truce by offering royal pardons. Several pirates accepted defeat gracefully, but the most notorious left to continue their depredations elsewhere: the Indian Ocean now became a new theatre of pirate activity.

THE 'PIRATE ROUND'

The route used by pirates who travelled from Caribbean bases to the Indian Ocean and the Red Sea to plunder ships, before returning to sell the goods to colonists in North America, became known as the pirate round. Its heyday was the 30-year period between 1690 and 1720.

From 1498 when the Portuguese had sailed into the Indian Ocean and found that local communities had little use for their objects of trade—wool, olive oil, and minerals—the European strategy in the region became one of dominating trade routes by force and attacking local merchant and pilgrim ships. One of the first examples of European piracy in Indian Ocean waters was Thomas Cavendish's taking of a Manila galleon during his circumnavigation of 1586–8.[4]

By the mid-sixteenth century, Spanish and Portuguese domination of trade and empire was being challenged by the English, Dutch, and French; in that race state sponsorship of marauders, and the licensing of pillagers was not uncommon. Thus the early pirates of the Indian Ocean were often men of high station, like Sir Robert Rich, who went into partnership with a Genoese merchant in 1616, and sailed the *Francis* and the *Lion* to the Red Sea, where they attempted to capture a Gujarati ship. Charles I himself commissioned a privateering voyage in the Indian Ocean in 1630. The *Seahorse* had been sent to the Red Sea to capture Spanish ships. However, 'on sighting a heavily laden Indian ship, captain and crew abandoned their plans and snapped up the prize. The East India Company was furious, because the Mughal government held it liable for the ship and its cargo. The company petitioned the king, who heard the complaints, uttered soothing words, and pocketed his share of the profits'.[5] The French also joined in the general mayhem: in 1642 François Cauche and Régimond left their recently established base in Madagascar for the Red Sea in the hope of gaining prizes—they seized two Indian ships with cargoes of cloth, and 200,000 ecus (unit of currency in seventeenth century) in coins. In 1660, Laurent David seized the treasures of the queen mother of Vijapur, off Perim island. François Martin wrote ruefully from India that the French name was synonymous with pirate there at that time.[6]

Thus, between the sixteenth and eighteenth centuries, traders in the Indian Ocean often themselves engaged in piratical acts, as Das Gupta and Pearson have noted:

all countries, whether European or Asian, with subjects in the Indian Ocean area contributed their share to piracy... Asians whose trade was taken from them by local cartels or European monopolies turned to piracy, but many European pirates seem also to have been people frozen out of Asian trade by the monopolies enjoyed by the Dutch and English companies.[7]

Over the course of the seventeenth century, however, as the Dutch, French, and English East India Companies established trading posts known as 'factories' in the region, piracy by officials and merchants gave way to more legitimate forms of trade and marauding became a distinctly renegade activity. Ironically, just as it was becoming increasingly important for European traders to establish proper credentials, their status was undermined by pirates from the Caribbean, who sailed into the Indian Ocean, having realized that the Mughal and Arab vessels trading between India and the Red Sea often carried treasure even more valuable than the Spanish fleets.

The transfer of focus from the Caribbean to the Indian Ocean brought the North American colonies into the 'pirate round'. From New York to North Carolina, merchants profited greatly from purchasing the goods captured, supplying in turn, clothes, guns, food, and medical stocks for the pirates. In 1693, the Lieutenant Governor of Jamaica, Sir William Beeston, warned:

several privateers and pirates have found their way into the Red Sea, where they have committed unheard-of piracies, murders and barbarities. These are now returned with vast wealth to most of the northern plantations in America where they quietly enjoy their ill-gotten riches, but whether with or without the knowledge of the Governments I do not know.[8]

The last phase of pirate activity in the Indian Ocean followed the expulsion of pirates from their Bahamas stronghold in 1717. However, by the mid-1720s, the heyday of piracy was over: the Madagascar-based pirates had either been reclaimed by French and British amnesties, or disappeared back into European and American society; a few unfortunates—scapegoats for the rest—swung on gibbets above the Thames of London.

PIRATE RECRUITS

The typical pirate was an experienced mariner who had been discharged or had deserted from merchant or naval service. Men who had been press-ganged, or who had been embittered by the harsh discipline of shipboard life, might consider escape to the relative egalitarianism of a pirate vessel a preferable option. They might also subsequently enact revenge on fellow mariners or officers who had ill-treated them. Since ex-seamen made up a significant proportion of pirates, their crews tended to be dominated by northern Europeans, but in the Indian Ocean, captured Indians and Africans might also be converted into, or used by pirates.

Despite the popular image of a pirate as a rebel, more men became pirates when the merchant vessels on which they were employed were captured, than had originated as mutineers who seized control of their ships.[9] Recruits were also gleaned from the less fortunate members of colonial society—indentured servants who were condemned to work for low wages in return for their passage out, petty criminals, and adventurers. Above all they attracted men who aspired to earn more than the pittance paid to ordinary workers. As Kevin Rushby has pointed out: 'in 1700 an East India Company man sailing east for 18 months might hope to earn himself £30. In stark contrast are the figures for piratical returns: an average expedition produced a staggering dividend of £50 to £3,000 per man'.[10]

Edward Barlow, a mariner from 1659 to 1703, described how ignorant country folk in London could get tricked into embarking for the colonies. He himself was offered a job on a ship trading in the Caribbean, but his uncle warned him of kidnappers

who used to entice any who they think are country people or strangers...promise them great wages and good fortune at such places as they will help them to: and many times they give them money and entice them along with them to their houses.... And in this manner they would drill them on till they got them aboard of a ship... they cannot get away, not one out of a hundred of them; for they always keep them on board and will not let them come on land, nor send the least note to any of their friends to come and get them clear. And so carrying them to Barbados and to Virginia, and some to Jamaica, sell them for servants for four years.[11]

Darby Mullins of Londonderry had been an indentured servant, dockhand, and tavern keeper in Jamaica before moving to New York where he enlisted on William Kidd's 1696 privateering expedition that subsequently became a pirate cruise in the Indian Ocean. He was hanged on the same day as Captain Kidd.[12]

A considerable number of the men on Indian Ocean pirate ships were black. Christian Tranquebar was on a ship attacked by two vessels commanded by Bartholomew Roberts in 1721 and reported that Roberts' ship was manned by 180 white men and 48 'French Creole blacks'; while his consort was manned by 100 whites and 40 French blacks.[13] Avery and other pirates who captured Indian ships kept the native crews, known as lascars, on board for considerable periods of time. While blacks who became full-fledged pirates might achieve a status equal to their white confrères, in general, the white outlaws were little different from their contemporaries, making use of slaves and lascars for the menial tasks on board their ships, and using their linguistic skills derived from years in Madagascar, not to better the lot of the natives, but frequently to profit from slave trading. Although Rogozinski's recent study projects a romanticized view of the Indian Ocean pirates, asserting that unlike white colonists, 'most pirates accepted the Malagasy as they were...they adopted the Malagasy way of life as much as they could', there is a wealth of other evidence which demonstrates that pirates operating off the coast of Africa routinely took slaves and sold them on along with other goods captured.[14]

THE MODUS OPERANDI OF PIRATES

There was a semblance of hierarchy on board the pirate ship. The most famous of the pirates were usually also the commanders or captains of the ships which they brought into this notorious service. They were assisted by a 'quartermaster' as on a naval vessel. This officer would be responsible for disciplining the crew and, where necessary, could eject a turbulent crew member from the vessel to languish on some lonely shore. However, the fact that the vast majority of pirates were from the lower social classes ensured a more muted hierarchy aboard the ship than was common in the merchant or naval service: pirate captains had fewer privileges than their legitimate counterparts.[15]

Pirate ships tended to be overcrowded, as for fighting purposes they often carried three or four times as many crew as a merchantman. The pirate deckhand would be expected to combine the ability to caulk the boat and repair sails with good fighting skills. The ship's carpenter might also act as surgeon. Once a sufficient crew had been recruited and provisions were aboard, the search could begin for prizes. Men who had risked their all to join a pirate ship were keen to make captures and if a pirate captain showed reluctance to go after a well-armed merchantman, a crew might vote to overthrow him, appointing a more daring leader in his place.

Pirates needed fast, manoeuvrable vessels, and often preferred small sloops and schooners that they had themselves captured and then armed. Occasionally, pirates joined forces to create a fleet of formidable proportions and power. More usually, acting alone or in twos and threes, they relied on surprise, speed, and cunning to pounce on their victims. It was not unheard of for pirates to trick ships into approaching them. They often carried several flags to deceive their victims into thinking they represented friendly nations.

Swooping in on relatively poorly armed merchantmen or pilgrim ships and even defenceless fishing sloops, they used the minimum firepower necessary and all the means at their disposal to terrify opponents: from fearsome flags, to loud screams, and music, such as drum beats. Pirates aimed to subdue their victims quickly and the weapons they used to attack ships were equally designed to cause panic. They fired lethal, anti-personnel shot from their cannons, peppering the decks with sharp, jagged items as diverse as nails and broken crockery.[16]

It was the level of violence used by pirate crews that determined their notoriety. Whilst some pirates treated their victims with relative courtesy, simply holding them until the ship had been looted and then allowing them to depart, others subjected their unfortunate captives to all manner of indignities, humiliations, and occasionally torture in an attempt to ascertain the whereabouts on board of suspected caches of money and valuables. Pirates who had been in naval service might likewise exact revenge on their former superiors or officers known for sadistic disciplining of sailors.

Pirates' bravado in pursuing a ship and in boarding it once within close range was often fuelled by alcohol. If the attack succeeded, the rum and wine found on board a prize was commonly among the first items to be liberally indulged in by the pirates. Much of their loot was generally quickly dissipated in the extravagant prices paid for goods and for the favours of local women at each port of call, and in gambling sprees.

PIRACY IN THE INDIAN OCEAN

By the late seventeenth and early eighteenth centuries marauding had become a worldwide phenomenon, and the conjuncture of European trade and exploration and local political weakness created a particularly fertile hunting ground for pirates in the Indian Ocean in this period. A complex network of shipping lanes had been developed, carrying precious goods to and from the colonies to Europe. Increasingly policed in the Caribbean, the pirates turned their attention to the Indian

Ocean which now promised the greatest prizes. By the 1690s many of the Caribbean pirates were cruising the Red Sea looking for profitable pickings while a ready market for their plunder was found in the North American seaports, chafing under the protectionist policies of their British masters.[17]

European pirates in Indian Ocean waters had a number of options: they could sail northward to lie in wait for the Mughal fleets at the mouth of the Red Sea, turn northeast to raid coastal shipping off India, or intercept European ships stopping for wood and water at the southwestern islands of the Comores, Madagascar, and the Mascarenes. The East Indiamen were heavily armed by 1700 and sailed well out to sea, whilst the pirates preferred to hug the coasts, but three notable captures of merchant ships were made by pirates between 1696 and 1720. However, the easiest pickings of the European pirates were the 20 or so Gujarati ships which sailed each year from Surat to Mocha and Jedda, carrying wealthy Muslim pilgrims and traders. They were notoriously ill-equipped for battle. The pirates targeted, in particular, the returning Indian ships, which, having sold their goods for money were going home from Arabia laden with silver and gold. In the last decades of the seventeenth century these pirate captures caused serious disruption to the trading activities of the English, French, and Dutch factories at Surat and elsewhere in India, subject as they then still were to the whims of Mughal governors. Mughal retribution for attacks on the Red Sea shipping was swift—they locked up the European officers at the Company factories and demanded restitution for lost cargoes. Letters home from the outraged officials demanding an end to the pirate incursions forced the British to take action: American governors who connived at trade with the pirates were recalled, questioned, and removed from office, while the rules governing privateering operations were tightened up.[18]

PIRATE BASES IN THE INDIAN OCEAN

In between cruises pirates needed a safe haven. In the Indian Ocean, they favoured the islands of the southwest, which were situated in the path of the ships trading with India; could provide a source of timber, water, and provisions; and were too sparsely populated with European colonists to provide any serious resistance to the marauders. Madagascar became the chief resort of European pirates, while the islands of Comores, Mauritius, and Bourbon (present day Réunion) were frequently visited by them.[19]

In the late seventeenth century, Madagascar and the Comores were ruled by warring princes, largely outside the influence of European colonizers. The French, driven off Madagascar by hostile natives in 1674, had shifted to the island of Bourbon, while the Dutch, already established at the Cape, had sent a small party of colonists to occupy the neighbouring island of Mauritius. The embryonic Mascarene colonies were in no position to resist the demands of visiting pirate ships, while European commerce to and from the East Indies was severely embarrassed by their attacks. Increasingly aware that the misdemeanours of European pirates had serious repercussions on their own trading posts in the region, the responses of European governments to the issues raised had to take into account the practicalities of life on their tiny settlements in the southwestern Indian Ocean.

The Dutch governors of Mauritius and the French administrators of Bourbon struggled to discipline their colonists who benefited from trading with pirates, while themselves occasionally proving not averse to such dealings, offering amnesties to the marauders and encouraging them to settle. Their ambivalence is typified by local Governor Van der Stel's comments to the home government with regard to dealings of the Dutch in Mauritius with pirates: 'I believe that certainly a profitable trade might be opened with those people on the island, but in what manner is it to be established? It is most unchristian to go hand in hand with robbers'.[20]

PIRATES AND THE MADAGASCAR SLAVE TRADE

Europeans made several attempts to convert Madagascar into a way station on the Indies trade route, but its colonization proved difficult. In the 1640s small settlements established by the English were defeated by drought, disease, and hostile natives. Around the same time, a French colony at Port Dauphin was decimated by a massacre with the rump of the settlers fleeing to India and Bourbon. Visiting Europeans did, however, succeed in exacerbating local conflicts with their arms and slave trading, and paved the way for pirates to win the support of rival princes by engaging themselves as mercenaries for one side or another.

By the close of the seventeenth century, Madagascar, as Ritchie reports, had become the principal base for Indian Ocean pirates. It offered several advantages, having 'neither local merchants nor company servants to interfere with the buccaneers...a number of fine harbors and supplies of beef and rice'.[21] The pirates' skill in the use of firearms brought them friendship from the locals and a supply of slaves to trade with visiting European merchants. Significantly, their knowledge of local conditions and language would render them increasingly valuable intermediaries.[22]

The pirates established a number of settlements on Madagascar but were chiefly located along the stretch of coast from Tamatave to the Bay of Antongil. A few acquired the status and title of petty kings, such as King Samuel of Ranter's Bay (Antongil). Accounts of their numbers and the size and strength of their fortified settlements varied widely, as mariners and travellers posted accounts about them throughout Indian Ocean trade centres. The Cape Dutch informed their home government in 1699 that the pirates had three fortified posts at Madagascar. By 1705 Van der Stel was writing that the Madagascar pirates 'are about 830 strong, or perhaps 1,000. ... It is not certain where they mostly live, as they go from one place to another on the island, when they think that booty can be obtained from ships arriving'.[23]

By all accounts, their time on the Red Island was relatively short. Visiting Cape Town in 1711, Captain Woodes Rogers was informed that the Madagascar pirates were still trading slaves, but were in a pitiful condition: 'those miserable wretches, who had made such a noise in the world, were now dwindled to between sixty or seventy, most of them very poor and despicable, even to the natives among whom they had married'.[24] In 1717, Robert Drury, who had spent more than a decade in Madagascar in a state of slavery himself, reported that only around 20 were left, hoping for an amnesty. These few held on for several more years: in 1719 Captain Lewis noted that two pirates had come aboard his ship at Madagascar, and claimed to each have 500 negro subjects, while in 1727 the Dutch fort on Delagoa Bay was pillaged by English pirates whose base was said to be at Madagascar.[25]

When on shore, the pirates took local wives, established coastal fortifications, and, above all, dealt in slaves. Arthur Gardiner, a pirate based at St Augustine, for example, was reportedly paid £100 by the English slave ship *Eugenie* for his services in 1718. The pirates also undertook slaving voyages themselves around Madagascar and sometimes delivered them over long distances—Bourbon, Barbados, and America. The Abbé Rochon went so far as to credit the Madagascar pirates with introducing the slave trade, but their role may rather be seen as one of having acted as agents in this branch of commerce. Brown believes that it would be wrong to attribute to the pirates major responsibility for the Madagascar slave trade which, he states 'was already flourishing before Madagascar became an important scene of pirate activity'. He also argues convincingly that contemporary accounts of the 'pirate kings' were exaggerated, and that they were simply 'living as princelings or village chiefs in little communities along the north-east coast or some little distance in the interior, owing their position to their martial reputation and their ill-gotten wealth which often enabled them to marry the daughters of Malagasy chiefs'.[26]

THE TRIANGULAR TRADE IN GOODS FROM ST MARY'S ISLAND

It was on St Mary's islet,[27] 10 miles from the northeast coast of Madagascar, that pirates established their largest trading settlement. The British naval captain Thomas Warren heard in 1697 that here the pirates 'have built a regular fortification of forty or fifty guns. They have about 1,500 men, with seventeen sail of vessels, sloops and ships, some of which carry forty guns. They are furnished from New York, New England and the West Indies with stores and other necessaries'.[28]

Rogozinski has stressed the importance of St Mary's in the history of Indian Ocean piracy, stating that it was from here that the richest pirate cruises set out:

Henry Every in 1695 captured an Indian warship carrying gold and gems with a value of $200 million in modern currency. Three years later, the crews of the *Soldado* and *Mocha* split $65 million in cash taken from the *Great Mahomet*. At the mouth of the Red Sea in 1700, John Bowen and his men shared out $50 million from another Indian vessel. In 1721, John Taylor and Oliver La Buse took a Portuguese carrack with diamonds, gold, and cargo worth more than $400 million.[29]

While the significance of the settlement as a 'pirate colony' is questionable—Ritchie has concluded that it was probably 'a ramshackle affair [consisting] of a few houses, a low palisade, and a couple of cannon'—it is certainly the case that pirates conducted a thriving trade from the islet.[30]

It was from St Mary's, where he arrived in 1691, that Adam Baldridge, believed to have formerly been a pirate in the Caribbean, set up a lucrative trade with New York merchant Frederick Philipse, supplying slaves and luxury items looted by pirates from the pilgrim ships and the Indiamen in return for clothes, alcohol, and other necessities demanded by the marauders when they returned from their cruises. In 1697, Malagasies— who did not appreciate the indiscriminate slave raids conducted by pirates—attacked the post, killing several men and destroying stores. Baldridge survived to return to America where he supplied a detailed account of his trading activities with the pirates. He was replaced at St

Mary's by Edward Welsh; in 1699 Dutch skipper Jan Coin provided an eye-witness account of continuing pirate activities on the islet:

various Europeans live there and drive a big trade with the ships coming from New York or New Netherland, New England and the Bermudas.... There is no fort on the island, but about forty-five or fifty guns lie scattered about on the ground. In this harbour lie various wrecks of pirate ships and of the Moorish prizes captured by them.[31]

The Comores: Banditry and Barter

As in Madagascar those European pirates and mariners who were prepared to lend a hand in warfare between the islands of Mohilla and Anjouan were welcomed by their inhabitants, and rewarded in the usual way, with the favours of local women and privileged trading facilities. However, relations with the inhabitants of the Comores were not always cordial. Pirates were not above making hostile visits to the islands: in 1701, the pirate Nathaniel North is reputed to have caused the evacuation of the inhabitants of Grande Comore, where he attacked the house of the local sultan and destroyed crops and cattle, before making off with bales of cloth and silver jewellery.

More usually, however, pirates simply used the islands—as did passing European ships—as a convenient lay-by to repair and careen their vessels, and to barter for food with the natives. William Kidd is supposed to have made a lengthy stopover at the Comores during his notorious cruise, bringing his ship the *Adventure* there when it needed repair, and earning some money by lending it to shipwrecked French soldiers at Mutsamudu who used it to recover their cargo. Pirates Thomas White, Booth, and Bowen spent six months at Mayotte in 1702–3, where they sheltered their ships the *Speedy Return* and *Prosperous* in the lagoon.

More ominously for Company ships trading in the region, the Comores were also the setting for some notable pirate attacks. The pirates used the sheltered bays to conceal their presence from Europeans who habitually stopped there to take on fresh supplies. It was here that the East India Company ship *Pembroke* was captured. The pirates were able to procure a 12-oar rowing boat that came from another Company ship, the *Ruby*, which had earlier been shipwrecked near the island. Captain Wooley was kept prisoner aboard his ship—which the pirates renamed the *Prosperous*—while they cruised off India, and left an account of the events.

In 1704 the *Severn*, a British naval warship under Captain Richards arrived at Johanna (Anjouan). Sent to hunt down the pirates, the

Severn had on board pirates David Williams and John Pro, delivered up to Captain Richards a few weeks earlier by a Malagasy chief. However, before continuing on his voyage, Captain Richards succumbed to an offer of money made by the sultan of Anjouan who needed help to repress a rebellion of islanders from Moheli. Williams and Pro took advantage of the ensuing engagement to escape their bonds. They then offered assistance to the rival group of rebels on Moheli, who agreed to hide them from the British. When the *Severn* had left, the pirates went to Anjouan and then to Mayotte where they were employed by the local sultan as carpenters. They later constructed a small sail boat and were able to get to Madagascar and regain their base on St Mary's island. Another attack on Company ships *Cassandra* and *Greenwich* took place around 1720 at Mayotte where they were moored. The fleet of the English pirate Edward England arrived to attack them, and the *Cassandra* fell into the hands of the pirates, who were assisted by 15 others from the crew of Olivier Le Vasseur's ship, *The Indian Queen* which had a short time before been lost on the reef at Mayotte.[32]

PIRATES AND COLONISTS IN THE MASCARENES

In the last decades of the seventeenth century, when European pirates surged into the Indian Ocean, the Mascarene islands were only sparsely populated. Both the French commandant of Bourbon, and the Dutch governor on Mauritius had strict instructions against fraternizing with pirates, but did not have the resources or manpower to engage with marauders. Their strategy was, therefore, to treat with them. Occasionally some pirates would be disembarked at the islands to rest, recuperate, and sometimes to settle. Pirate captives were also on occasion landed at the Mascarenes, where they were obliged to work for their keep until they could board a passing ship.[33]

Bourbon was, in the seventeenth century, settled by a small group of French colonists who had survived the massacre of their confreres in Madagascar, with some Malagasy women and slaves. The island's population slowly increased by the arrival of a trickle of settlers from India and the metropolis, with the addition of a few score of pirates whose money and skills were welcomed on Bourbon, provided they agreed to marry and renounce their marauding habits. In such a small community, the presence of 30 or more pirates was a significant addition to the colony—it has in fact been estimated that they constituted one fifth of the early settler population, and a quarter of heads of household.

Thus around three-quarters of the present-day 'white' population of Réunion have pirate forebears.

The first recorded pirate visit to Bourbon dates from 1687 when 70 flibustiers disembarked from Avery's successful cruise with plenty of gold. A number of them settled on the island. Among a further group of pirates who disembarked in November 1695 and later became settlers was Englishman Dennis Turpin.[34] John Bowen made several visits to Bourbon with his pirate crew before deciding to settle there in 1704, but died soon afterwards. In 1705 and 1706 Thomas White and his crew made stopovers there; in 1707 a Bermuda pirate ship visited the island on its way to St Mary's as did a supply ship of pirates in May 1709. Despite orders from France which initially prohibited their reception, the governors tolerated pirates, at the behest of the settlers, who were often outnumbered by their visitors.[35]

Some of the pirates who settled in Bourbon were trying to avoid retribution for their crimes of plunder; others were Protestants, a persecuted minority in France, who consequently had little desire to return. A few were English, and Rogozinski points out that one reason for their choosing a French colony, apart from the availability of women, was that they were embittered by the British failure to adhere to pardons which the pirates believed had been accorded them:

By the 1700s, Réunion was the favorite refuge for pirates who did not want to remain on Madagascar. After the English courts reneged on an offer of pardon in 1699, the men were leery of English colonies. French officials on Réunion, in contrast, were eager to accept pirate settlers as long as they ceased from robbery and recognized the Roman Catholic faith.[36]

The manuscript diary of Governor Villers, written between 1701-9, preserved in the New York Public Library, provides a graphic demonstration of the decisions that confronted officials in the diminutive settlement when pirate ships arrived. On 19 August 1702, learning of the arrival of a pirate ship, the Governor ordered the inhabitants to defend themselves. The latter retorted that they had wives and children and that they did not wish to get their 'heads broken' in defending what the pirates were willing to pay for. Further, since they had no money with which to buy goods for themselves, they 'needed to take it where they could get it'.[37]

Over succeeding years, it became routine for the governor to refuse, and for the colonists to petition that visiting pirates be supplied. Moreover, it is noteworthy that pirate settlers very often led the demand for lenient treatment of their confreres. Thus when on 19 May 1707 a pirate ship originating in Bermuda and commanded by Jon Jovis arrived, it was pirate settlers Noel, Thomas Elgar, and Edward Robert who signed the formal request that they be allowed to take wood, water, and some refreshments.[38]

Finally, in 1716 the Navy Council in France agreed to a general amnesty for the Indian Ocean pirates, and instructed the colonial administration to receive all those pirates who presented themselves and even to attract others to settle where possible. A measure of the change in attitude of the French Company Directors in Paris to the pirate settlers is shown by a letter addressed to their representatives in Bourbon on 3 April 1722. They approved an amnesty proposed to the remaining rump of Madagascar pirates, stating that while the men concerned did not deserve to be pardoned, it was 'the best means of making them give up piracy'.[39] They advised that the best course of action to ensure their settlement was to marry them off in Bourbon. They had sharp words for the missionaries on the island, who objected to the irreligious pirates, reminding them that their own funds derived in part from sums deposited by the pirates, and even declaring that 'the best inhabitants of Bourbon were once pirates!'[40]

Mauritius, the sister island of Réunion, was not permanently settled until the French took possession in the early eighteenth century. However, the Dutch established themselves on the island at the beginning of the seventeenth century and settled colonists there between 1638 and 1658, and again from 1664 before finally abandoning the colony in 1710. During this period, the island was always vulnerable to hostile visits from pirates.

Indeed European pirates pre-dated the arrival of the first group of Dutch colonists. One of three ships fitted out for a voyage of pillage along the Indian coast and in the Spice Islands by Sir Robert Dudley was shipwrecked in the Indian Ocean at the close of the sixteenth century, and five survivors eventually washed up in a boat at the southeast bay of Mauritius. Merchants-cum-pirates like Gilles de Regimond of Dieppe also visited Mauritius when the French ships en route to missions of plunder in the Red Sea would leave a few men behind to chop ebony trees on the island before being picked up on the return voyage. In 1634 information reached Surat from the captain of a Dutch ship which had stopped at Mauritius of finding 14 men ashore there, who were found to have 'Venetians' and 'Ibrahims' on them, which coins they confessed to have taken from a prize in the Red Sea the previous year.[41]

Towards the end of February 1697 Mauritius received a visit by 108 pirates sailing in the *Welcome* from Bombay to London. The pirates anchored off the southwestern settlement of Black River, landed some of their crew, and forced the Dutch colonists to give them refreshments. The Governor, Diodati, learning of their arrogant behaviour went to meet them, but the pirates rowed back out to their ship, having boasted of their pirate cruise to the inhabitants. In any event, as Moree points out, 'Diodati could do little about it as he had only twenty-five VOC servants and fifteen slaves'.[42] The men of the *Welcome* stated that they had captured five Moorish vessels and two French ships. The Governor concluded that the fact that the men seemed to have as much say as their commander, and that they were all heavily armed, carrying their weapons in their bedding, was proof that they were indeed pirates.[43]

In November 1701 a French pirate ship was seen off Mauritius—a rowing boat came close in to shore and threw three lascar sailors into the sea. The men, picked up from the west coast, were identified as Mallinsick, Issop, and Adam, and claimed to have been aboard a Moorish vessel, the *Fitebos* of Muscat, taken by the pirates three months earlier. They informed the Dutch in Mauritius that the French pirates had a crew of 30 French, four captured Dutch, nine English, four Portuguese, and 11 blacks from Calabar and Brazil. The ship mounted 24 cannons and had already made prizes of English, Portuguese, and Dutch vessels. The Muslim sailors reported that the pirate ship was en route to Madagascar where the crew intended to abandon their vessel and return to France. In early 1702 the pirates were caught in a cyclone, and their ship was reportedly wrecked off Saint Denis in Bourbon.[44]

The Dutch authorities gave frequent instructions to the small settlement in Mauritius as to how to deal with aggressive visitors, usually English sailors and pirates:

only use violence when indispensable, and overpower them should you see a chance, selling them nothing except trifles. Should any pirate visit you, and leave any men behind, they are to be brought to the lodge, to work there for their daily food and clothing until they can be sent to Batavia or the Cape. They are to be carefully watched and examined, and their statements sent to us.[45]

Despite their difficulties, the Dutch were reluctant to leave the island for fear it would fall into the hands of the English, or the pirates. As Diodati wrote to the Cape authorities in February 1698:

It is true that it would be more profitable for the Company, seeing the heavy expenses hitherto incurred, to abandon this island, but then the English would be the first to take possession of it, whilst the New Netherlands pirates, who have seven ships, and are settled on St Maria before the Bay of Antongil, would consider it a very convenient place for themselves and ships, and make a fine thieves' nest of it. This would greatly prejudice our ships.[46]

However, the authorities in Amsterdam, feeling that the station could not defend itself from pirates, decided for that reason, around 1708, to abandon Mauritius:

the garrison and the ships are not safe there, because of the pirates who call there, and other ships in great numbers which do what they like. One of these days it may happen that one of these pirates, one of which only lately visited the place with 200 men, may seriously injure the station. We therefore consider it high time to release ourselves from our responsibilities there by abandoning the island.[47]

After the Dutch finally left Mauritius in 1710, that island was again deserted, but continued to be visited by several pirates and by the fleets of warships that were hunting them. The sister island of Bourbon then decided to take possession of Mauritius, by sending a small contingent of its colonists in 1721. Among them were certainly some relations of the retired pirates who had settled in Bourbon and married local women. Thus, the beginnings of French Mauritian society were also inextricably tied up with the adventures of the European pirates who had ventured from the Atlantic into Indian Ocean waters.[48]

FROM MARGINALS TO MEN OF SUBSTANCE: PIRATE SETTLERS

In 1721 when Father Le Cheron d'Incarville stopped at Bourbon, he noted that there were few workers or artisans among the white population. Consequently labour was expensive.[49] The number of pirates among the settlers must surely have been in part responsible. Ex-seamen with fighting skills, they had few agricultural or artisanal talents. So what use were pirates to the embryonic European settlements in the Indian Ocean?

The use made of those men who disembarked from pirate ships at Mauritius gives us some clues. In 1706, the Dutch at the Cape reported that their flute *Oestgeest* had picked up one Jan de Wit of Amsterdam, who had run away from a pirate ship which stopped at Mauritius. He was a mariner by profession, but was reported to know Madagascar and its local rulers well 'having wandered about on it for a long time.... He also speaks the language perfectly'.[50] He was therefore employed on the Dutch yacht *Ter Aa* which made regular trips to Madagascar for slaves.[51]

Similarly, Thomas Elgar, a Londoner by birth and a pirate by trade, was made an offer in 1704 by the French on Bourbon to take command of a ship which the settlers proposed to establish for trade with Madagascar. This arrangement fell through and Elgar briefly returned to piracy before settling permanently in Bourbon in December 1706, purchasing, with fellow pirate Edward Robert, an estate for the considerable sum of 3,500 ecus. The colonists later made use of Elgar's knowledge of the Malagasy language by sending him on a trading voyage to Madagascar on the *Courrier de Bourbon* in 1718. Elgar was described as well educated, and an experienced pilot, but also as a drunkard and quarrelsome man. He died in Bourbon in June 1735.[52]

John Clayton, who arrived with a number of other pirates, in Bourbon in a small bark in January 1724, hoping to benefit from the French amnesty, was immediately singled out by the Governor, Desforges-Boucher, who offered him the title of captain in the service of the Company and sent him on a mission to take rice and slaves from Madagascar, at the same time bringing back any further pirates who were prepared to accept the amnesty. Unfortunately, the distinction given to Clayton infuriated his fellow pirates, who murdered him and escaped with the bark.[53]

Jacques Delattre, a pirate who originated from Ostend and who also settled in Bourbon in 1704, was said to be able to speak six or seven languages, and was employed as an interpreter for several of the English who had established themselves in Bourbon. At the time of his arrival he was believed to be worth 2,200 ecus, but became by 1710, 'poorer than Job', having reportedly dissipated in gambling and drunkenness a fortune in gold worth 20 times what he had retired to Bourbon with. He died there in 1719. Scottish pirate, Robert Tarby, known as 'Robin', became a cultivator in Bourbon, producing rice, maize, tobacco, bananas and vegetables, but was described as a 'poor farmer' and a man of no means in his later years.[54]

Some pirates were men of education and status. Guy Dumesnil, born in Flanders, was of noble descent and declared that he had received a military training at Tournay. The date of his leaving Europe and of his subsequent career is unknown until he disembarked at Bourbon on 9 April 1704 from the pirate ship commanded by John Bowen. Soon after arriving, Dumesnil and two of his crew mates jointly purchased a landed property and several houses. Guy married the Bourbon-born daughter of a former pirate and by 1709 he was a substantial landowner. Described, unlike many of his confrères, as a peaceful, charitable and generous man, and a good neighbour, he was made 'Capitaine' of the Sainte Suzanne district of Bourbon by Governor Villers. Another pirate with an unusual background was Joseph de Guigné of Saumur. From a merchant family, Joseph was a cavalry officer before leaving the service and becoming involved in slave voyages to Madagascar where his ship was taken by pirates and he was co-opted to be their pilot and surgeon. Disembarking from Bowen's ship in 1704, by the end of that year he had already married a white Creole Françoise Carré, but possessed nothing according to the 1705 census, suggesting that he had not accepted pirate loot. Guigné acquired a house at Butor and plots of land at Rivière des Pluyes and Sainte Suzanne which he farmed. He was made 'enseigne' of the district and 'greffier' of St Denis Council between 1707 and 1718. He was later promoted Capitaine of the district and offered a gold medal with the portrait of the king in 1727 for his exemplary conduct.[55]

Even those pirates who were not forced men like De Guigné, were not necessarily wealthy. The property owned by pirate settlers, as their Acts of Decease in the Réunion Archives indicate, was often pitifully small: a few shirts and a handful of coins, in many cases. However, this may have been, at least in part, because they were so easily fleeced by the senior colonial officials who secured their amnesties. It is clear that one of the key attributes of pirates as far as the colonists—and their governors— was concerned, was their wealth on arrival. The story of the lost pirate treasure of Jacobus Van Laar is a case in point. John Tarver, the first mate of an English galley, the *Stringer*, captained by Isaac Pyke, which visited Mauritius on its homeward journey in 1708, kept a journal, which related that Van Laar, who disembarked from Bowen's ship *Defiance* in February 1704 along with five others, had hidden his money in a bottle and buried it in Mauritius before leaving for Batavia, where he obtained a pardon for his crimes. Laar then returned to Mauritius where he learned that his treasure had been found and removed by the slave of a Dutch settler, Carstense, who was in turn found out after paying for a bottle of arrack (spirits) with a gold rupee. Governor Momber, according to Tarver, then extorted a confession from the slave, recovered the money that was reputed to be worth 6,000 dollars in silver and gold coins, and kept the hoard for himself.[56]

That more than one governor of the Mascarene islands benefited from the loot of pirates is also evident. Desforges-Boucher of Bourbon did not resort to outright robbery, but instead gained his wealth by organizing card games with newly arrived pirates (no doubt keeping the tables well fortified with spirits) winning such a considerable sum that he returned to France and made a good marriage on the strength of his new-found assets. Another pirate settler, Dennis Turpin, complained about the seizure and sale ordered by Villers of two of his slaves, in payment for a gambling debt contracted with the governor himself. When Clayton and his men arrived on Bourbon to be amnestied, they were informed that they had to pay 20 piastres per man, and asked to deposit their jewels, gold, and silver with the local authorities. Alongside their loot, the pirates were welcomed for the number of slaves each brought with them, and which were quickly sold to the labour-hungry colonists.[57] These accounts reveal that the pirate settlers were by and large exploited and that few benefited long term from their maritime careers. Their chief asset in the colonial context was their rarity in status as white males with some useful local knowledge.

As David Starkey has remarked, 'long waves of piratical activity were inextricably linked to the political and economic aspirations of the states, colonies or communities from which they emanated'.[58] In the case of the vulnerable Indian Ocean colonies, marginal men such as pirates could make a significant difference to their economic well-being and indeed, on settling, become important contributors to these fledgling communities. The influence of the pirates, furthermore, stretched beyond the borders of Indian Ocean states to that other geographic periphery: the North American colonies. Pirates, in short,

fitted into the scheme of things, as North American merchants conceived that scheme. They looted the Grand Mogul's shipping but stayed out of the way of the English; they fetched in saleable goods, paid off the right people, behaved themselves ashore, strengthened the colonial economy in general and enriched their New England backers in particular.[59]

Scammell has pointed out that there were also 'major markets in Dutch Cochin and English Bombay, where the pirates had European accomplices, and in western Indian ports where they dealt with local merchants'.[60] On the geographic periphery of empire, therefore, piracy was not so much an irritant, but a temporary solution to unfavourable trading conditions. For the pirate settlers themselves, the most they gained, seemingly, was a young wife and a small freeholding on a sparsely populated French outpost.

NOTES AND REFERENCES

1. C.H. Haring, 1966, *The Buccaneers in the West Indies in the XVII Century*, Hamden, CT: Archon Books, p. 13; J.S. Bromley, 1987, *Corsairs and Navies, 1660–1760*, London: The Hambledon Press.
2. D.J. Starkey, 2001, 'Pirates and Markets', in C.R. Pennell (ed.), *Bandits at Sea: A Pirates Reader*, New York: New York University Press, pp. 107–24.
3. D. Marley, 1995, *Pirates: Adventurers of the High Seas*, London: Cassell, pp. 130–1.

4. G.V. Scammell, 1995, 'European Exiles, Renegades and Outlaws and the Maritime Economy of Asia c. 1500–1750', in K.S. Mathew (ed.), *Mariners, Merchants and Oceans*, Delhi: Manohar, p. 129.

5. M.D.D. Newitt, 'The East India Company in the Western Indian Ocean in the Early Seventeenth Century', *Journal of Imperial and Commonwealth History*, vol. 14, 1986, p. 23.

6. R.C. Ritchie, 1986. *Captain Kidd and the War Against the Pirates*, Cambridge, MA: Harvard University Press, p. 14.

7. A. Das Gupta and M.N. Pearson, 1999, *India and the Indian Ocean 1500–1800*, New Delhi: Oxford University Press, pp. 16–17.

8. Calendar of State Papers, America and West Indies 1693–1696, Beeston to Lords of Trade and Plantations, 10 June 1693, p. 114.

9. M. Rediker, 2001, 'The Seaman as Pirate Plunder and Social Banditry at Sea', in Pennell (ed.), *Bandits at Sea*, pp. 140–2.

10. K. Rushby, 2001, *Hunting Pirate Heaven*, London: Constable, p. 9.

11. B. Lubbock (ed.), 1934, *Barlow's Journal of His Life at Sea in King's Ships, East & West Indiamen & Other Merchantmen from 1659 to 1703*, 2 vols, London: Hurst & Blackett, vol. 1, p. 27.

12. J. Rogozinski, 1995, *Pirates, Brigands, Buccaneers, and Privateers in Fact, Fiction and Legend*, New York: Facts on File, p. 233.

13. D. Cordingley, 1995, *Under the Black Flag. The Romance and the Reality of Life among the Pirates*, New York: Random House, p. 16.

14. J. Rogozinski, 2002, *Honor Among Thieves: Captain Kidd, Henry Every, and the Pirate Democracy in the Indian Ocean*, Pennsylvania: Stackpole Books, p. 64.

15. A. Lougnon, 1956, *L'Ile Bourbon Pendant la Regence*, Paris: Larose, p. 162.

16. Cordingley, *Under the Black Flag*, p. 119.

17. J.L. Anderson, 2001, 'Piracy and World History: An Economic Perspective on Maritime Predation', in Pennell (ed.), *Bandits at Sea*, pp. 93–110.

18. A. Das Gupta, 2001, *The World of the Indian Ocean Merchant, 1500–1800*, New Delhi: Oxford University Press, pp. 257, 308–10; Rogozinski, *Honor Among Thieves*, pp. 24–6.

19. At this time, Madagascar was still occasionally called by its former name, St Lawrence, while Bourbon was chiefly known as Mascarin to visiting sailors.

20. H.C.V. Leibbrandt, 1896–1903, *Precis of the Archives of the Cape of Good Hope*, Cape Town: Western Cape Archives, 3 vols, vol. II, 1696, no. 14, vol. III, pp. 242–5, 261–2.

21. Ritchie, *Captain Kidd*, pp. 82–3.

22. Ibid.

23. Leibbrandt, *Precis*, vol. III, pp. 108, 261–2.

24. Cordingley, *Under the Black Flag*, p. 147.

25. J. Biddulph, 1995, *The Pirates of Malabar*, Delhi: Asian Educational Services, p. 147; Lougnon, *L'Ile Bourbon Pendant la Regence*, p. 164; J. Macau, 1973, 'La Suede et Madagascar au début du 18ème siecle', *IHPOM, Etudes et Documents*, vol. 7, p. 118.

26. M. Brown, 1978, *Madagascar Rediscovered*, London: Tunnacliffe, p. 95.

27. St Mary's was also known as Nossi Ibrahim, and today is called Ambodifototra.
28. Calendar of State Papers, America and West Indies 1697-8, Captain Thomas Warren of HMS Windsor to the East India Company, 28 November 1697.
29. Rogozinski, *Honor Among Thieves*, p ix.
30. Ritchie, *Captain Kidd*, pp. 112-13.
31. Leibbrandt, *Precis*, vol. II, p. 228.
32. J. Martin, 1983, *Comores: quatre îles entre pirates et planteurs*, Paris: l'Harmattan, vol. 1, pp. 24-8.
33. A. Toussaint, 1972, *Histoire des Iles Mascareignes*, Paris: Berger Levrault, pp. 35-6.
34. D. Vaxelaire, 1999, *Histoire de la Réunion*, 2 vols, St Denis, Reunion: Editions Orphie, p. 92.
35. A. Lougnon, 1958, *Sous le Signe de la Tortue, Voyages anciens à l'Ile Bourbon, 1611-1725*, Paris: Larose, p. 151.
36. Rogozinski, *Honor Among Thieves*, pp. 236, 159.
37. Journal of Occurrences, 1701-9, New York Public Library, Compagnie des Indes Orientales, Records, vol. 3.
38. Vaxelaire, *Histoire de la Réunion*, p. 106.
39. Archives Départementales de la Réunion (ADR) C 11Conseil du Marine, Paris to Conseil of Bourbon, 31 May 1721.
40. Ibid.
41. P.J. Barnwell, 1948, *Visits and Despatches, Mauritius 1598-1948*, Port Louis: Standard Printing Establishment, pp. 10-12.
42. P.J. Moree, 1998, *A Concise History of Dutch Mauritius, 1598-1710*, London: Kegan Paul, p. 89; Leibbrandt, *Precis*, II(31).
43. Ibid.
44. A. Pitot, 1947, *T'Eylandt Mauritius*, Port Louis: Coignet Freres, p. 298.
45. Leibbrandt, *Precis*, vol. III, pp. 265-7.
46. Leibbrandt, *Precis*, II(22 and 32), pp. 168-74.
47. Ibid.
48. Ibid. The third island of the Mascarene group, Rodrigues, then known as Diego Ruis, was largely uninhabited during this same period. Around 1700, pirates attacked a French ship which had stopped to take on turtles at Rodrigues, but as the island was generally deserted, there are few accounts of pirate visits. For further information see A. North-Coombes, 1994, *Histoire des Tortues de Terre de Rodrigues*, Port Louis: Service Bureau, p. 7.
49. Lougnon, *Bourbon Pendant la Regence*, p. 163.
50. Leibbrandt, *Precis*, vol. III, p. 278.
51. Ibid.
52. India Office Library and Records (IOL) E/3/65 No. 8057. The declaration, on 2 November 1702, of the former carpenter of the pirate ship *Speaker* mentions a Thomas Elgrave on board. For further details of Thomas Elgar's life see J. Barassin (ed.), 1978, *Mémoire pour servir à la connoissance particulière de chacun des habitants de l'isle de Bourbon*, Aix en Provence: IHPOM, pp. 188, 380-2.

53. National Archives Paris, C3/4 no. 18 Desforges-Boucher to Maurepas, 30 November 1725; ADR Procès Verbal de depot 27 January 1724, p. 105.
54. Barassin, *Mémoire*, pp. 97–8, 106–7, 263–4, 273–4.
55. Ibid., pp. 64–5, 70–1, 229–35; H. Bourde de la Rogerie, 1998, *Les Bretons aux Iles de France et de Bourbon*, Paris: Editions La Decouvrance, p. 288.
56. Barnwell, *Visits and Despatches*, pp. 114, 127; Leibbrandt, *Précis*, vol. II, p. 359.
57. ADR Judgment of the Provincial Council, 22 September 1716; Deliberation du Conseil provincial of 26 January 1724, p. 103; Procès Verbal de depot, 31 January 1724, p. 105.
58. Starkey, 'Pirates and Markets', pp. 107–24.
59. A. Winston, 1969, *No Man Knows My Grave, Privateers and Pirates 1665–1715*, Boston: Houghton Mifflin, p. 35.
60. Scammell, 'European Exiles', p. 133.

'Tracing lines upon the unknown areas of the earth'

Reflections on Frederick Jackson Turner
and the Indo-Tibetan Frontier

Alex McKay

THE TURNER THESIS

At a meeting of the American Historical Association in 1893, a young historian from Wisconsin named Frederick Jackson Turner presented a paper on the European settlement of the American 'West'.[1] Turner described a process in which successive waves of settlers had moved gradually westwards, transforming the wilderness of the 'moving frontier' into agricultural and pastoral land. That frontier consisted of overlapping zones of European impact, so that at any one time there was not one frontier, but many; a frontier of exploration, a frontier of settlement, a military frontier, and so on. The most enduringly controversial aspect of Turner's thesis was his claim that European social structures, practices, and understandings had proved inappropriate in the new lands and that the pioneers' encounter with the frontier environment had not only given a 'frontier character'[2] to the transformed lands, but had produced a new American national character, with innovative and self-sufficient individuals who were mistrustful of government and restrictions on their freedom. The paper was in many ways an elegy for a recently past era. The frontier, Turner proclaimed, no longer existed; the United States now stretched from the Atlantic to the Pacific and the age of the 'Old West' was over. As Ronald M. Davidson observed, Turner's study, 'must be the single most influential conference paper in the history of American academia'.[3] Unlike the many academic theories that have come and gone in the course of more than a century, Turner's thesis, while frequently critiqued, has persisted as a stimulating device through which to engage with the history of the American West. That it might have wider implications has also been recognized,[4] and what follows is an attempt to discuss the most significant section of the Indo-Tibetan frontier, the region lying between the tea gardens of northern Bengal and the hinterlands of central Tibet, in the light of Turner's insights. It would also be of interest to compare the settlement of this region by indigenous groups at various times in history with Turner's model, but for reasons of space, the focus here is on the British period and my concern, as was Turner's, is with European expansion. The application of some aspects of his theories to indigenous peoples and histories will be considered in the final section; in the wider context our concern is not with a particular race or social group, but with the question of whether Turner's theories have wider implications or describe only a particular historical process. In the confines of this essay only selected aspects of Turner's theory and a fraction of the relevant sources can be drawn upon, but I believe that this is sufficient to indicate that his insights provide a stimulating theoretical device through which we may derive new understandings of the Himalayan frontier in the colonial period.

INDO-TIBETAN FRONTIER ZONES

In 1900 the northern border of British India stretched along the Himalayan foothills for more than 2,000 miles. Beyond the border were a variety of different polities that separated imperial territory from Tibet, a state which the British recognized as part of the Chinese empire but also regarded as a 'buffer state' separating the British from the Russian and Chinese empires. Among the different polities between India and Tibet were Indian 'princely states' such as Kashmir and 'protected states' such as Sikkim, as well as the 'independent' kingdom of Nepal, a friendly neighbour whose troops served in the Indian Army. These states effectively formed a political and diplomatic frontier zone between Tibet and British India because although none of them were administratively part of India, they were under imperial influence and their foreign relations were effectively under the control of India's diplomatic service, commonly known as the 'political' department. The latter was achieved by assigning a Political Officer (along with a supporting staff of medical, military, and communications specialists) to each Himalayan state in order to ensure that they followed policies acceptable to the Government of India.

That the Government of India recognized the transitional and zonal nature of this frontier is illustrated by the case of a European tourist wishing to travel up to Tibet. While they could travel freely through British India to places such as Kalimpong and Darjeeling, they required permission from the British Political Officer in Gangtok (theoretically in consultation with the Durbar) to enter Sikkim. The Political Officer (after 1905) also had the authority to issue further permission allowing a tourist to travel across the border on the main trade route as far north as Gyantse and could, in consultation with the Tibetan government, provide additional permission to travel on to Lhasa.[5] But restrictions were imposed on specific types of visitors, who were seen as potentially disruptive influences on indigenous society. While a few missionaries were permitted to practise in Sikkim, none were allowed to enter Bhutan or Tibet, and prospectors and miners were only allowed into any of these states under official auspices.

There were thus a series of zones of authority lying north of the British Indian border, and although the Tibetan border was the official boundary of 'India', even that border did not mark the full extent of either official British power and influence or a boundary for European initiatives. Indeed we may identify a whole series of frontiers that existed in relation to particular categories of Europeans, consistent with the Turnerian model in which there were a number of European frontiers in advance of the frontier of settlement. For example, the system of political department posts located in the zone beyond the imperial border enables us to speak of a diplomatic frontier. After the Younghusband mission in 1903-4, the British advanced that diplomatic frontier beyond the Himalayan states, stationing Political Officers in Tibet itself, although that state had no common border with British India. Initially they were limited to Gyantse in southern Tibet, but in 1936-7 that diplomatic frontier was unilaterally extended when a British mission was established in Lhasa.

As the Younghusband mission of 1903-4 demonstrated, there was also a military frontier that could be advanced beyond India's boundaries when necessary. Indeed the Gyantse post (although not Lhasa) had its own small military establishment to 'escort' the political department official posted there under the Sikkim Political Officer's command. British India's military frontier zone can thus be seen to have extended to Gyantse. The Political department official in Gyantse was termed a 'Trade Agent' (trade having been the principal public justification for the Younghusband mission) and Gyantse might thus also be seen as a frontier of trade,[6] as could the tiny 'Trade Agency' maintained at Gartok in far-off western Tibet. But in practice, trade remained in indigenous hands. Failed efforts by a handful of European traders who visited Gyantse in the immediate post-Younghusband years meant that Gangtok (Sikkim) remained the frontier of European trade and commerce.

Even before Tibet was reached there were transport frontiers; the railway reached no nearer to Gangtok than Jalpaiguri and the motorable road, for all practical purposes, ran out at Gangtok even in the 1940s. Neither road nor rail reached into Bhutan or Tibet, and although a communications frontier reached Gyantse (and later Lhasa) in the form of a telegraph line and the Indian postal service, it did not penetrate Bhutan. This was also the case with other aspects of western science and modernity. Biomedicine (allopathy, or 'western medicine'), for example, similarly reached Gyantse and, after 1936, to Lhasa, where Indian Medical Service officers established biomedical clinics in association with the political department posts.[7]

The frontier of European settlement, however, did not extend as far as these frontiers. Although the British maintained an official presence in the Himalayan states, and individuals remained in places such as Sikkim most of their working life, Europeans were not actually permitted to settle there permanently.[8] Indeed, India itself was never subject to European settlement in the manner of countries such as America, Australia, and New Zealand. But during the nineteenth and early twentieth centuries, the northeastern frontiers of India did attract European settlers engaged in the tea industry and there was a frontier of settlement in this region, although it was limited to British Indian territory, particularly the *terai* in the north of Bengal and the hill station towns of Darjeeling and Kalimpong.

It is important to remember that the number of Europeans in the region of this essay, and their economic and social impact, was extremely limited by comparison with Turner's subject area. The number of Europeans resident in Sikkim, for example, never exceeded forty. But, with few exceptions, these Europeans congregated in urban centres, towns which in Turner's thesis were seen as the advance guard of European civilization, providing the security that attracted further settlers. This was certainly the case with the establishment and development of Darjeeling in the 1830s, which was an essential step towards the subsequent expansion into Sikkim, Bhutan, and Tibet, drawing Europeans into the region and creating centres for the further expansion of medical, military, and other frontiers.[9]

In addition to the army cantonments and the growing body of civil officials residing there, this region was also a fertile ground for Christian missionaries and for European explorers, traders, botanists, and so on. Despite obvious differences of scale with the American West, the imposition of European government and civilization proceeded in a manner that resembles Turner's 'shifting frontier' and there were parallels with the settlement of the American West in regard to overlapping zones of expansion. Here we might note the work of the mid-twentieth century economic historian, W.K. Hancock, whose concept of diverse frontiers in Australia and South Africa forming 'the moving fringes of an expansionist society',[10] came, he states, 'without any conscious borrowing from American historians, with whose work I was not then familiar'.[11] Like Turner, Hancock described the process of European expansion as involving the movement of a succession of overlapping frontiers, among which he identified frontiers of settlement, farming, mining, trade, and investment, as well as political frontiers. But Hancock refined the Turnerian model of the missionary frontier, drawing a distinction between sects catering to Europeans and those that focussed on the indigenous peoples[12] (the latter frontier being the more advanced).

This distinction is applicable to the Indo-Tibetan frontier where different Christian preachers catered to European and indigenous audiences. In the 1930s, for example, a missionary such as Mary Scott in Sikkim lived in the 'native' quarters and engaged almost exclusively with the local people, including both the aristocracy and the poorer communities.[13] At the same time, a separate church existed for European worshippers in the Sikkimese capital of Gangtok, with the ministers there devoting most of their time to the European (and Anglo-Indian) congregation.

Following Hancock, these 'established' churches at urban centres such as Gangtok and Darjeeling can be seen as forming what we might call an 'official' Christian frontier, while the missionaries formed another, more geographically advanced frontier. Approaches to the different indigenous groups in northeast India were divided on a more-or-less formal basis among various nationally-based Christian missionary organizations (although 'poaching', particularly by American evangelicals, was not unknown). Thus Welsh missionaries worked farther east among the tribal peoples of the Assam region, while Scottish missionaries had almost exclusive 'rights' to the Lepchas of Kalimpong district and the Finns had exclusive access to northern Sikkim at one point. This missionary frontier was, therefore, in advance of the 'official' Christian frontier, and was expansionist in the sense that the missionaries sought to proselytise across the Himalayas despite official restrictions on their access to Tibet.[14] They considered themselves to possess a higher calling that freed them from national boundaries, and while both the Tibetan and the British imperial governments sought to exclude them from Tibet, missionaries such as Annie Taylor made arduous journeys through the Tibetan hinterlands in an attempt to reach Lhasa.[15]

Other groups similarly disregarded national boundaries. Particularly in the nineteenth century, there was a frontier of espionage, with British spies such as Major Hamilton Bower and the famous pandits carrying out information-gathering missions throughout Tibet.[16] There was also an unbounded frontier of exploration, with explorers and scientists (often difficult to distinguish at this distance from spies), seeking to map Tibet within European knowledge systems. We may also identify a zone beyond the official border in which hunters travelled in search of *shikar*, a zone avoiding urban and monastic centres of the Tibetan state. The Government of India turned a blind eye to these journeys as long as the Tibetan authorities were not alerted to them, particularly if the sportsmen (who were generally civil or military imperial officials) were able to provide intelligence on the regions they traversed. It is difficult, however, to speak generally of a frontier of intelligence gathered by diverse types of travellers because the different groups did not always share information; missionaries and sportsmen, for example, advanced their information in different outlets and even the most assiduous of frontier officials did not have access to the entire body of knowledge collected by the diverse sources.

Two other aspects of Turner's thesis may be considered here; first, Turner's contention that the frontier acted as an economic 'safety-valve' in that the westward movement of workers in search of new opportunities left vacancies in the settled eastern regions and, by reducing the pool of available labour, raised the wages of those who remained.[17] Turner later moved away from this position, one of the more disputed areas of his thesis, but the role of the British empire in providing employment is widely recognized. This was particularly so in regard to the Scots, who were strongly represented on the Indo-Tibetan frontier, and in general terms Turner's ideas do appear applicable to our region, although the number of Europeans involved is far fewer and their economic impact on both the periphery and the metropolis was miniscule.

It seems difficult to suggest parallels with Turner's primary thesis of the 'nationalizing force of the frontier'[18] when the British in India retained such a strong sense of their separate identity and actively promoted that identity through a variety of means—architecture, dress, diet, symbols, and so on—typical of the reinforcement of national identity in both pre-modern and modern states. But as I have previously noted elsewhere,[19] a distinct colonial frontier identity was established within the wider British imperial identity. This separateness was recognized in official discourse,[20] and was very much part of the identity of what I have termed the 'Tibet cadre', that group of Political Officers who served lengthy terms as diplomatic representatives in Sikkim and Tibet.[21] That differing identity was seen by them as deriving from the frontier environment, on the Turnerian model, and given the cultivation of this distinct identity (with its characteristic contempt for central government),[22] the seeds of the emergence of a specific, new, identity that might have taken on national characteristics in different circumstances and time frames, can perhaps be discerned.

IMPERIAL FRONTIER THEORY

The official acknowledgement of a distinct frontier identity fitted within the wider framework of imperial frontier theory. Frontiers were recognized as a potential source of dispute between states and in the nation state system, agreed frontiers were seen as a step towards both the security and the stability necessary for progressive government, global capital, and the nationalizing projects.

As British power in India developed in the early nineteenth century, it had been confronted by a potential threat to the security of India from the expansion of the Russian empire. In 1844 an Anglo-Russian agreement was reached that 'the Khanates of Central Asia should be left by Russia to form a neutral zone between the two empires, so as to preserve them from dangerous contact'.[23] Russia subsequently breached the agreement and annexed Turkestan, but Prince Gortchakoff, the Russian Minister for Foreign Affairs (1856–82) then issued his famous circular of 21 November 1864. This articulated a particular process with which the British could find little argument. Gortchakoff argued that

The position of Russia in Central Asia is that of all civilised states which are brought into contact with half-savage nomad populations possessing no fixed social organisation. In such cases, the more civilised state is forced in the interest of the security of its frontier, and its commercial relations, to exercise a certain ascendancy over their turbulent and undesirable neighbours. Raids and acts of pillage must be put down. To do this, these tribes on the frontier must be reduced to a state of submission. This result once obtained, these tribes take to more peaceful habits, but are in turn exposed to the attacks of the more distant tribes against whom the State is bound to protect them. Hence the necessity of distant, costly, and periodically recurring expeditions against an enemy whom his social organisation makes it impossible to seize. If, the robbers once punished, the expedition is withdrawn, the lesson is soon forgotten; its withdrawal is put down to weakness. It is a peculiarity of Asiatics to respect nothing but visible and palpable force. The moral force of reasoning has no hold on them. In order to put a stop to this state of permanent disorder, fortified posts are established in the midst of these hostile tribes, and an influence is brought to bear upon them which reduces them by degrees to a state of submission. But other more distant tribes beyond this outer line come in turn to threaten the same dangers, and necessitate the same measures of repression. The State is thus forced to choose between two alternatives—either to give up this endless labour, and to abandon its frontier to perpetual disturbance, or to plunge deeper and deeper into barbarous countries, when the difficulties and expenses increase with every step in advance. Such has been the fate of every country which has found itself in a similar position. The United States of America, France in Algeria, Holland in her Colonies, England in India; all have been forced by imperious necessity into this onward march, where the greatest difficulty is to know where to stop.[24]

Although the takeover of Khiva in 1873 revived British fears of Russia's intentions, the moral imperatives and political inevitabilities of the expansion process described by Prince Gortchakoff were acknowledged by subsequent British imperial strategists. They too understood that the 'Turbulent Frontier'[25] was inevitably expansionist until it reached the limits of another great empire, when a permanent border might be achieved by agreement. But they recognized that until that agreement was reached there was a risk of a major conflict between empires over border issues, and that the presence of so-called 'buffer states' separating empires could postpone the consideration of those issues.

As the wider implications of the Central Asian frontiers of their empire became apparent, British imperial thinkers became increasingly concerned with frontier theory. There were lengthy treatises on the subject by the former India Foreign Secretary, Sir Alfred Lyall, and the Superintendent of Frontier Surveys, Sir Thomas Holdich.[26] Most famously, George Nathaniel Curzon (Viceroy of India, 1899–1905), gave a lecture at Oxford in 1907 that remains a fundamental source. In its subsequent published form the lecture retains not only Curzon's ringing oratorical style,[27] but also the atmosphere of the high imperialism of that age when, as the former Viceroy put it, the frontier, 'its incidents and... incomparable drama are the possession of a few silent men, who may be found in the clubs of London, or Paris, or Berlin, when they are not engaged in tracing lines upon the unknown areas of the earth'.[28]

Like Turner, Curzon understood a frontier as a series of zones. His particular concern was with the nature of statehood that had developed in the zone between the British and Russian empires. He identified three types of states there: [a] a 'buffer-state', which was a 'deliberately neutralized' polity, 'possessing a national existence of its own, which is fortified by the territorial and political guarantee, either of the two Powers between whose dominions it lies...or of a number of great Powers';[29] [b] a 'protectorate', which was a state beyond the administrative frontier of an imperial power but under their political and strategic influence; and [c] a 'sphere of influence', which was an autonomous polity where 'commercial exploitation and political influence are regarded as the peculiar right of the interested Power'.[30]

These categories were not considered permanent, but represented stages of a process. Indeed, Curzon observed that it 'has been by a policy of Protectorates that the Indian Empire has for more than a century pursued, and is still pursuing, its as yet unexhausted advance'.[31] The process as Curzon described it was that, 'the uniform tendency is for the weaker to crystallize into the harder shape. Spheres of Interest tend to become Spheres of Influence; temporary leases to become perpetual; Spheres of Influence to develop into Protectorates; Protectorates to be the forerunners of complete incorporation'.[32]

Curzon's understanding of the frontier was not limited to political aspects, however, but revealed a wider vision. While he did not specifically refer to Frederick Jackson Turner, he was clearly familiar with his work. He acknowledged a 'modern school of historians in America [that] has devoted itself with patriotic ardour to tracing the evolution of the national character as determined by its western march across the continent ...'[33] and gave a colourful retelling of Turner's thesis.

First comes the trapper and the fur trader tracking his way into the Indian hunting-grounds and the virgin sanctuaries of animal life. Then the backwoodsman clears away the forest and plants his log hut in the clearing. There follow him in swift succession the rancher with his live-stock, the miner with his pick, the farmer with plough and seeds, and finally the urban dweller, the manufacturer, and the artisan. On the top of the advancing wave floats a scum of rascality that is ultimately deposited in the mining camps of California and the gambling dens of the Pacific Coast...from this tempestuous cauldron of human passion and privation, a new character, earnest, restless, exuberant, self-confident, emerged...the entire nation, purified and unified in its search for the Frontier.[34]

The former viceroy supported Turner's concept of the national-izing force of the frontier with his own examples,[35] arguing for the transformative nature of the frontier on the character of the British who served there:

The British Empire may be seen shaping the British character.... Outside of the English Universities no school of character exists to compare with the Frontier; and character is moulded there...in the furnace of responsibility and on the anvil of self-reliance. Along many a thousand miles of remote border are to be found our twentieth-century Marcher Lords. The breath of the Frontier has entered into their nostrils and infused their being. Courage and conciliation...patience and tact, initiative and self-restraint, these are the complex qualifications of the modern school of pioneers. To these attainments should be added—for the ideal Frontier officer—a taste for languages, some scientific training, and a powerful physique...there may await him either the knife of the Pathan fanatic, or the more deadly fevers of the African swamp. But the risk is the last thing of which he takes account.[36]

Curzon's rhetoric suggests a construction of the ideal frontiersmen indistinguishable from that of imperial mythology as promulgated in popular magazines such as *Boys Own* paper and in the novels of Rudyard Kipling and his less sophisticated imitators. But this 'ideal type' was precisely the sort of officer who was actually sought for service on the frontier, particularly by the political department which described the desired character and capabilities of its recruits in very much the same terms as those used to describe the heroes of imperial legend. The myth and the reality thus informed each other.

A specific early model of the ideal frontiersman was Sir Robert Sandeman, who was responsible for taking Sind into the British empire. That his methods and achievements were honoured is indicated by the fact that his biography was one of four texts on which later would-be Political Officers were examined. Although Sandeman was clearly an officer whose actions sometimes exceeded officially-sanctioned limits, both Lyall and Curzon contributed to the biography, giving it an *imprateur* of approval from the highest levels. Curzon wrote that while 'the [Sandeman] sometimes acted upon the frontier in a spirit of somewhat greater independence of the central government than a rigid officialism either encourages, or readily condones...I do not set this down to his discredit, believing that a certain freedom of action is necessary to men occupying the position he filled'.[37] Foreign Secretary Lyall similarly eulogized Sandeman, stressing that he fitted

the special characteristics of the men of action who have contributed so greatly to the enlargement of our Indian Empire...indefatigable...plans and policies always bold and forward...temperament...positive and practical...with little interest in rules and regulations...[He was] never satisfied with quiet administration behind a settled frontier, but continually discovered excellent reasons for advancing beyond it and annexing fresh territory.[38]

This description of Sandeman as the ideal frontiersman parallels the view of a contemporary pioneer officer in Alaska, Lieutenant (later Brigadier-General) 'Billy' Mitchell, who stated that 'An officer who always follows the letter of the Books of Regulations instead of the spirit seldom gets anywhere'.[39] Their ideal concept of the frontiersmen was, therefore, of an individual very similar in nature to Turner's frontiersmen, so 'impatient of any governmental restriction upon his individual right to deal with the wilderness'.[40]

Thus, while the British sought to bring India's northeast frontier under increasing administrative control, the individuals chosen to serve on the frontier were actually those who valued initiative above regulations, a situation with parallels elsewhere in British India such as the Punjab and the Northwest Frontier. The frontiersmen themselves regarded their own paternal methods of government as more suited to local conditions than government based on codes of law and regulation, although, in practice, the two methods constantly overlapped. The paradox that frontiersmen with little regard for rules and regulations were seen as best suited to bringing settled administration to the frontier reflected a wider sense of understanding among the British in India that they served in a zone which both required, and produced, special traits of character among the successful.[41]

The British imperial understanding of the frontier was, therefore, very similar to that expounded by Turner. Both saw the frontier as a series of zones, and as an environment that produced a particular type of character, one most appropriate to deal successfully with the conditions there. But whereas Turner's model implies that the key factor shaping the character of *any* settler was the frontier environment, the British considered that certain individuals potentially possessed the qualities necessary to deal successfully with frontier conditions, and they sought to select such individuals for service there.

THE PROBLEM OF DEFINITION

The use of the terms 'frontier' as referring to the zones on both sides of a political border, and 'border' as relating to boundary lines as demarcated[42] on a map has been established in the geographical field, most comprehensively by J.R.V. Prescott.[43] Locating the concept of the frontier more specifically in time, Prescott recognized that the 'width of a frontier zone will be dependent on topography, the culture and the period in the state's history which is being studied'.[44] Following Turner, he concluded that 'no one can doubt that "frontiersman" denotes a particular kind of philosophy and character'; one whose behaviour has been 'influenced by both government regulations and their perception of the possibilities offered by the frontier'. But in a refinement of Turner's work, Prescott identified a specific agency integral to the character of the frontier as responsible for producing that type of frontiersman recognized by Turner and his British imperial contemporaries. He concluded that the predominant characteristic of the frontier was its distinct transitional nature in which the absence of fully-developed legal and administrative systems resulted in those conditions Turner identified on the American frontier, which encouraged 'those who were self-reliant, and capable of improvisation'.[45]

Yet in accepting these definitions as established and supportive of Turner's conclusions, it is important to note that in proposing his 'Frontier thesis', Turner resolutely avoided precise definition of the term 'frontier'. While noting that census reports used the term to denote a density of two or less persons per square mile, Turner concluded that 'the term is an elastic one, and for our purpose does not need sharp definition'. The nearest he came to definition was to write in almost metaphysical (or Curzonian!) terms of how, 'the frontier is the outer edge of a wave—the meeting point between savagery and civilization'.[46] Clearly Turner's frontier was to be understood in the widest sense.

This refusal to define his key term is crucial to the application of Turner's theory to our region, as this lack of definition not only allows for multiple facets of historical interpretation to be incorporated into our analysis, but is also appropriate in that it was a defining characteristic of imperial responses to the Indo-Tibetan frontier. Despite a counter trend towards the collection of positivist knowledge, geographic, legal, and linguistic imprecision was regarded as a valuable political device in the maintenance and expansion of the British empire in this region. Tibet was never precisely defined geographically and terms such as 'Trade Agent' and 'Head of British Mission (Lhasa)' were specific to Tibet and had no administrative place outside the Tibetan context. Even the description of the legal status of Tibet as being under Chinese 'suzerainty' had no agreed meaning in international law. British officials on the Tibetan frontier considered such linguistic imprecision as politically useful, and understood the frontier as a zone in which precise definition was often best avoided. This imprecision at a practical level was allowed for within the development of a grand theoretical structure surrounding imperial frontiers, as we have seen.

Turner's imprecise use of the term 'frontier' was to be one of the most criticized aspects of his thesis. His detractors argued that his 'sweeping generalisations did not meet the rigorous standards of scientific analysis',[47] and that they resulted in a frontier that was 'a hazy and shifting concept, riddled with internal contradictions'.[48] Yet it is just these 'hazy and shifting...contradictions' that are, I contend, essential to the proper understanding of 'the frontier'. While the prevailing academic tendency is to search for definition, the nature of the frontier is such that it requires a different approach. In dealing with the unbounded systems of the frontier we might adopt the term 'fuzzy logic' from the physical sciences to describe the manner in which Turner's methodology allows us to avoid precision in an area where precision can only be in error.

In recognizing that the term 'frontier' implies a dimension that cannot be precisely measured or defined, we are reminded of C.C. Elridge's point in regard to the Victorian understanding of empire; that 'political and economic arguments alone would never have secured the almost universal support of the Victorian governing classes. What is missing is the emotional context, for belief in empire was never entirely rational... it was often the sense of mission...which convinced the doubtful and placed the empire above rational argument'.[49]

Just as there was an 'emotional context' to empire, so was there a dimension to the understanding of the frontier that cannot be classified in positivist terms. Although the mythology of the American West was a European construct with few, if any, obvious indigenous elements, in our region the mythology of the frontier had deeper roots. In the indigenous understanding the Himalayan frontier zone was the setting for much of the foundational mythology of the elite regional cultures; within Indic culture it was the homeland of the major Brahmanical deities, while in Tibetan Buddhist culture it not only housed the retreat centres of the great religious renouncers, but was considered to shield the 'hidden valleys' of apocryphal revelation. At a more popular level it was a region associated with magic and mystery, a worldly location of other-worldly power that was understood to have been drawn on by cultural 'heroes' such as Arjuna and the Pandava brothers, Padmasambhava, and Milarepa. This pre-modern understanding of the Himalayas as an other-worldly zone was widespread, reaching China and the European readers of Marco Polo's accounts of Tibetan 'necromancers'. More recently this belief underpinned the nineteenth century European construction of 'mythos Tibet'; that 'mysterious land on the Roof of the World'.[50]

That indigenous mythology affected colonial perceptions of the region. As the northern frontiers of the British presence in India developed, the British increasingly came into contact and conflict with previously unknown Himalayan cultures and polities and it was that new environment, allied to the dynamic nature of the expansion process, that made the frontier the prime location for an imperial mythology that combined both traditional indigenous and fresh European elements. As a result of this process a new 'hero' emerged in British imperial culture, the 'frontiersmen', who, in imposing British political and cultural hegemony, operated in constant confrontation with the paradoxes of social structures and systems alternative to their own. This encounter with the Himalayan 'wilderness' generated a 'heroic mythology' in imperial discourse, which situated the frontiersmen as an idealized hero in the legends of empire.[51]

This understanding of the Himalayas as an 'other-worldly' location and the construction of the imperial frontiersmen as 'heroes' affected the actions of the frontiersmen and thus the course of history.[52] We are faced with the problem of how to locate that dimension of historical causation into a wider history of the region.

EMBRACING THE MYTHOLOGICAL

In a previous study I have examined how the Tibet cadre became an integral part of British frontier mythology, a status that was part of their collective identity. They had absorbed the imperial legends in their youth and their service training and the glamour of service on the frontier was enhanced in this setting by the popular mystique associated with Tibet and the Himalayas.[53] While there was considerable mythology associated with the European settlement of the American West, and in some senses Turner contributed to that myth, his thesis largely excluded imaginary constructions of the frontier and focused on a purely physical environmentalist determinism.[54]

A more comprehensive analysis might, however, attempt to include the mythological aspects of the frontier location.

In seeking to locate the mythological aspects of the frontier within historical analysis, the application of Frederick Jackson Turner's model to the Indo-Tibetan frontier may be enhanced through consideration of the work of a later twentieth century namesake, Victor Turner, the American scholar of pilgrimage. Victor Turner drew on the anthropologist Arnold van Gennep's work on 'rites of passage', locating the pilgrims' status as within van Gennep's central transitional phase of 'liminality' (from the Latin *limen*, a threshold),[55] an ambiguous state 'betwixt and between' customary social categories. He used the term 'liminal' to emphasize a zone which though outside normal social structures and location was entered by choice, and his work stressed those aspects of freedom and ambiguity that prevailed at the interface of cultural change.[56]

In seeking to describe the many-faceted implications of a transitional location such as the Indo-Tibetan frontier in both historical time and imperial (and indigenous) imagination, the term 'liminal' is appropriate as it implies both the environmental and the mythological aspects of this zone; the latter aspect being difficult to otherwise quantify in historical terms. The works of Prescott, and Victor and Turner indicate that we may regard a frontier as a liminal zone of transition, where the absence of defined place and identity produced new responses by individuals, whose character was affected by the freedom and ambiguity of their location. Being on or outside the limits of a cultural centre, with its established identity and codes of meaning, this liminal zone becomes the setting for experience to be expressed as myth and legend.

The liminal status of the frontier implied a place which transformed the character of individuals entering the zone. This was an essential part of the wider belief in frontiers as zones of transformation. This effect of the frontier on the individual was generally portrayed in wholly positive terms in British India.[57] Lord Curzon considered that character was 'moulded' on the frontier by 'responsibility and...self-reliance', and that those with 'courage...patience and...initiative' found the frontier 'ennobling and invigorating'.[58] Similarly Melody Webb, in a study of the Alaskan frontier based on F.J. Turner's methodology, quotes an Alaskan pioneer as claiming 'nothing will test our men as to their real character, resourcefulness, courage and endurance...as...that hard frontier country'.[59]

The frontier zone·was a sphere of human encounter, a transitory process between cultures, races, and religions. For the imperial officer heading north from the colonial political and cultural centre of Calcutta towards the Tibetan political and cultural centre of Lhasa there was no abrupt change from 'familiar' to 'other'. Rather, they passed through a zone of transition between the two, the frontier zone that lay between the Indian terai and the Tibetan plateau. The process of transition was at once physical, cultural, and imaginary.

That an imaginary dimension of understanding 'the frontier' may exist has also been recognized by Ron Davidson in a recent article analysing Central Asia as a historical frontier of Indic Buddhism. Drawing on Turner's model of the frontier as a zone of encounter, he notes that the zonal nature of Central Asia as a frontier of China, as understood by Owen Lattimore and others, may be applied to the Indic frontier with that region. Lattimore described how Central Asia was occupied by 'a graduated series of social groups, from partly sinicized nomads and semibarbarized Chinese, in the zone adjacent to China, to steppe peoples in Mongolia, forest peoples in North Manchuria and Urianghai, and the peoples of the plateau in Tibet, of whom the more distant were virtually unmodified by such attenuated contacts as they had with China'.[60]

Davidson notes that if we replace 'China' with 'India', and speak of the Kusanas, the Sogdians, and others in the Western Tarim and Western Turkestan in the terms that Lattimore spoke of Mongols, Manchus, and others, 'much the same analysis would hold true', with environmental factors shaping economic and social processes. But he also identities a less quantifiable factor; the place of Central Asia in the Indic imagination. While Indic culture spread to other regions, not least Sri Lanka and Southeast Asia (Burma, Cambodia, and so on), without those regions attaining any particular imaginal resonance in India culture, many Indic 'missionary monks...became enamored of the paradoxical presence of metropolitan sophistication and rural isolation that Central Asia afforded'.[61] As a result

In aggregate...there is no other area of the world that has maintained a visibility so great in the literature and landscape of South Asia...the romantic aura of the desert oasis or isolated culture, encountered after a period of hard travel by merchants (who were secured by their own wealth and influence in India), has been an important factor. All the influential areas are difficult to visit, easily the objects of romantic fantasies, and exceptional primarily in the disparities between their verdant cities and the surrounding desert. The lack of understanding of these areas contributed to their legends.[62]

We may, therefore, identify a dimension to the history of the Indo-Tibetan frontier that augments Turner's thesis. The character of the frontiersmen both affected and was affected by the Himalayan frontier mythologies, indigenous and imperial. The lack of definition of the frontier gave it a freedom from fixed identity and place which made it a potential location for the transformation of experience into legend, a process which parallels the frontier experience elsewhere. Turner's rejection of precise definition is appropriate for the liminal experience of the frontier, but on the Indo-Tibetan frontier that experience cannot be divorced from its imaginary associations, which were integral to the character of the frontiersman.

IMPLICATIONS FOR INDIGENOUS HISTORIES

Having focused on the British experience of the Indo-Tibetan frontier, let us briefly consider examples of how aspects of Turner's thesis might be relevant to the study of indigenous Himalayan frontier history. The issue has been previously raised by Todd Lewis, who applied a centre-periphery model of analysis to Himalayan history.[63] He describes a historical process in which centres of Himalayan civilization[64] (particularly the Indic and Tibetan cultures, but including secondary core areas such as Kashmir, the Nepal Valley, and Assam),[65] radiated their influence outwards towards the periphery. The integration of the periphery into the socio-economic culture of the centre was facilitated by a nexus of religious and economic processes that included central political control of peripherally-located monasteries and the actions of moneylenders, merchants, and soldiers.[66] On the Turnerian model, Lewis identifies frontier zones of politico-cultural interpenetration that existed at the cultural periphery, noting particularly the religious compromises essential for survival in new locations and circumstances and the importance of ritual as means of cultural transformation and legitimization.[67] His frontier history is, anthropologically, 'multi-variant, contended by migrating hunter-gatherers, pastoral nomads, diaspora merchants of diverse origins, missionaries (Hindu, Buddhist, Muslim, Christian), pioneering generals and state officials. There were also ascetics, pilgrims, refugees and, in recent years, international development officials who have been key figures in frontier history'.[68]

We may, therefore, locate indigenous frontier zones of politics, culture, and religion in the Indo-Tibetan Himalayas, and here we might note that religion was at least as important a factor as economics was in sending people westward in America. But although the mythic aspects of Tibet were a considerable draw to Europeans, religion was not an explicit factor in the European movement into the Indo-Tibetan region, with the obvious exception of the missionaries. Similarly, while for logistical and security reasons the Himalayan frontier zone actually attracted few conventional religious practitioners or pilgrims before the British period, it did attract one group frequently ignored in Himalayan histories; the *sanyasis*, Indic religious renunciates and their Buddhist equivalents. Margaret Walsh has noted that in the American West 'mountain men' and fur trappers were at the end of an economic network;[69] so too were the sanyasis, who were both religious and economic agents of cultural penetration. Like the Christian missionaries, they recognized no political boundaries, and sought to extend their teachings beyond even the periphery of their culture. We may, therefore, utilize Hancock's distinction between official and missionary religious frontiers in considering indigenous religious histories of the region.

Questions of identity are more complex. Turner's account of the 'nationalizing force of the frontier'[70] involves a process determined by interaction with a *new* environment. It does not, therefore, seem applicable to the indigenous peoples of the American West (with whom Turner was not concerned), nor to the settled Himalayan communities in our period. But we have suggested a possible parallel between Turner's process and that where the imperial frontiersmen's separate identity potentially represented a preliminary stage in the development of a new political identity. What then were the processes that affected indigenous nationalism and identity in the same period; were they environmentally determined? Peter Robb's recent analysis of events and processes in the northeast of India in the 1880s suggests that for the indigenous peoples there, government initiatives played a key role in establishing an 'Indian identity'. He concludes that

[a]t least three elements of colonial administration seem likely to have helped create an Indian identity. The first is the establishment of fixed borders, the second the assertion of undivided jurisdiction or sovereignty within those borders, and the third the assumption of state responsibility for the well-being of the people in a kind of contract between ruler and ruled.[71]

Robb implies a wider process at work in that region, as the 'motive behind the closer definition of the frontier and the administration was not just the need to defend and define British territory; it was also the need to identify the peoples who were to be treated as British subjects'.[72] This 'need to identify' required the deliberate gathering of knowledge of the indigenous peoples,[73] and the equally deliberate use of what

Ranajit Guha called 'strategies of improvement';[74] initiatives aimed at various social groups as a means to bring them into identification with the state. Government initiatives led to the development and creation of national structures (state organizations, institutional frameworks such as boundaries, and so on), and social processes (community values, economic relationships, and the like) that constructed a nation state within the external border of 'India'.[75]

That external border, however, existed both in the 'narrow' sense of a line on the map and in the 'broad' sense in which 'there were various layers or zones of contestation and influence rather than a definite line of demarcation between one jurisdiction and another'. Within the external border there were 'various realms of transitional sovereignty' (princely states, tribal territories, and others), although these exceptions were gradually reduced. 'Thus the narrow internal frontier advanced, implying the spread of definite, measured and recorded categories, and their subjection to a single, centralized rule or sovereignty'.[76] We might also note here that the imperial government sought to encourage a similar process in Tibet. Implicitly recognizing the play of cross-border forces, they tried to encourage the Tibetan government to develop as a nation state, one with fixed borders, national institutions and symbols, and a sense of national identity, that would take on similar responsibilities for its citizens.[77]

The imperial frontiersmen were, therefore, engaged in a process that not only affected their own identity, but also that of the indigenous peoples of the region. It was, however, not a spontaneous result of interaction with the environment, but part of a wider process of definition, control, and political modernization on the nation state model. In demonstrating the processes instituted on the frontier by government action, Robb sheds light on a dimension ignored by Turner, and suggests a more complex pattern of interaction with the indigenous peoples in our region than Turner allows. By not situating his theories within studies of imperialism, Turner may have understated the extent to which political and legal initiatives on the frontier were the result of deliberate government strategies. As Mary Holdsworth has noted in regard to Russian expansion in Central Asia in the nineteenth century, 'The terms most often used in the despatches of the Russian governors of the border territories, in reports of emissaries, traders, and in discussions of ministers, etc. mean, to arrange, stabilize, organize, settle, quieten, suppress, pacify. These evoke overtones of deliberate decision'.[78]

APPLYING THE TURNER THESIS IN THE HIMALAYAS

While never precisely defined, the Indo-Tibetan frontier in the British imperial understanding consisted of a zone between the north Indian terai and the Tibetan town of Gyantse, just 120 miles southeast of Lhasa. The zone was a geographical one in that it occupied the Himalayan mountain range, while culturally it represented a frontier of encounter between Indic and Tibetan civilizations that had recently come under British influence. As we have seen, following Turner, we may identify a series of particular imperial frontiers that existed within that zone during the period under consideration—frontiers of trade, diplomacy, technology, and so on. It would be possible to represent these frontiers on a map which would show that most of them extended beyond the official border, some fell short of it, and while a few were fixed in time, the others waxed and waned throughout the colonial period, albeit with a general tendency to northward expansion. While the reverse would be true in that the Tibetans had frontiers of trade and pilgrimage within British India, the general tendency was for their frontiers to be broadly established while the British were expansionist. Given that a series of such expanding frontiers has been identified as making up a wider frontier zone of expansion both by Turner in the American West, and independently by Hancock in regard to Australia, this would appear to be characteristic of frontiers during the expansion into the region by a particular population group. Political and cultural advancement is made by a number of different agents, both independently and in collusion.

Although there were very different factors driving British expansion on the Indo-Tibetan frontier and the European settlement of the American West, the character of the frontiersmen described by Turner closely equates to the ideal frontiersman described by Curzon and his British contemporaries. Further studies, however, would be required to isolate the extent to which the two mid-nineteenth century constructs of the ideal frontiersmen informed each other. We are left to ponder the extent to which the ideal did actually represent the most appropriate type of person for the environment, and whether, or to what extent, it was the environment that produced that type of character.

Frederick Jackson Turner's refusal to define his frontier demonstrated his awareness of the wider implications of the term, and while he was not engaged with such issues, his avoidance of precise definition allows the inclusion of the indefinable influences of mythology and imaginary constructs. The very process of history has been affected by these constructs, as Davidson has indicated, and as we can see, for example, from the consequences of the lack of precise definition of the legal status of Tibet in the colonial period. Victor Turner's insights suggest a means of including these elements by understanding the frontier as a liminal zone of transition, in which aspects of myth and legend are a part of the regions' identity, and shape its history.

Thus it appears that Turner's American frontier experience has parallels with the essential features of the British imperial experience on the Indo-Tibetan frontier in regard to the zonal nature of the frontier and the construction of an idealized 'frontiersman' in response to the environment. Although the factors shaping indigenous identities in the same period were very different, both indigenous and foreign actors on the Himalayan field were aware of their location within mythical and legendary constructions of history, and their character and actions were affected by that understanding. While these were issues which Turner felt able to ignore in his history of the American West, any attempt at a 'totalizing history' of the Indo-Tibetan frontier must take these factors into account.

NOTES AND REFERENCES

1. The paper was based on his 1890 doctoral thesis from The Johns Hopkins University and was first published in the 1893 annual report of the American Historical Association (AHA) (1894). It is now most easily accessible reprinted in Ray A. Billington (ed.), 1966, *The Frontier Thesis: Valid Interpretation of American History?* New York: Krieger. For a summary of Turner's career, see Amy Craven, 1956, 'Frederick Jackson Turner', in R. Taylor (ed.), *The Turner Thesis: Concerning the Role of the Frontier in American History*, George Boston: Heath, pp. 76–86.
2. Craven, 'Frederick Jackson Turner', p. 11.
3. Ronald M. Davidson, 2003, 'Hidden Realms and Pure Abodes: Central Asian Buddhism as Frontier Religion in the Literature of India, Nepal, and Tibet', *Pacific World Journal of the Institute of Buddhist Studies*, 3 (4), p. 168. I am indebted to Geoffrey Samuel for drawing my attention to this article.
4. See Richard Hofstadter, 1966, 'The Thesis Disputed' in Billington (ed.), *The Frontier Thesis*, p. 103; Todd Lewis noted a decade ago that the American frontier historiographical tradition might profitably be applied to South and Southeast Asian contexts; see Todd T. Lewis, 1994, 'Himalayan Religions in Comparative Perspective: Considerations Regarding Buddhism and Hinduism Across their Indic Frontiers', *Himalayan Research Bulletin*, XIV (1–2), p. 25.
5. A few individuals obtained permission directly from the Tibetan government. For more details on this process, see Alex McKay, 1998, 'Tibet: The Myth of Isolation', in Paul van der Velde and Alex McKay (eds), *New Developments in Asian Studies: An Introduction*, London: Kegan Paul, pp. 302–16.

6. Hancock notes that the frontiers of 'economic empire...do not coincide with the frontiers of political allegiance'. W.K. Hancock, 1964, *Survey of British Commonwealth Affairs Vol. II; Problems of Economic Policy 1918–1939*, part 1, London: Oxford University Press, p. 27. For a wider examination of 'economic empire', see Peter Cain, 1980, *Economic Foundations of British Overseas Expansion 1815–1914* (Studies in Economic and Social History), London: Palgrave MacMillan.

7. In discussing the impact of these initiatives in Tibet, we might speak more generally of a frontier of modernity. In many senses the Himalayas remained a 'natural frontier' of disease, with most of the endemic diseases of tropical India absent from the mountain environment.

8. With the exception of official visitors, Bhutan remained entirely free of Europeans.

9. On the role of hill stations, see Dane Kennedy, 1996, *The Magic Mountains: Hill Stations and the British Raj*, Berkeley: University of California Press.

10. W.K. Hancock, 1942, *Survey of British Commonwealth Affairs, Vol. II, Problems of Economic Policy 1918–1939*, Oxford: Oxford University Press, part 2, p. ix.

11. Ibid., part 1, p. 4, n2.

12. Ibid., pp. 19, 22–3, 53–4; also see N. Etherington, 1984, *Theories of Imperialism: War, Conquest and Capital*, London: Croon Helm, p. 221.

13. See Albert Craig, n.d., *A Scot in Sikkim*, Edinburgh: Board of World Mission and Unity, pp. 10–13.

14. With their willingness to operate in a clandestine manner the missionaries did have some success in this regard. David Macdonald, a political department employee stationed just across the Tibetan frontier in Yatung during the 1909–24 era, was at that time of his life a particularly active Christian, and probably uniquely had even preached in Lhasa during the Younghusband mission; National Library of Scotland, Dep 298 (13), Minutes of the Church of Scotland Foreign Mission Committee 1903–6 (p. 300), David Macdonald to Dr Graham, 17 August 1904. On the missionary endeavour see also, Louis M. Fader, 2002 and 2004, *Called from Obscurity: The Life and Times of a True Son of Tibet, Gergan Dorje Tharchin*, Vols 1 and 2, Kalimpong: Tibet Mirror Press.

15. Regarding Annie Taylor, see William Carey, 1902, *Travel and Adventure in Tibet*, London: Hodder and Stoughton.

16. Regarding Bower, see Hamilton Bower, 1976 [1894], *Diary of a Journey Across Tibet*, Kathmandu: Ratna Pustak Bhandar. Regarding the Pandits, see P. Waller, 1990, *The Pandits: British Exploration of Tibet and Central Asia*, Lexington: University of Kentucky Press.

17. Billington, *The Frontier Thesis*, p. 5. Also see Margaret Walsh, 1981, *The American Frontier Revisited* (Studies in Economic and Social History), London: Palgrave MacMillan, pp. 15–17.

18. Taylor, *The Turner Thesis*, p. 79.

19. See Alex McKay, 1997, *Tibet and the British Raj: The Frontier Cadre 1904–1947* (SOAS London Studies on South Asia, 14), London: Curzon Press, especially chapter 5, pp. 77–85 and chapter 13, pp. 183–94.

20. Ibid., pp. 183–4.
21. Ibid.
22. This was frequently indicated in personal correspondence, see for example, Royal Geographical Society, Bailey correspondence, 1921–30; Irma Bailey to Arthur Hinks (RGS Secretary), 9 October 1924.
23. Alex Krausse, 1900 [1899], *Russia in Asia: A Record and a Study 1558–1899*, London: Curzon Press, 2nd edn, pp. 222–3.
24. Quoted in ibid., pp. 224–5.
25. See J.S. Galbraith, 1960, '"The Turbulent Frontier" as a Factor in British Expansion', *Comparative Studies in Society and History*, 2 (2), pp. 150–68.
26. Sir Alfred Lyall, 1891, *The Rise and Expansion of British Dominion in India*, London: John Murray; Sir Thomas Holdich, 1916, *Political Frontiers and Boundary Making*, London: Macmillan.
27. Curzon's extravagant phrases are only the most extreme example of a frequent tendency for frontier discourse to embrace excessive rhetoric, perhaps implying the articulation of a vision.
28. George Nathaniel Curzon, 1907, *Frontiers* (The Romanes Lecture, 1907), Oxford, p. 5.
29. Ibid., pp. 28, 30–1.
30. Ibid., pp. 42–3.
31. Ibid., pp. 37–9, 42.
32. Ibid., p. 47; Curzon's lecture drew heavily on the work of Alfred Lyall, a standard text of the period with which he was undoubtedly very familiar. Lyall had described how 'We surround ourselves...with a zone of land...under political taboo so far as concerns rival powers and thus our political influence radiates out beyond the line of our actual possession. The true frontier of the British dominion in Asia...does not...tally with the outer edge of...territory over which we exercise administrative jurisdiction...The true frontier includes... large regions over which the English crown has established protectorates...its object is...excluding a rival influence, and the right of exclusion carries with it the duty of defence. The outer limits of the territory which we are prepared to defend is what must be called our frontier.' Lyall, *The Rise and Expansion of the British Dominion in India*, pp. 336–7.
33. Ibid., p. 55.
34. Ibid., pp. 55–6
35. Ibid., pp. 28, 54–5.
36. Ibid., p. 57.
37. T.H. Thornton, 1895, *Sir Robert Sandeman*, London: John Murray, pp. 294–5.
38. Ibid., pp. 288–92.
39. Quoted in Melody Webb, 1985, *The Last Frontier: A History of the Yukon Basin of Canada and Alaska*, Albuquerque: University of New Mexico Press, p. 160.
40. Billington, *The Frontier Thesis*, p. 28.
41. In this section I draw on Alex McKay, 1995, 'Tibet and the British Raj 1904–1947: The Influence of the Indian Political Department Officers', London University SOAS (unpublished) PhD thesis, p. 236.
42. As Curzon notes (*Frontiers*, p. 51), 'delimination' refers to the processes for

determining a boundary including the associated treaty, while 'demarcation' refers to the actual work on the ground.

43. T.S. Murty, 1978, *Frontiers: A Changing Concept [sic]*, New Delhi: Palit and Palit, p. 14. Murty provides a good survey of the historiography of frontiers. Also see C.B. Fawcett, 1918, *Frontiers: A Study in Political Geography*, Oxford: Clarendon Press, pp. 5–6; J.R.V. Prescott, 1965, *The Geography of Frontiers and Boundaries*, London: Allen and Unwin.

44. Prescott, *The Geography of Frontiers*, p. 208.

45. Ibid., pp. 15, 30, 102; J.R.V. Prescott, 1972, *Political Geography*, London: St Martin's Press, pp. 54–5, 59–60.

46. Billington, *The Frontier Thesis*, p. 10.

47. Walsh, *The American Frontier Revisited*, p. 14.

48. George W. Pierson, 1966, 'Turner's Views Challenged', in Billington (ed.), *The Frontier Thesis*, p. 40.

49. C.C. Elridge, 1984, 'Sinews of Empire: Changing Perspectives', in C.C. Elridge (ed.), *British Imperialism in the Nineteenth Century*, London: Macmillan, pp. 188–9.

50. On 'Mythos Tibet', see, for example, T. Dodin and H. Rather (eds), 2001, *Imagining Tibet: Perceptions, Projections & Fantasies*, New York: Wisdom Publications.

51. L.D. Wurgaft, 1983, *The Imperial Imagination*, Middletown, CT: Wesleyan University Press, p. xvii.

52. See McKay, 'Tibet and the British Raj'.

53. Ibid., pp. 19–92.

54. Harry C. Allen (1966, 'The Thesis Upheld', in Billington (ed.), *The Frontier Thesis*, p. 117), does refer to the 'Go west young man' mythology of the American West, noting that the fact that an ideal of freedom existed was important even if the opportunity was not actually taken, in that it acted to some extent as a social 'safety valve'.

55. We might think here of parallels with the Sanskritic term for a pilgrimage place, *tirtha*, deriving from the meaning 'river ford/crossing'.

56. Turner came to favour 'liminoid' over 'liminal' but his later terminology is not more specific for our wider purpose; see Victor Turner, 1969, *The Ritual Process: Structure and Anti-Structure*, Chicago: Aldine, pp. 94–5; Victor Turner, Victor, 1973, 'The Center Out There: Pilgrim's Goal', *History of Religion*, 12 (3), especially pp. 199–200, 213–14; Victor Turner and Edith Turner, 1978, *Image and Pilgrimage in Christian Cultures: Anthropological Perspectives*, New York: Columbia University Press, especially, pp. 2, 35, 231, 249. As Murty, *Frontiers*, p. 78 notes, Arnold Toynbee had used the term 'limen' to describe a geographically located 'conductive cultural threshold' between a civilization and the 'barbarians' beyond: see Arnold Toynbee, 1960, *A Study of History*, abridgement by D.C. Somervill, Oxford: Oxford University Press, p. 678.

57. Paradoxically there is a parallel image of the frontier as a region of decay and degeneracy in which the worst aspects of surrounding cultures are expressed. For an example of this in the Central Asian context see Donald Rayfield, 1976, *Dream of Lhasa: The Life of Nikolay Przhevalsky*, London: Elek, pp. 39–40.

58. Curzon, *Frontiers*, pp. 56–7.
59. Webb, *The Last Frontier*, p. 96. We are reminded of Rama, emphasizing to Sita in the Ramayana, the hardness of the renunciate's life in the 'forest'.
60. Davidson, 'Hidden Realms', p. 170.
61. Ibid., p. 171.
62. Ibid., p. 172.
63. Lewis, 'Himalayan Religions', p. 25.
64. Also see Geoffrey Samuels, 1994, 'Tibet and the Southeast Asian Highlands; Rethinking the Intellectual Context of Tibetan Studies' in Per Kværne (ed.), *Tibetan Studies: Proceedings of the 6th Seminar of the International Association for Tibetan Studies, Fagernes 1992*, Oslo: The Institute for Comparative Research in Human Culture, vol. II, pp. 696–710.
65. Lewis, 'Himalayan Religions', pp. 33–4.
66. Ibid., pp. 28–32.
67. Ibid., pp. 26, 30, and 37.
68. Ibid., p. 39.
69. Walsh, *The American Frontier Revisited*, pp. 45–6.
70. As cited in Taylor, *The Turner Thesis*, p. 79.
71. Peter Robb, 1997, 'The Colonial State and Constructions of Indian Identity: An Example on the Northeast Frontier in the 1880s', *Modern Asian Studies*, 31 (2), pp. 245–83; the quotation is from pp. 248–9.
72. Ibid., p. 262.
73. Ibid., p. 267.
74. Ranajit Guha, 1989, 'Dominance Without Hegemony and its Historiography', in R. Guha (ed.), *Subaltern Studies VI*, New Delhi: Oxford University Press, p. 242, discussed in Robb, 'The Colonial State', pp. 251–2.
75. Robb, 'The Colonial State', pp. 251–2.
76. Ibid., pp. 249–51.
77. See McKay, *Tibet and the British Raj*, pp. 195–211.
78. Mary Holdsworth, 1959, *Turkestan in the Nineteenth Century: A Brief History of the Khanates of Bukhara, Kokand and Khiva*, Oxford: Central Asian Research Centre, St Antony's College Oxford Soviet Affairs Study Group, p. 46.

Inventing a Frontier

Imperial Motives and Sub-imperialism on British India's Northwest Frontier, 1889–98

Sameetah Agha

In 1886, the Commander-in-Chief of India Frederick Roberts declared in a memorandum that the advance of Russia in Central Asia called for a new policy. What was at stake was not just the defence of the Northwest Frontier but of the Indian empire itself. It was essential for the British to have command of the northern passes so they would be able to see 'the other side of the hill'. Roberts proposed that it was crucial in any scheme for the defence of the Northwest Frontier to have the tribes who occupied the intervening countries as allies:

> It is of such vital importance that we should get hold of the tribes, that I strongly advise a reconsideration of the policy which has guided us during the last thirty-eight years, and which has resulted in our knowing little more about our neighbours in the hills, than we did when first we occupied the Panjab, and in our being absolutely uncertain as to whose side they would be upon, in the impending struggle between Russia and England. Such an unsatisfactory state of affairs should not be allowed to continue longer'.[1]

Thus ensued a series of correspondence which led to a debate between the Government of India and Punjab on the state of affairs in the Frontier and the called-for departure in policy. The new more 'active' policy that the Government of India insisted upon adopting has been called the forward policy.

Based on unpublished archival sources, this essay examines the imperial motives behind this new policy and how it was actually played out in Waziristan. In the process, it offers a new view of the era in which the policy was undertaken leading up to the Great Tribal Revolt of 1897. Further, this study reveals the crucial role of sub-imperialism on this intractable fringe of the British empire in India. The term 'sub-imperialism' was conceptualized in the 1970s by the Brazilian economist Ruy Mauro Marini within the Marxist framework as 'the form that dependent capitalism assumes on arriving at the stage of the monopolies and finance capital.'[2] For Marini, sub-imperialism is characterized by the exercise of an autonomous expansionism and an increase in military expenditures and militarization of society. In world-systems theory, sub-imperialism is the semi-periphery which is used by the core to exploit the periphery. The concept has also been increasingly applied to South Africa's imperialist role in southern Africa. Here, I use sub-imperialism to describe the local machinery of imperialism and its driving role in how colonialism operated on the fringes of empire.

This essay is divided into two parts. In the first part, we will consider the imperial motives behind the forward policy and in the second part we turn to the question of sub-imperialism in Waziristan. No secondary sources have provided a microcosmic view of the forward policy nor have they examined how the policy was played out on the ground. Some of the imperial debates on the forward policy are well known from contemporary sources that discuss the distinction between the previous policy known as the close-border system or contemptuously as 'masterly inaction' and the forward policy. Elsewhere I argue that the distinction between the two was not as great as is made out in the historiography on the subject.[3] However, it is beyond the scope of this essay to focus on that debate. Instead, by focusing on the micro-history of a policy that attempted to carve out a frontier out of a thousand miles of mountainous terrain inhabited by tribes that embroiled the British in continuous warfare, this essay brings forth a different view of the colonial encounter on the Northwest Frontier of British India and gives us an understanding of how policy was made and played out on the remote geographic fringes of empire.

IMPERIAL MOTIVES

The forward policy called for bringing the tribes that inhabited the Northwest Frontier region under British influence and enlisting them as allies for the purposes of imperial defence. By 1889, two things had occurred. Lord Roberts was the Commander-in-Chief of India and Russia was expanding in Central Asia. Roberts was first and foremost a soldier and he remained convinced that 'we have won India by the sword, we hold it by the sword, and with the sword we must defend it'.[4] His military nature and his conviction of an impending conflict with Russia in Asia led to the defining of defence policy in terms of modern military science. Both these factors had an impact on thinking and policy in Frontier affairs. If Russia and England clashed in Asia, the likely scene of military operations would be the Northwest Frontier with the point of contact along the Kandahar–Ghazni–Kabul line. Thus, passes and approaches leading up to this line needed to be opened up and the militarized Pukhtun tribes inhabiting the region needed to be enlisted as allies for purposes of defence against the invading army.

The tribes that the British were now most concerned with enlisting consisted of the 'independent or semi-independent communities' that held the 'chain of almost impenetrable mountains' immediately outside the British administrative frontier line. The British divided these tribes into three broad divisions and regarded the Pathan division as the strongest and most important of the three: 'It contains several great tribes, such as the Afridis, Orakzais, and Waziris, inhabiting a rough mountainous country; and with the exception of a few non-Pathan Swaits and Kohistanis in the north, and some of the softer Pathan tribes in the south, all its million-and-a-quarter or more of inhabitants belong to hard untamed races. They are fanatical, brave, fairly armed, and inured to hardship and warfare from their childhood; and they can turn out at least 200,000 very formidable fighting men'.[5]

British relations with Pathan tribes were conducted, up to this point, by officers of the Punjab frontier districts, with the aid of two special Political Officers—Colonel Warburton stationed in the Khyber and an Assistant stationed at Thal. The Pathan division was not only the most important to the British, it was also the most difficult to control:

> With regard to the second or Pathan division, we find a totally different state of things. Except at one or two points, e.g., Kurram and the Khyber, our officers cannot cross the frontier; the tribes are thoroughly independent; and our own territory is frequently troubled by their raids. Except the Khyber we have no roads, and of course we have no railways, through their country; and though some of their men enlist in our regiments, and many live on our side of the border, we cannot be said to have gained any controlling influence over them.[6]

This was the crux of the 'problem' on the Northwest Frontier. Many in the Government of India thought it appalling that British control stopped at the foothills and the area beyond was off-limits.[7] But any forward move had to be justified as necessary for imperial defence. After much internal debate the Government of India concluded that the policy of pushing British influence across the Frontier would best be effected by the Punjab government. However, the Punjab government was wary about pushing a policy that called for interference amongst the tribes. On 17 October 1889, a letter was sent by the Government of India to the Punjab authorities instructing them on how to proceed:

The Government of India cannot consider its present relations with the trans-frontier tribes on the Punjab border as either suitable or satisfactory, and the absence of any friendly understanding between them and the neighbouring British Officers may at any time prove a source of serious danger and anxiety. The country within a day's ride of one of our most important garrisons is indeed almost a *terra incognita*, and there is no security for British life a few miles beyond the border. Punitive expeditions have been frequent, but have been attended with very few permanent results, and there is probably no other spot in the world where, after 35 years of peaceful occupation, a great civilized power has obtained so little influence over its semi-savage neighbours or has acquired so little knowledge of them.[8]

The Government of India felt that it was important that British control be established in the Kurram valley and that the lines of communication, such as the roads through Dir to Chitral and through the Tochi and the Gomal passes, be thoroughly explored. At the same time, they were unwilling to engage in direct annexation or confrontation: 'nothing...should be attempted nor should any step be taken likely to lead to a collision'.[9]

In 1896, the Government of India reviewed with satisfaction the results of the forward policy. The then Commander-in-Chief, George White, summed up the progress made since 1889:

1) Zhob has been brought under our protection; the long dreaded Sherani hills including the Takht-i-Suleiman, at which the Punjab Frontier Force had been looking for 40 years since the annexation of the Punjab, have been turned and the tribes, who formerly found safe sanctuary in their fastnesses, have been dominated and brought under control: 2) the Gomal has been traversed by our troops from Domandi to its eastern gate, and has since been rendered safe by 3) the conquest and occupation of Waziristan: 4) the Tochi has been annexed and direct communication opened between it and Bannu: 5) the Dir-Chitral route has not only been opened as a tribal postal route to Chitral, but a British right of way has been established and British forces have moved from the Peshawar valley to Chitral, and from Chitral to the Peshawar valley along roads held on our interests by tribal levies....7) the Durand Mission has settled a line of influence between Afghanistan and India, and it now remains to us but to safeguard the interests thus secured to us against Afghan repudiation of a bargain which entailed on us the payment of an extra subsidy of six lakhs a year, besides gifts of arms and numerous other benefits.[10]

These forward moves summed up by White are evidence of a clear contradiction to the stated policy, which did not seek to interfere with the independence of the tribes or annex their territories but only sought to foster close and friendly relations with the tribes so as to render India safe in the event of foreign aggression. Thus, despite the stated goals of the forward policy, the British were in effect undertaking a policy of annexation, all the while stating that this was far from their intention.

In 1897, the British faced one of the most formidable revolts in colonial history on the Northwest Frontier. The first outbreak occurred in Tochi in north Waziristan. The case of Waziristan provides us a glimpse of how the stated policy of bringing the tribes into close and friendly relations was actually implemented. This, in turn, offers a clear view of the contradiction between imperial motives and the events on the ground.

SUB-IMPERIALISM IN WAZIRISTAN

In January 1894, the Government of India wrote to the Secretary of State at Whitehall, 'We wish it to be clearly understood that nothing is further from our intentions than the annexation of tribal country on our frontier.'[11] But that was not all. While the Government of India did not want to annex the Wazirs and their territory, they wanted to show them that they were 'our men'.[12] So, the same telegram continued: 'We believe, however, that without annexation, and without interference in the internal affairs of the tribes, it will be possible to bring them further within our influence, and to induce them to regard themselves as owing allegiance to us.'[13] The Secretary of State agreed and replied:

I trust that the tranquillity of the border, especially in the neighbourhood of the Gomal, will now be secured. I observe that your Government emphatically repudiates all intention of annexing tribal territory, but desires to bring the tribes whom this settlement concerns further within your influence. I approve generally of the policy thus described; but I trust that in carrying it into effect your Government will carefully abstain from taking any steps to extend your influence which may tend to bring about a collision with the tribesmen, or to the establishment of fresh posts beyond the frontier which may require armed protection.[14]

The cleverness with which the instructions of Whitehall and the declared policy in Waziristan were violated demonstrate the power of sub-imperialism. This led to a series of events which culminated in the Tochi attack in 1897.

Early in 1894, a heated debate took place among the upper echelons of the British Government of India about their policy towards Waziristan. The question arose due to the agreement that the British had concluded with the Amir of Afghanistan in November 1893, which would demarcate the territories of British India and Afghanistan. The settlement to demarcate, which the Amir had yielded to unwillingly, was in turn the result of a struggle for dominion between the British and the Amir. The essence of the problem was that the British realized and stated that the territories in question were in no way theirs. But they did not want the Amir laying claim to them either. However, this problem was an imperial invention on the part of the British because tribal areas such as Waziristan may have had at some time owed a nominal allegiance on their own terms to the Amir but, by the 1890s they were independent.

However, the undefined and constantly shifting nature of the tribes' relationship with the neighbouring powers was something that was unacceptable to the British in India. In January 1894, Lord Lansdowne, the Viceroy of India, declared:

I take it to be an axiom of frontier administration that a tribe, or group of tribes, situated between two comparatively powerful States must be under the influence of one or the other of those States. There may be moments when the tribe finds it convenient to face both ways and to keep up simultaneous relations with two rival Courts or Governments. We have had illustrations of this in the case of the Waziris themselves, who, while affairs were in suspense, held constant communications with Kabul on the one side, and with our Frontier officials on the other.... Such a condition of things is, however, fruitful of intrigue, and dangerous to all concerned.... It is necessary that there should be a clear understanding with the Waziris, as well as with the Amir, that they are, to use a very convenient expression, 'our men', and no one else's, or, as we should put it in an official paper, that they fall within our sphere of influence, and not within that of any other Power.[15]

Having decided without their wishes that they were 'our men' the British government had to figure out what this policy meant and how best to implement it. The debate on the new forward policy in Waziristan was waged during much of 1894.

As a result of the agreement reached between the British government and the Amir of Afghanistan, the latter was precluded from all interference in Waziristan except a small portion of it called Birmal. What would the state of affairs be in the rest of Waziristan, which the British now claimed lay within their sphere of influence? The British insisted that it was 'absolutely necessary that this block of country should not be allowed to fall under Afghan influence.'[16] This was because the colonial military authorities had decided that in case of a Russian advance into Afghanistan, the best response for the British would be to advance to the Kabul–Ghazni–Kandahar line. In order for advance to be made rapidly, it was necessary to control and be able to use the principal approaches leading from British India to that line. As the Government of Punjab was in charge of the local administration of the frontier regions, the Government of India referred the question of Waziristan to Punjab for input.

The first reports on the question from Punjab were provided by three local officers—R.I. Bruce, Commissioner and Superintendent, Derajat; L.W. King, Deputy Commissioner, Dera Ismail Khan; and H.A. Anderson, Deputy Commissioner of Bannu. Bruce was the seniormost of the three and for several years had proposed a forward policy. However, he was sceptical of the tribes' eagerness to ally with the British: 'I do not for a moment say that the hill sections on the Tochi–Thall side are waiting to rush into our arms and say "Mark out your boundary and our country; its routes and resources are open to you and we are your submissive subjects".'[17] On certain terms, though, Bruce believed they could be brought around.[18] He advised that the tribes would 'eagerly welcome' the establishment of military posts as they are 'alive to the fact that nothing can prosper amongst themselves, and that they will be constantly in hot water with the British Government and with the Amir unless they are constrained by some controlling authority to maintain peace towards one another'.[19] In terms of resigning their independence, Bruce concluded that their idea of independence meant 'a title to be free of all wholesome controlling authority, with a general license to cut throats, maintaining a state of anarchy in the country, making it useless for all practical purposes and an actual source of danger and weakness in times of trouble...'[20]

Bruce proposed that the government pursue three objectives, all in line with past imperial declarations:

1–To bring the tribes into line with ourselves by the establishment of intimate and friendly relations identifying their interests with ours, rendering the resources of the country available for our requirements, and thus making our border land and its tribesmen a factor of strength in the great scheme of imperial frontier defence, instead of a source of weakness as it is while left in the normal condition of anarchy. 2–The opening of the Tochi, Gumatti–Thall, and other routes, and the establishment of safe lateral communication between the Gomal and Kurram beyond the Mahsud hills. The latter may be said to be more particularly the local object and follows the first as a matter of course. 3–The amelioration of the condition of the frontier tribes by the extension of humanising influences over them, redeeming them from their semi-barbarous condition and putting them in the way of earning an honest livelihood.[21]

In order to attain these objectives, Bruce pushed for the Sandeman policy to be applied to Waziristan.[22] Essentially, this involved establishing a military station in the area with an outpost and giving the tribesmen and their leading headmen allowances. While the other two Punjab officials, King and Anderson, largely concurred with Bruce and proposed an immediate demarcation of the boundary, they also warned of indications that the tribes were not wholly pleased with the agreement reached with the Amir, which had 'sold' their territory without their consent to the British. The territory in question was Birmal, which was considered joint country of all the Darwesh Khels. The tribe encamped there in the summer to graze their cattle. As Anderson stated in his report:

In the first place, until the Darwesh Khel have given us a mandate to align the boundaries of Waziristan, they not unnaturally question our right to fix their boundaries. Waziristan is a perfectly independent country according to their views, and they should be consulted before any portion of what they claim is assigned to a third party...It needs little argument to show that if the Waziris are dissatisfied with the boundary, they being headstrong hillmen, will not only be unwilling to assist in demarcating their boundary, but will do their best to throw difficulties in the way of the Commission appointed to do so.[23]

Both Anderson and King warned against demarcating the boundary without coming to some sort of arrangement with the tribes first. By giving them subsidies and raising levies from among them to keep the routes open, all three officers, and especially Bruce, advocated the 'pacification' of Waziristan. The fact that 'pacification' amounted to annexation and was counter to the stated policy was not lost on some.

Sir Dennis Fitzpatrick, the Lieutenant Governor of Punjab, strongly disagreed with Bruce and tried to persuade the Government of India not to pursue what amounted to a policy of occupation.[24] He argued that the policy would backfire and instead of the tribes becoming allies of the British, would come to resent them. The case was extensively discussed in the Governor General's Council. Some of the members of the Council also pointed to the contradiction in policy advocated by the local officers. C.B. Pritchard made a forceful case:

If we push forward our military posts beyond the Gomal, make roads through Waziri territory, levy tribute from the tribes, interfere in their quarrels, and undertake to prevent them from raiding into Afghanistan, we shall destroy the independence of the Waziris and be practically assuming the administrative control of their country, in whatever terms we may choose to describe our action....The cost of these operations will be enormous. In carrying them out we shall have to encounter and overcome much stubborn resistance; and, if the new line of posts along the Afghan border is laid, we shall find ourselves in contact with a fresh set of tribesmen who are likely to prove quite as troublesome neighbours to deal with in the future as the Waziris have proved in the past. A forward movement and a policy of the nature just described seems to me to transgress alike the declarations of policy made in our despatches to the Secretary of State, and the instructions of that authority.[25]

However, Pritchard, along with other dissenting members, was brushed aside when the Council drafted a despatch to the Secretary of State in England proposing a policy along the lines of Bruce's scheme. While the details of how the policy was to be implemented were not completely clear, it was decided that: a) it was necessary to establish a strong military post in the country; b) a Demarcation Commission would proceed to mark out the boundary in October accompanied by troops; c) a Political Officer would be deputed to explain to the Wazirs the nature of the relations which the British government intended to establish with them as it was 'desirable that these negotiations should be carried on at a time when we are able to make a strong display of force';[26] and d) allowances would be given to the headmen to enlist inferior men for service in levy posts.

Dennis Fitzpatrick of the Punjab government continued to argue against this policy before the Government of India insisting that Bruce, whether 'by hook or by crook', was attempting to draw the government on. He feared that the leading men of the tribes whom Bruce wanted to subsidize and through whom the British worked were ultimately 'too weak to control their people' in a country where the tribes were organized on an extremely democratic basis. 'This will, I fear be one of our greatest difficulties, if we undertake the pacification of Waziristan.'[27] In August, Henry Fowler, the Secretary of State reluctantly approved the policy on the condition that interference with the tribes and the outlay of money in Waziristan would be kept within the narrowest practicable limits.

On 25 October 1894, Bruce, having been appointed Commissioner of the Delimitation Commission, arrived with a brigade of all arms in Wana. A few days before his arrival he had received a letter from Mullah Powindah stating that troops should not be stationed at Wana and that the British should abstain from interfering in the country as these areas were under Mahsud limits.[28] He also demanded the release of five prisoners who had been taken in 1893 for the murder of a British officer. Bruce sent back a reply to the Mullah saying that he declined to have any communications with him except through the tribal Maliks.

On 3 November, Mullah Powindah and an estimated 3,000 followers attacked the British camp at night. The British force, 'considered strong enough to suppress such opposition as any sections of the Waziris might be inclined to offer,'[29] was unable to ward off the attack. At the break of daylight, the Wazirs retreated. The resulting loss to the British was 120 killed and wounded, including several officers. The government offered the tribes terms to make reparation, which included: (a) the surrender as hostages of 18 of the principal men engaged in the attack; (b) the banishment from the country of Mullah Powindah; and (c) the surrender of every rifle, horse, and the money stolen from the British camp. The Maliks were set the task of getting the Mahsuds to comply with the terms. They failed to do so.

Therefore the government decided to sanction a punitive expedition against the Mahsuds. On 15 December, political control was transferred from Bruce to Lieutenant General Sir W.S.A. Lockhart and two days later, he assumed command of the Waziristan Field Force. In order to punish the Mahsuds for the attack, the troops blew up their houses, carried off their forage and grain, and captured their flocks and herds. The Mahsuds had taken refuge in the higher valleys along with their families. The village of Marobi belonging to Mullah Powindah was completely destroyed with the exception of a mosque. The Lee-Metford rifle together with cordite was used for the first time in frontier warfare.[30] In February, the Field Force also started the work of demarcating the boundary.

So far the Waziristan policy had not proved successful. It had become clear that the delimitation was not approved by the tribes and they did not want the British in their country. Following these events, Bruce wrote a report to the government attempting to explain the situation. He stated that since the opening of the Gomal Pass in 1889, 'a uniform and consistent policy' had been pursued in regard to the Wazirs:

The foundation on which this entire policy rests, which is the same as that which has so successfully been pursued in Beluchistan, is support and encouragement to leading headmen who throw in their lot with and range themselves on the side of Government, the controlling through them of the marauding factions and bad characters, and the consequent maintenance of peace and order.[31]

He stated that it would be 'an unfortunate mistake' to conclude from this punitive expedition that the policy had been a failure. To prove that the policy had not failed, he pointed to the 'friendly attitude' of the Maliks who wanted the British in their country. The fact that there was a large proportion of 'marauding factions' who wanted otherwise made it difficult to make the case. Nevertheless, Bruce pressed that 'if persevered in and reasonable support is afforded by the Government, there is no obstacle that can not be overcome.'[32] Again, he advocated the permanent occupation of Wano.

At this point, the British entered Tochi and began their dealings with the Madda Khel. This led to a series of events, which I would argue culminated in the Maizar outbreak over two years later. In December, one of the columns attached to the Field Force marched through northern Waziristan to reach its destination of Razmak. In February, the troops entered Tochi with the purpose of demarcating the northern portion of the boundary. Anderson, the Deputy Commissioner of Bannu, then summoned the Madda Khel and the Dawar in order to explain to them the objects of the government. Commander Lockhart commended Anderson for making it possible for the troops to march through the Darwesh Khel country and 'succeeded in overcoming all objections on the part of the inhabitants to my advance up the Tochi valley.'[33]

Sadda Khan was one of the main Maliks with whom Anderson dealt. The Tochi Maliks met with Anderson in Bannu and said they did not wish the British to enter Tochi as they were afraid that their country would be occupied. Anderson assured Sadda Khan and other Maliks that the purpose of the government was just to delimit the boundary and not to occupy Tochi. Sadda Khan arranged for supplies and sent men to escort the troops during the delimitation.

Anderson and Bruce were confident that the Maliks of Tochi were friendly and open to the occupation of Tochi by the British:

The Darwesh Khels of the Tochi, the Tori Khel, Mohmit Khel and Madda Khel, have shown conclusively by the friendly way in which they welcomed us that they are exceedingly well disposed to us, and that they do not in any way resent our coming into the valley. All sections have expressed their willingness that our occupation should continue. They are quite ready to accept allowances and to observe the conditions in return for which they are granted.[34]

Anderson presented a scheme for the permanent occupation of Tochi that included the distribution of allowances and the establishment of military posts. Not only was Anderson misrepresenting the feelings of the Darwesh Khel to the government, he was also deceitfully misleading the tribes as to the true intentions of the British presence in Tochi. The events that followed made it clear that the tribes were not well-disposed to British troops.

On 13 May, the troops moved up to Boya, a cooler part of the valley. On the same day, a British officer of the sixth Punjab Infantry, Mr Limond, a sepoy, and a syce were attacked by four men. Limond and the syce were killed, the sepoy recovered. Three of the assailants were bayoneted or shot by the British troops and the fourth ran away. He was soon discovered and shot two days later. The houses of all four were blown up. And to inflict the utmost retribution for this attack, the bodies of the first three assailants were burnt, an act of defilement that the tribes regard as being worse than mutilation. Muslims believe that if the body of a person is burnt and not buried in accordance with Muslim custom, then the person is denied paradise. A few days later, Anderson received a petition from the Maliks of the Tochi valley documenting their dismay:

The bodies of the three persons of Khare Killa Amzoni who attacked a British officer on the 13th near camp Boya were burnt which was quite contrary to our religious ordinances. No such action was ever taken during Pushtu times, and this has been greatly disapproved of both by the Darwesh Khel and the Dauris of the Tochi valley. It has brought shame on us. We request therefore that the Government should suitably compensate us for this shame which we endured, as the burning of dead bodies is objectionable and prohibited according to the Muhammadan Law.[35]

Anderson decided against compensation but reported that the burning of the bodies had 'created so great a stir throughout the Tochi Valley'[36] that such an action should not be repeated in future. Bruce also remarked that 'the Muhammadans regard the burning of bodies as hitting below the belt and I must say I have some sympathy with the feeling and not think that assassination, being amongst their methods, is sufficient reason for our resorting to such measures.'[37]

As for the attack itself, Bruce hastened to assure the government that it should not conclude 'from the acts of a few individual fanatics that the general feeling and wish of the people for our occupation of the Tochi, so frequently expressed, had changed, and should recommend that they should have no effect on the Government policy.'[38] Anderson also dismissed the attack as one inspired by 'pure fanaticism'[39] by a gang of bravos and assassins.

However, a few days later, on 18 May, another attack occurred in Miran Shah where a Pathan Lance-Naik of the Second Punjab Infantry was killed by Wazir herdsmen. One of the herdsmen was killed in retaliation and 10 people found in the vicinity of the attack were taken prisoners and their flocks detained. Reports also started coming in that a change had come over the people of Tochi as they had become strongly hostile towards the British taking possession of their country. There were also reports that the troops harassed the people in Tochi: 'The camels graze on and injure their trees and nobody takes the matter into consideration. They say Shaftala [grass], &c., are not paid for at all. The sepoys take fruit from the gardens by force.'[40] There were also reports that the tribes were looking to Mullah Powindah for leadership to help them oppose the British. The Mullah was attempting to effect peace between the Mahsuds and the Darwesh Khels so that they could resist the British.

Anderson and Bruce discounted these reports. Bruce claimed that 'popular feelings could be accurately gauged by Sadda Khan'[41] and other leading Maliks who approved of the British presence. Anderson stated that the feeling of discontent was due to the fact that allowances had not been granted as yet. Once the allowances were distributed, he assured, the feeling of dissatisfaction would disappear.

The government went along with their assessment. Anderson submitted a scheme of 13 posts to be established in Tochi. Meanwhile, several difficulties arose over the question of how best to distribute the allowances. Anderson proposed handing over the allowances to the tribes and letting them decide how to make the distribution among individuals and different sub-sections. Bruce pointed out that their entire policy was aimed at singling out certain Maliks and strengthening their position so that they would be able to control their tribes in the interest of the British:

I would also point out that in my opinion the granting of small allowances to a great number of big and little Maliks on the basis of tribal distribution will not of itself secure an efficient hold on any tribe. At any time when the tribe's relation with the Government become strained in any way, the individual Maliks having only small interests in the allowances will not as a rule mind risking them, while we cannot safely reckon in working on the tribe as a whole merely through these allowances. It is therefore most desirable that the self interests of the men of note and leading in the country should be bound up with ours, so that in times of trouble or difficulty we may be able confidently to reckon on their ranging themselves on the side of Government.[42]

Meanwhile shots continued to be fired into the British camp and a few days after the attack in Miran Shah, another attack occurred inside the post when two sepoys were stabbed. Anderson explained to the government that

it is impossible to expect that in a highly fanatical country like Dawar fanatical outrages will not occur, and in the same way we cannot expect savage young Waziris to become at once orderly and obedient subjects. It is likely enough, too, that intriguers will make foolish efforts to organize against us the unruly elements in the tribes of the valley and their brethren, not with the object of driving us out of the country, but with the view of increasing the allowance.[43]

However, Anderson was getting lists made of the 'more turbulent characters' and a careful watch would be maintained on them. The higher authorities went along with Bruce and Anderson's views. The

Chief Secretary to the Government of Punjab wrote to Bruce in reply to his reports:

It may of course be that whatever feeling there is against us in the Tochi at this moment worth speaking of is due merely to the delay in granting the allowances, and some of those untoward incidents which must, in spite of all care and vigilance, occur from time to time when a military force is in camp in a strange country, but we must be on the lookout for and carefully study any symptoms going to indicate more deep-lying and permanent causes of ill-will against us.[44]

The British stayed on in Tochi and the military posts continued to be built. The government accepted the views of the 'men on the spot' that in order to open up the Tochi route, it was necessary to establish permanent military posts there. The policy in Tochi was based on strengthening the hands of Maliks such as Sadda Khan, who approved of the British presence in their country. Bruce and Anderson, the 'men on the spot', also indicated to the government that except for a few 'turbulent spirits', the inhabitants of Tochi approved of the British being there. The allowances were finally distributed to the tribes in November and December 1895. The success or failure of Bruce's policy, with Anderson in close step, can be assessed after looking at the event that occurred next.

In February and March 1896, 'tribal agitation and demonstrations'[45] occurred in Tochi. On 9 February, there was a 'riotous demonstration'[46] in the Sheranni post by the Madda Khels. About 100 members of the tribe had gathered there to discuss the allowances. Several 'minor Maliks' had gathered who had not been given any allowances and according to Anderson, 'excitement followed the discussions, and some of the more turbulent spirits threatened to turn the Munshi out of the temporary Sheranni post and also threatened some of the levies.'[47] The mob also threatened the posts. Piyal and Nur Muhammad were leaders in the discussions that preceded the riot, but they restrained the mob and assisted the Munshi. The gathering dispersed.

On 14 February, Anderson reported that an 'extremely aggressive'[48] letter was sent to the Political Officer, Mr Casson. He did not discuss the contents of the letter but attributed it to a 'fanatical writer'.[49] Anderson reported that the Maliks represented to him that 'a certain amount of agitation prevailed', and that Sadda Khan ascribed the agitations due to 'insufficient and incorrectly distributed allowances.'[50] Furthermore, Sadda Khan 'persistently represented that the agitation had grown beyond his control, and he asked that troops should be sent up the valley to assist him in suppressing it'. On 16 March, during the religious festival of Id, another demonstration occurred. A large number of people had assembled at the ancestral tombs of Sadda Khan's family, as was the usual custom. The gathering turned into an agitation when the Mullahs charged the Maliks with bringing British troops into their country. The people dispersed, but various 'alarmist reports'[51] were received by the Muharrirs of the posts. Anderson discredited these reports because he felt that the Muharrirs 'were being utilized by the intriguing Maliks for their own ends.'[52] He felt that the Maliks, including Sadda Khan, were at the root of the agitation, the cause of which he attributed to the desire of the Maliks and tribesmen to put pressure on the government to make a substantial increase to the allowances. He believed that Sadda Khan had instigated the agitation. Anderson stated that this belief was shared by 'that shrewd and well-informed observer, Gholam Muhammad Khan, Assistant District Superintendent, Police.'[53] But he concluded that he did not doubt Sadda Khan and the other leading Maliks' 'loyalty as a body and individually to their promises made to Government.'[54] 'I do not doubt that Sadda Khan in asking for troops really wishes the support of troops to strengthen his authority over his section.'[55]

Casson did not agree with Anderson and Ghulam Muhammad Khan that Sadda Khan was responsible for the agitation. On the last day of March, Anderson met with many of the Maliks who demanded certain conditions:

The Maliks, however, unanimously pressed me to obtain for them some written assurance for the satisfaction of their tribesmen that the government will not take revenue from them; they will be exempt from Court Fees; their jungle and grazing grounds will not be interfered with; that their mines will remain their own; that cases regarding women will be decided according to their own customs and offenders will be confined in jails in the Tochi.[56]

The event that occurred next is the one that was most immediately connected to the Maizar outbreak. On 9 June, Honda Ram, the Muharrir of the Sheranni post, was murdered by Waris Khan, who belonged to the Ali Khan Khel section of the Madda Khels. Mr Gee had by then taken over the position of Political Officer of Tochi Valley, Anderson having been promoted to Bruce's former position as Commissioner and Superintendent of Derajat. Waris Khan escaped soon after into Birmal, which was now Afghan territory. The British could have demanded his surrender from the Afghan authorities. However, Anderson decided that if such a demand were made, the Afghan authorities would be entitled to make a reciprocal demand on the British 'which may be inconvenient'.[57]

This showed that the object of British policy of delimiting the boundary and occupying Tochi with a view to facilitating the solving of raids and 'outrages' across the border was unsuccessful. Instead of pursuing the known murderer, Gee called upon the Maliks (none of whom were present in Sheranni on the day of the murder) to surrender several people who had 'incited' Waris Khan to commit the murder even though he was alone when he had committed the murder. These people were supposed to be religious students of Mullah Ghain-ud-din, who according to Anderson had been regularly preaching against British occupation and 'promising paradise to any one who should kill a servant of Government'.[58] The Maliks expressed to Gee their inability to comply with his demand.

Anderson submitted a report on the general situation in Tochi in which he noted that it had become unsafe for the levies to move around the area. Further, he stated:

Intrigues against the Maliks and their authority are at work, and in fact the control of the Maliks over the turbulent characters of their sections has been relaxed. Offences have been committed in which the offenders have not been brought to justice, such as the looting of the contractor's fir poles near Dre Vasta, the destruction of bricks at the Muhammad Khel Post, the murder of two coolies of the Muhammad Khel Post, the theft of the Kanirogha Muharrir's property, the killing of a levy sowar's horse, the attack on the dak sowar near Pakki Killa, and the theft of his horse. The Maliks find themselves growing weaker and unable to control the bad characters.[59]

The new policy in Waziristan, which had been based on strengthening the Maliks essentially by bribing them, had proved unsuccessful. And Anderson's constant urgings that the inhabitants of Tochi approved of British presence, if true, was working in a strange way—unless the majority of the inhabitants had turned into 'turbulent spirits'.

Anderson and Gee submitted to the government that the only way to remedy things was to advance troops into the upper Tochi to strengthen the hands of the Maliks. Gee proposed that a fine of Rs 2,000 be inflicted on the Madda Khels to punish them for the murder of Honda Ram and a fine of Rs 1,000 for the agitation that had occurred in February. The reason why Gee added the latter fine, even though it had not been inflicted at the time of the agitation, was that by now the Muharrirs of other posts, all of them Hindu, had resigned and refused to serve. Gee and Anderson's logic was that the Muharrirs having withdrawn, they had no employee in that tract whose safety for which they were responsible. So they could now 'realize fines by putting additional pressure on the tribe, and this is a reason for imposing fines now which did not exist before.'[60] Of course the infliction of fines would not mean the exemption of suspected persons from arrest.

In February 1897, the suspected men including Mullah Ghain-ud-din were produced before Gee and tried. They were exonerated from the murder of Honda Ram and released. Gee reported that the Mullah appeared to be 'a quiet retiring man with more learning than the ordinary run of Mullahs usually possess, and I regard his coming in and taking the oath as most satisfactory.'[61] Gee reduced the fine from Rs 2,000 to Rs 1,200.

Following Gee and Anderson's recommendation, after the murder of Honda Ram, troops were moved into Tochi at Datta Khel. However, Anderson reported that something more was needed:

We cannot expect to get the Darwesh Khels well in hand for our purposes unless we undertake to establish peace and order in their country, and this can not be effected without interfering in their internal disputes. Admitting then that we must interfere in the settlement of internal disputes, the question arises whether we are in any way bound not to interfere in their internal concerns. At the time we concluded our settlement with the Darwesh Khels in 1895 we told them that we did not want to take possession of their country, nor to interfere in their internal affairs, and so long as they behaved themselves and did not force us to do so, we should not interfere, nor take possession of their country.[62]

Asked by the Lieutenant Governor 'whether this interference in the internal disputes of the Darwesh Khels is not a breach of faith with the tribe', Anderson responded that even if they had led the tribe to believe that they would not interfere in their internal disputes, 'their subsequent conduct has been such as to absolve us from any obligation to abstain from doing so.'[63]

The next 'outrage' to occur was the Maizar attack. When the attack occurred, Gee and Anderson reported that it was fanatical. This fit perfectly with the pattern of their past explanations that whenever an 'outrage' was committed it was the work of 'fanatical' and 'turbulent spirits' and did not represent the majority of the people. But in the case of Maizar they could not argue that it did not represent the feelings of the people, as almost all the inhabitants had taken part.

The series of events in north Waziristan discussed reveal a complex network of sub-imperialism that entangled and drew the government on, in spite of its stated objectives. The Government of India went along willingly (apart from a few voices of dissent), and Whitehall somewhat reluctantly. The local Government of Punjab was a sullen bystander and attempted to provide a restraining hand at times, but was ultimately brushed aside. The question is why was the government continually drawn in, when that is the last thing it stated it wished to do? My answer is that ultimately the logic of this sub-imperialism coincided with the logic of the vast imperial machinery of the nineteenth century. The government had two options before it in this case: to be drawn in (in one way or another) or to say that the Frontier and the Pukhtuns were beyond its grasp. It chose the former.

NOTES AND REFERENCES

1. Frederick Roberts, 1887, 'Extract from a Memorandum on the desirability of making a Military Road through the Kohat Pass', 17 August 1886, *Proceedings of the Government of India* (hereafter *PGOI*), *Foreign Frontier* (hereafter *FF*), 1887 (Directorate of Archives, Peshawar, North-West Frontier Province, hereafter DOAP).

2. Ruy Mauro Marini, 1972, 'Brazilian subimperialism', *Monthly Review*, 23 (9), pp. 14–24.

3. Sameetah Agha, manuscript in progress, 'The Limits of Empire: British-Pukhtun Encounter on the North-West Frontier of British India'.

4. J.L. Morison, 1936, *From Alexander Burnes to Frederick Roberts: A Survey of Imperial Frontier Policy*, Raleigh Lecture on History, 15 July 1936, (Proceedings of the British Academy, 1936), p. 200.

5. Lord Lansdowne, 1889, 'Proposed New Arrangements for the Administration of the N.W. Frontier Districts and the Management of the Trans-Frontier Tribes', *PGOI*, Secret Frontier (from hereon Sec. F), (DOAP).

6. Ibid.

7. As far back as 1877 Lord Lytton had proposed a great Frontier Chief Commissionership to deal with the trans-frontier tribes and to administer the frontier districts of the Punjab. In another proposal, the Commander-in-chief recommended that the political work of the Frontier should be placed under the orders of a single high officer reporting directly to the Government of India. In one way or another all these schemes revolved around removing the authority of the Punjab government so that India had more power.

8. 'From—The Secretary to the Government of India, Foreign Department, To—The Secretary to the Government of Punjab, 17 October 1889', *PGOI*, Sec. F, 1889 (DOAP).

9. Ibid.

10. G.S. White, 15 June 1896, 'Administration of the Frontier Districts of the Punjab and the Management of the Trans-Frontier Tribes', *PGOI*, Sec. F, August 1896 (National Archives of India, New Delhi, hereafter NAI).

11. 'From—GOI, To—The Secretary of State, 3rd January 1894', *PGOI*, Sec. F, Keep With (from hereon KW), April 1894 (DOAP).

12. Ibid.

13. Ibid.

14. 'From—Secretary of State, To—GOI, 2nd February 1894', *PGOI*, Sec. F, April 1894 (DOAP).

15. 'Arrangements for the demarcation of the Amir's frontier from the vicinity

of Wakhan to the Persian border by joint British and Afghan commissions in accordance with the agreement concluded with His Highness in November 1893', *PGOI*, Sec. F, KW, April 1894 (DOAP).

16. Ibid.
17. 'From—R.I. Bruce, Esq., CIE, Commissioner and Superintendent, Derajat Division, To—The Officiating Chief Secretary to the Government of Punjab, 28th February 1894', *PGOI*, Sec. F, April 1894 (DOAP).
18. Ibid.
19. Ibid.
20. Ibid.
21. Ibid.
22. Bruce was a disciple of Sandeman and believed his methods in Baluchistan for pacifying the tribes would work well in the Pukhtun areas as well. The policy was one of working with headmen. However, critics pointed out that there were no headmen among Pukhtuns and the policy would not work.
23. 'From—H.A. Anderson, Esq., Deputy Commissioner of Bannu, To—The Commissioner and Superintendent, Derajat Division, 25th February 1894', *PGOI*, Sec. F, April 1894 (DOAP).
24. Dennis Fitzpatrick, 'Note by His Honor the Lieutenant-Governor of the Punjab on the demarcation of the Waziri boundary, 14 March 1894', *PGOI*, Sec. F, KW, 1894 (DOAP).
25. C.B. Pritchard, 6 June 1894, *PGOI*, Sec. F, KW, 1894 (DOAP).
26. 'From—The GOI, To—The Secretary of State for India', *PGOI*, Sec. F, July 1894 (DOAP).
27. Extract from a letter from Sir D. Fitzpatrick, KCSI, Lt Governor of the Punjab, to the Viceroy, dated Camp Thal, 20 March 1894, *PGOI*, Sec. F, July 1894 (DOAP).
28. Mullah Powindah had emerged as a leader of the Mahsud Wazirs in 1889, when the British first started encroaching in Waziristan. He set himself up and was seen as a leader in opposition to the Maliks who the British had been subsidizing and whose influence they sought to strengthen. By 1894, Mullah Powindah had gathered a formidable following which included those Maliks who did not support the British. Mullah Powindah used the banner of religion to rally support to his movement. However, his goals were political—to resist the British in order to preserve the independence of Waziristan. He emerged as a charismatic political-religious leader, because of which it was even more difficult for the Maliks, subsidized by the British, to oppose him.
29. Ibid.
30. H.C. Nevill, 1911, *Campaigns on the North-West Frontier, 1849–1908*, London: John Murray, p. 154.
31. 'From—Bruce, To—Lockhart, 19th March 1895', *PGOI*, FF, June 1895 (DOAP).
32. Ibid.
33. 'From—Lieutenant-General Sir W.S.A. Lockhart, KCB, CSI, Commanding the Waziristan Field Force, To—The Adjutant-General in India, d. 30th March 1895', *PGOI*, FF, June 1895 (DOAP).

34. 'From—H.A. Anderson, Esq., Deputy Commissioner, on Special Duty, Waziristan Delimitation Commission, To—The Commissioner and Superintendent, Derajat Division, 21st April 1895', *PGOI, FF,* November 1895 (DOAP).

35. 'Translation of a Petition presented by the Darwesh Khel and the Daur Maliks of the Tochi Valley, to H.A. Anderson, Esq., Political Officer, Tochi Valley, dated the 17th May 1895', *PGOI,* Sec. F, August 1895 (DOAP).

36. 'From—H.A. Anderson, Esquire, Deputy Commissioner, on Special Duty, Waziristan Delimitation Commission, To—The Commissioner and Superintendent, Derajat Division, d. 17th May 1895', *PGOI, FF,* June 1895 (DOAP).

37. 'From—R.I. Bruce, CIE, Commissioner and Superintendent, Derajat Division, To—The Chief Secretary to Government, Punjab, d. 20th May 1895', *PGOI,* Sec. F, June 1895 (DOAP).

38. Ibid.

39. 'From—Anderson, To—Commissioner, 17th May 1895', *PGOI,* Sec. F, June 1895 (DOAP).

40. 'Extract from Waziristan Diary for the week ending 4th June 1895', *PGOI, FF,* August 1895 (DOAP).

41. 'From—Bruce, To—The Chief Secretary, d. 20th May 1895', *PGOI, FF,* June 1895 (DOAP).

42. 'From—R.I. Bruce, Esq., CIE, Commissioner and Superintendent, Derajat Division, and Chief Political Officer, Waziristan, To—H.A. Anderson, Esq., Deputy Commissioner, on Special Duty, Waziristan Delimitation Commission, d. 18th July 1895', *PGOI, FF,* November 1895 (DOAP).

43. 'From—H.A. Anderson, Esq., Deputy Commissioner on Special Duty, Waziristan Delimitation Commission, To—R.I. Bruce, Esq., CIE, Commissioner and Superintendent, Derajat Division, d. 8th June 1895', *PGOI, FF,* August 1895 (DOAP).

44. 'From—H.C. Fanshawe, Esq., Officiating Chief Secretary, to the Government of the Punjab, To—The Commissioner and Superintendent, Derajat Division, d. 28th May 1895', *PGOI, FF,* August 1895 (DOAP).

45. 'From—H.A. Anderson, Esquire, Political Officer, Superintendent, Derajat Division, T—GOP, d. 10th April 1896', *PGOI, FF,* June 1896 (DOAP).

46. Ibid.

47. Ibid.

48. Ibid.

49. Ibid.

50. Ibid.

51. Ibid.

52. Ibid.

53. Ibid.

54. Ibid.

55. Ibid.

56. Ibid.

57. 'From—Commissioner, Derajat, To—Simla & Punjab, d. 13th June 1896', *PGOI,* Sec. F, October 1896 (DOAP).

58. 'From—H.W. Gee, Esquire, BCS, Political Officer, Tochi Valley, To—The Commissioner and Superintendent, Derajat Division, d. 25th June 1896', *PGOI*, Sec. F, October 1896 (DOAP).
59. 'From—H.A. Anderson, Esquire, Commissioner and Superintendent, Derajat Division, To—The Chief Secretary to Government, Punjab, d. 4th July 1896', *PGOI*, Sec. F, October 1896 (DOAP).
60. Ibid.
61. 'From—H.W. Gee, Esquire, CS, Political Officer, Tochi Valley, To—The Commissioner and Superintendent, Derajat Division, d. 23rd February 1897', *PGOI*, *FF*, May 1897 (DOAP).
62. 'From—H.A. Anderson, Esquire, Commissioner and Superintendent, Derajat Division, To—The Chief Secretary to Government, Punjab, d. 11th January 1897', *PGOI*, *FF*, March 1897 (DOAP).
63. Ibid.

A Hindu Kingdom on the Colonial Periphery

Forging State Legitimacy in Late Nineteenth Century Kashmir

Mridu Rai

As it was of the utmost importance to weaken the Sikh nation before its Government should be reestablished I considered the appropriation of this part of the ceded territory to be the most expedient measure I could devise for that purpose by which a Rajpoot Dynasty will act as a counterpoise against the power of a Sikh prince... and both will have a common interest in resisting attempts on the part of any Mahomedan power to establish an independent state on this side of the Indus or even to occupy Peshawur.[1]

This was the justification offered by Henry Hardinge, Governor General of India (1844–7), for the Treaty of Amritsar of 16 March 1846, which 'constructed' the princely state of Jammu and Kashmir, under the protection of the British government.[2] Kashmir's new rulers were fitted thus into the *dramatis personae* of a colonially construed political world in which religious differences between indigenous sovereigns presupposed also the irreconcilability of their temporal aspirations. From this perspective, it was his twin credentials as a Hindu and a Rajput that qualified Raja Gulab Singh most eminently to serve as the first maharaja of Kashmir (r. 1846–56) and a guarantor of British interests in the sensitive northwestern reaches of their Indian empire.

In this sense, the emphasis on the religious identity of Kashmir's rulers was prompted by their physical location on this crucial fringe of the empire—the theatre of the long drawn-out and intricately plotted 'Great Game'. However, while the new maharajas became central in British geo-political strategy, as rulers within their state they stood on the edge of legitimate power. This marginality stemmed from their newness as a dynasty and the uncertainty of their right to govern the vast majority of their subjects with whom they had had no previous association as rulers. Their key role in the geographical frontier of the empire dictated the urgency of 'mainstreaming' them in other ways. Therefore the new maharajas' Hindu–Rajput identification was also deployed to provide them access to a 'central' store of symbols with which to legitimize their rule. Focusing on the reigns of the first two maharajas, Gulab Singh and his son Ranbir Singh, lasting from 1846 to 1885, this essay examines how the rulers of Kashmir and their colonial overlords forged a state ideology, constructed from and between fringes, which turned a state ruled by Hindus into a Hindu state. What made this exercise particularly notable was that it was carried out notwithstanding a preponderantly Muslim subject population.

FOUNDING THE STATE

As mentioned earlier, the state of Jammu and Kashmir was brought into being by the Treaty of Amritsar of 16 March 1846 signed between the East India Company and Gulab Singh, a former 'vassal' of the Sikh kingdom of Lahore. The outcome of the first Anglo-Sikh war fought to a draw earlier that year, disparate territories stripped from Lahore's sway, including Jammu, Kashmir, and Ladakh,[3] were amalgamated to create this new dominion. Its redrawn boundaries mapped the history of colonial geo-political schemes rather than any commonality of experience shared by the people encompassed within them. While the rulers were drawn from the Dogras[4] of Jammu, the state obtained its primary identity from control over the valley of Kashmir. While the rulers were Hindu, the vast majority of their subjects were Muslim.[5] Although such differences in religious affiliation between rulers and the ruled was neither unique nor in itself politically consequential in either pre-colonial or colonial India, in Kashmir it acquired sharp edges owing to the narrow ideological and cultural arenas from which the Dogra maharajas derived their legitimacy to govern. So much so that in a popular upsurge beginning in the early twentieth century that ended the princely rule there in 1947, a demand for long-denied rights by Kashmir's Muslims could not but express itself in a religious idiom. Yet before its dissolution, this state so awkwardly constructed and so lacking in cultivated consensus except from a minority of its subjects, had managed to last for all of century and a year. This needs explaining. The death in 1839 of the powerful Sikh Maharaja of Lahore, Ranjit Singh, shattered a status quo in the Northwestern Frontier carefully nurtured since the 1809 Treaty of Perpetual Friendship, by which the Punjab ruler and the East India Company had set the river Sutlej as the limit of their respective territorial expansions.[6] The passing of the 'Lion of the Punjab' triggered factional infighting at the Lahore court and within the Sikh army, endangering the delicate frontier with Afghanistan whose stability the Company considered the only guarantee against the ever-imminent threat, as perceived by them, of Russian advance into their Indian empire. These new circumstances, untenable in light of British balance-of-power strategies, signalled the Company's intervention and led, in 1845, to the first Anglo-Sikh war. While the hostilities ended with Sikh defeat at the battle of Sobraon on 10 February 1846, the Company's victory was not decisive enough and its resources too strained to allow it to absorb fully Ranjit Singh's territories. Rather than acquire the volatile border with Afghanistan and mountainous territories such as Kashmir, too costly to defend or control, the British settled on the simpler expedient of maintaining a young puppet in Lahore and at the same time breaking up the extensive Sikh kingdom by parcelling out portions to an ally who could be relied upon to secure the more onerous areas.[7] Thus came to pass the transfer of Kashmir into the hands of Gulab Singh, until then raja of Jammu and a powerful subordinate of the kingdom of Lahore, whose decision to remain neutral in the recent war had been of capital importance in turning the tide against the Sikhs.

The cold calculation involved in effecting Lahore's diminishment through Gulab Singh, whose sobriquet of the 'Jammu fox' acknowledged his political cunning rather more than any nobility of personality, drew protest even from within British circles. Thus, Lord Ellenborough, Governor General of India from 1842 to 1844, forcefully repudiated the policy of 'rewarding' Gulab Singh's 'treachery to the Lahore State'.[8] And for all Hardinge's retort that the Jammu Raja 'had no cause of gratitude or attachment' to Ranjit Singh's successors 'by whose orders and intrigues his own family had been nearly exterminated, his possessions taken, and his own son slain', the older ties of collaboration and loyalty owed by Gulab Singh to his former overlords were not so easily shrugged off by the Company.[9] What was required was rather less transparency of strategy and rather more legitimating of its actions.

Quite as much as the British, Gulab Singh too felt keenly the need for establishing his legitimacy to rule. For one thing, his very assumption of power as Maharaja in Kashmir had met with an instant and embarrassing rebuff when, in utter disregard of the Company's treaties, the last Sikh-appointed governor of the valley, Sheikh Imam-ud-din, refused to relinquish charge. As the Sheikh had command of 'the whole resources of the country' and the support of 'all the Western Rajahs, Huzaras and Gukkars', as well as having 'popular feeling' behind him, his rebellion threatened the new state with failure at its very inception. It took the British bribing the erstwhile governor's more powerful allies with guarantee that their former privileges would be continued unhampered to wriggle out of this first crisis.[10] For another, as the Company was soon to discover, carving out territorially distinct political entities from regions that had formerly been integrated, albeit loosely, within one symbolic system of layered and hierarchical sovereignty, required rather more skill with the knife than it may have then possessed. Reflecting the complexities emerging from the political imbrication of the Sikh state and the Dogra Maharaja's new territories, Article VIII of the Treaty of Amritsar made Gulab Singh's accession to power conditional upon his respecting various 'Articles of Agreement' previously concluded between the Company and Lahore on 11 March 1846. Through them the British had undertaken to 'respect the *bona fide* rights' of those *jagirdars*[11] appointed by the Sikhs in territories now ceded to the Company and 'to maintain' them in 'their possessions during their lives'.[12] Since most of the territories in question, such as Kashmir, were then transferred to Gulab Singh, the Company's obligations also devolved upon him. The result, wittingly or otherwise, of this provision of the Amritsar treaty was to situate the first Dogra ruler as a 'successor' to the Sikhs in Kashmir rather than as an originally independent sovereign. It did so most obviously by placing Gulab Singh at the pinnacle of a hierarchy of land rights that had been granted by the Lahore durbar. From the new ruler's perspective, the deleterious political effect of this measure stemmed from *jagir* grants carrying with them duties of service and loyalty owed to the grantor. While Gulab Singh's responsibility to maintain the jagirdars was clear, the relationship was not a reciprocal one since the Amritsar and Lahore treaties froze these grants as Sikh gifts and so also the direction in which concomitant allegiances were to flow. What was blurred in this skewed association between the Maharaja and his 'inherited' jagirdars was more than the territorial limits of sovereignty but also the proper source of the legitimacy to govern. Even if the provisions of Article VIII were to apply technically only for the lifetime of the original jagirdars, it made the very founding of the state that much more perplexing for its new maharaja.

There is evidence aplenty that Gulab Singh attempted quietly to nullify this requirement of the treaty. Thus, in August 1847, a queen at the Lahore court complained that the Kashmir maharaja had confiscated one of her jagirs in Jammu.[13] This was clearly not an isolated incident since Gulab Singh had to be reminded officially that 'all jageers and dhurmurths...situated within the territory of [the] Maharaja...should remain in the possession of the present holders and that they should not be in any way interfered with.'[14] Conversely, a principal grievance of Gulab Singh was that 'all those about...[him] or in his service' who possessed jagirs now located in Punjab had been threatened by the Lahore durbar with the confiscation of these 'if they d[id] not quit the Maharajah's service and country.'[15] While the British were bound by their agreement of 11 March 1846, they were not unsympathetic to Gulab Singh's quandary. Indeed imperial strategy in the frontier had no interest in preserving arrangements which extended the influence of various layers of indigenous power-holders into each other's territories, particularly if it meant keeping Punjab alive as a symbolic arena from which the Dogra rulers would need to seek legitimacy to rule in Jammu and Kashmir. As Henry Hardinge had informed the Secret Committee of the East India Company three days after the signing of the Treaty of Amritsar, an officer had already been appointed to 'define the limits between the Sikh State in the Plains and the Rajpoot State in the Hills.'[16]

THE LEGITIMACY IN BEING RAJPUT

This largely arbitrary feat of state construction still needed legitimation. The old kingly practice of resorting to preservers of 'history' was tried but found inadequate. While a historically based claim to rule could be more convincingly made for Jammu, the 'home-base' of the Dogras, it proved more tenuous in the case of Kashmir. Ganeshdas Badehra, the author of *Rajdarshini*, a history of the Jammu rulers compiled in 1847, asserted that 'Kashmir had long before the era of *Kaljug* [dark ages], been favored by the Rajas of Jammu' where their rule had lasted for 'fifty-five generations'.[17] With the Treaty of Amritsar and thanks to the British, the 'entitlement' to Kashmir had 'reverted' to Maharaja Gulab Singh 'after the passage of a period of four thousand nine hundred and forty-seven years'.[18] Badehra's valiant effort notwithstanding, his claim rang hollow to any but the most determined consumer of 'invented traditions'. Badehra's failed attempt had shown that if history had to be creatively interpreted to validate Dogra rule in Kashmir, too much precision served little purpose since the 'facts' to support it clearly did not exist. Rather than attempt fruitlessly to justify the Dogras as rulers of Kashmir, it might be more profitable to legitimize the Dogras as rulers, *tout court.*

In turning the Dogras into the Rajput 'counterpoise' to Sikh and Muslim power in Punjab and Afghanistan respectively, the governor general had already suggested the line to be followed. By the time the Company deployed it strategically in this way, the term 'Rajput', translated as 'son of a king' and rich in prestige, had come to imply a royal lineage for all those it described, qualifying them generically for kingship whether or not they were in fact kings. But this had not always been the case, as Dirk H.A. Kolff has shown, and the emphasis on a genealogically derived cachet owed in large measure to the Mughals and the British whose own imperial authority was enhanced by augmenting that of their Rajput allies. In the pre-Mughal period, on the other hand, the term Rajput, far from designating an endogamous caste, was an open-ended category, which included individuals who had 'achieved such statuses as "horse-soldier", "trooper" or "headman of a village"'. Gradually the word was used generically as a name for 'this military and landed class as a whole'. By the sixteenth and seventeenth centuries, the more successful 'top layer' among these Rajputs, participating in the Mughal state and encouraged by its privileging of genealogy, began to 'close ranks' and to legitimize 'political power and social status' solely in the 'language of descent and kinship'. However, as Kolff further argues, this new genealogical interpretation of Rajput history emphasized by the bards of the elite Rajput families and 'inherited' by James Tod and other colonial administrators, ignores the fact that the older sociological open-endedness of the category Rajput in which members achieved status through 'service and fighting' continued elsewhere until late in the nineteenth century. The new 'genealogical orthodoxy' centred in Rajasthan led groups outside it to valourize matrimonial ties with the region's great families as well as Rajasthani bardic acknowledgment of their genealogical purity as the 'highest stage of Rajputisation'. For the few who accomplished this, there were many more that did not. Relegated to the category of 'spurious' Rajputs, their 'values and behaviour', however, 'kept alive a more ancient layer of Rajputhood'.[19] In fact, Norbert Peabody argues that the transition to 'ascribed' status among Rajputs was neither 'unidirectional' nor complete even in Rajasthan. Instead there was constant movement between the achieved and ascribed bases of Rajput status depending on strategic calculations of their political utility in any given context. The room for negotiation between these idioms was kept open in no small measure because bloodlines alone could not sort out contested 'hierarchies of rank among potential heirs'. The picture was not only complicated by the polygamous practices of Rajputs, which frequently complicated succession issues, but also because 'biological genealogies' were notoriously easy to invent. When genealogical status failed to provide clear legitimacy, older ideals of achieved status were relied upon.[20]

In the middle of the nineteenth century, then, at a time when the Dogras began to emphasize their aristocratic self-images with the help of their British-informed bards, both idioms of blood and achievement provided the foundation of the still-flexible category of Rajput. What is remarkable, however, is how the clear perception of the Dogras as Rajputs gained particular currency after the break-up of the Sikh kingdom appeared not only imminent but also began to appeal to the British as a desirable imperial strategy. Before then, European accounts were frequently unable to recognize their high status as 'sons of kings' either on the basis of their purity of descent or their achieved merit. Writing in 1842, G.T. Vigne had derived the etymology of 'Dogra' from the terms 'Do Rug', translated as two veins and therefore connoting an individual of 'mixed blood and low caste'.[21] It took a while for others to be able to tell Dogra apart from Sikh.[22] Nor was the official colonial assessment of their political achievements yet able to either separate their actions from those of the 'predatory' Sikhs or to endow them with any of the nobility later ascribed to them as Rajputs. Writing in 1844, Sir Frederick Currie, secretary to the Government of India, had suggested that

The Government knows generally that the extensive territory now under the Government of Raja Gholab Singh has in very recent times been conquered by him and his late brother Dhyan Singh and the Sikhs, and that the former chiefs of the country have been deprived of their rights of sovereignty and prosperity with every circumstance of treachery and cruelty. Attached as the inhabitants of the hills are to their ancient rajas it is impossible not to conclude that these acts of injustice and atrocity have left upon the minds of the people feelings of deep rooted animosity against the chiefs of Jummoo.... It cannot but be supposed that the rule of Gholab Singh is submitted to only from fear, and that he can really command the willing obedience only of the man he pays.[23]

This is not to suggest that the Dogras of Jammu were not Rajputs. Rather, the inability of the observers cited to recognize them as such arguably owed, at least partly, to the Dogras' own self-image not having set too much store by their 'Rajputness' alone as a measure of their distinction or distinctiveness. Indeed Gulab Singh and his brothers, who had risen to positions of great power in Maharaja Ranjit Singh's court, were known there simply as the Jammu or Dogra rajas. Descended only collaterally from the most illustrious of the Jammu rulers, Ranjit Dev (r. 1750–81), it was by dint of their military accomplishments rather than any prestigious bloodline that they had earned themselves places of honour in visual renderings of the splendour of the Sikh court.[24] And if it was by participating so fully and successfully in Lahore's sovereignty— one account suggested Gulab Singh's authority rivalled even that of Ranjit Singh at a distance[25]—that the Dogra brothers achieved eminence, can observers be entirely blamed for mistaking them for Sikhs?

After 1846, the political arena that sustained such blurring was removed by imperial strategy. On 3 February 1846 when the Governor General suggested that 'it may be politic and proper...to weaken the territorial power of the Government of Lahore' he also viewed this as 'rendering the Rajputs of the Hills independent of the Sikhs'.[26] With separation from the Sikhs, the earlier 'sociological openness' of the Dogras as a group was also gradually closed off and its leading members prompted to self-conscious enactment of the values generically associated with Rajput status. And like many 'fringe' Rajputs, they were encouraged to look up to the great lineages of Rajasthan as the manifestations of 'Rajputhood' par excellence and to emulate their practices. Indeed, when the British wished to persuade Gulab Singh to put down sati, they did so not only by suggesting that it was 'contrary to the Shasters' but also by pointing out that it 'had already been publicly forbidden by the [Jaipur] Durbar'.[27]

Simultaneously, with the waging of war against Lahore and the dismantling of the Sikh dominion in 1846, wide circulation was given to the lore of ancient Rajput ruling houses with deep-rooted claims to their territories in the region termed the Punjab hills and including Jammu, Chamba, and Kangra as its most powerful principalities. Thus, in 1846, the governor general's sons, Charles and Arthur Hardinge, visiting the new state of Jammu and Kashmir described the Dogras as 'the Rughoolbunsee [Raghuvanshi] Rajpoots descending from the old solar race' who had been 'in possession of this country since immemorial times'.[28] In 1847, Major G. Carmichael Smyth, a combatant in the first Anglo-Sikh war, included a 'Genealogical History of the Jummoo Family' in his book, *A History of the Reigning Family of Lahore*. Besides tracing the origins of the Dogras in a suitably remote antiquity, this account also found a common root for them with the great families of Rajputana—Jodhpur and Jaipur.[29] Furthermore, Major Smyth's account drew attention to the martial valour of the Dogra–Rajputs who had 'preserved the independence of the[ir] hill state' by 'stout opposition'. Gulab Singh and his brothers' involvement in Sikh conquests represented a temporary lapse, whereas the rest of 'the people of the country' had remained 'well disposed towards any one who had the will and power to harass and annoy the [Sikh] intruders'.[30] This portrayal of Rajputs chafing under the dominance of Lahore justified not only the Anglo-Sikh war but also the decision to place territories weaned from the Sikhs into Dogra–Rajput hands as merely a restoration of old freedoms to legitimate rulers.

A number of historical accounts also began to emphasize the religious basis of the authority of the Rajput raja who was 'the head of the State Religion, venerated as divine, either in his own right or as vice-regent of the national god'.[31] This ensured that his subjects rendered him 'a ready and willing obedience', making for the 'tranquillity' of these principalities in contrast to the chaos of 'contemporaneous Muhammadan and Sikh rule'[32] established by conquering outsiders of other faiths. Indeed, some writers suggested that when Muslims 'invaded India, Hindu culture, guarded by Rajput swords, retreated to the hills.'[33] In this sense, these Rajputs were deemed better custodians of the Hindu faith than those of Rajputana who, by partaking too freely of Muslim power and culture, had imbibed its adulterating alien influences. Truly indigenous in these various senses, the Rajput sentinels in the hills were seen as having founded 'legitimate' because, quite literally, 'natural' rulerships. 'It was not material force' we are told 'that has given them a perennial stream of vitality. They [had] struck their roots deep as trees grow in the rain and the soft air; they have, as it were, become one with nature, a part of the divine and established order of things, and the simple Rajput peasant no more questions their right to rule than he rebels against the sunshine which ripens his harvest.'[34]

THE LEGITIMACY IN BEING HINDU

In 1846, H.M. Lawrence, the agent to the governor general in the Northwestern Frontier, in defending the British decision not to take over Kashmir directly explained that while it

...would be a pleasant land for a man to dwell in...I am not a whit more satisfied after seeing it that we were wrong in not taking it.... Just now the people would be glad to have us for masters, but *being all Mussulmans or Brahmins* they *would* soon prove restive. About four fifths are Mahomedans and would *of course* kill cows while the minority *would* be hostile to the measure...between Moollas and Pundits our Raj would not long be declared to be Heaven sent.[35]

In territories with populations deemed so overpowered by religious sentiments that would inevitably set them on a course of mutual antagonism, governance was best left to others. However, Company officials still felt the onus of discouraging overt 'persecution' even if only by 'expostulation and indirect influence'. Thus Lawrence urged Maharaja Gulab Singh to 'make no difference between...subjects of different religions and sects but [to] look with equal favour on Hindoos, Sikhs, Sheeahs and Soonees and allow each and all to follow the precepts of their several religions.'[36] Gulab Singh's response was qualified by an important reservation that was apparently also accepted by the colonial government. He declared that he would 'treat all sects alike but there [were] certain practices among the Mohummedans distasteful to the religious prejudices of the Hindoos which [could] not be permitted.' In all other cases Hindus and Muslims would be 'equally at liberty to follow the precepts of their own religions agreeably to which also justice w[ould] be dispensed.'[37]

C.A. Bayly has described the rise of new eighteenth century Indian states in which rulers established their sovereignty through links with powerful symbols of their own faiths.[38] Yet, they were still based notably on traditions of 'religious compromise' as Hindu, Muslim, and Sikh rulers 'insisted not on the exclusiveness but on the primacy (or merely the equality) of their own form of worship' and a subject's belonging to a different faith did not preclude access to power.[39] In this sense, Gulab Singh's statement could be seen to be in harmony with the line of political legitimation followed by Bayly's eighteenth century rulers. The state of Jammu and Kashmir founded in the mid-nineteenth century, however, was of a different order. As already discussed, it was created by and for imperial strategic requirements which could be met ideally by a ruler already assigned a specifically Rajput–Hindu identity—one moreover that marked him off from both Sikh and Muslim rulers. Furthermore, it was created at a time when a specifically colonial sociology had established a powerful hold both on the functioning of the British Government of India and on the imperial cosmology into which India's princes more generally and the Dogra rulers of Kashmir more particularly were fitted, particularly after 1857. As Thomas Metcalf has put it, 'from the outset, the British had taken it for granted that there existed in India distinct "Hindu" and "Muslim" communities, and that these differences in religious belief shaped enduring differences in character.'[40] With such ideas moulding colonial understandings, the British could not have believed that any genuine 'representativeness' was possible for Indian rulers separated in their religious affiliation from their subjects. Constructing the Dogras as Hindu rulers, the imperial government encouraged them to legitimate their claims to sovereignty and kingship in the terms traditionally prescribed by and appropriate to their own community. This would also move them conceptually from the periphery of the empire to a Hindu cultural and ideological 'centre' in India.

In the aftermath of the rebellion of 1857, significant changes were ushered in the relations between the British and their princely allies. After that landmark year, the Raj and India's princes came to rely symbiotically on each other as sources of their respective legitimacy and political security. Acknowledging the key role many of them had played in salvaging British rule during the tumultuous months of 1857–8, the princes 'were accorded pride of place in a new imperial cosmology that recognized them as India's "natural rulers".'[41] This transformation in the world of the princes, their new role in it, and their relations with the paramount power were enacted in 1877 during the Imperial Assemblage held in Delhi to inaugurate Queen Victoria's assumption of the title of Empress of India. The ceremonies were presided over by the Viceroy and attended by princes, chiefs, and non-aristocratic notables identified as representatives of Indians. As Bernard Cohn has put it, the princes were present at the assemblage as 'fossilized embodiments of a past which the British conquerors had created.'[42] And this was a past coloured in clearly distinguishable religious shades. J. Talboys Wheeler, commissioned to document the event and the sociological assumptions underlying it, sketched a history of India divided into historical 'ages' associated with the religion of their respective ruling groups. Thus, a 'Muhammadan India' interrupted earlier 'Rajput' and later 'Mahratta' Indias.[43] An important purpose of the Imperial Assemblage was to derive the authority of the Queen–Empress and the British from the authority of these religiously identified sovereigns not only at the ceremonial itself but even afterwards.

Insofar as the Dogras are concerned, the assemblage not only confirmed them as legitimate rulers but also made manifest the sources from which this legitimacy had been derived during the preceding decades. Wheeler wrote of the Maharaja Ranbir Singh (r. 1856–85) in the following terms:

Another Chief presented a striking appearance at Delhi. This was the Maharaja of Kashmir, the ruler of the beautiful valley so often described by poets and travellers. He had been established in his present dominions ever since the close of the first Sikh war in 1846. There is an air of romance about the history of his family. He is the lineal representative of the old Rajput kings of Jummu, whose origin was lost in a remote antiquity before Mahmud of Ghazni invaded India. His father was a cadet of the house, but did not dare to ascend the throne until all the elder branches had died out. He is recognized by the hill tribes, not as a nominee of the Sikh government, but as a true representative of the ancient Rajput dynasty. He is a good ruler, and has shown on all occasions his loyalty and attachment to the paramount power.[44]

This representation of the Dogra maharajas rectified several 'flaws' in their history to reconcile it with the principles of legitimacy based on the antiquity of sovereignty that the British favoured. The recent provenance of the Dogra dynasty as rulers of Kashmir lay Ranbir Singh open to accusations of being the descendant of, and by association himself, a usurper-come-lately. This was glossed by pointing to the self-restraint exercised by Gulab Singh who assumed power only when it was suitable for him to do so. Attention is also drawn to Jammu and the 'hills' where Ranbir Singh's origins are appropriately lost in a time long gone. Interestingly, the word 'Dogra' is noticeably missing in this account and the rulers of Kashmir are identified only as Rajputs. This is particularly significant because Wheeler firmly coaxes the reader towards greater precision in other instances, as with the 'Maharaja of Mysore [who] is Rajput, or *akin to Rajput*'[45] or 'another prince of Rajputana...the Maharaja of Bhurtpur; *by race a Jat*'.[46] The legitimacy already established for the representatives of 'Rajput India' was reflected also upon Ranbir Singh, his ancestors and successors. As a 'loyal' and 'good ruler', Ranbir could draw on both idioms of Rajput status—of genealogy and achieved merit. Moreover, Wheeler's account treated as a settled fact the political separation of Dogra–Rajput from Sikh begun with the very formation of the state. Finally, a critical arena identified for culling legitimacy for the Dogras was in their being 'Hindu', qualifying them generically as original or more 'native' rulers, displaced by the 'Muhammadan empire'. The reference to Mahmud of Ghazni's incursions, although cursory, was calculated to evoke 'memories' of interrupted ancient Hindu rule. This was a fate shared with other Rajputs whose 'old heroes and heroines... were swept away by the Muhammadan invasions' and 'princes and nobles...driven out of their ancient thrones in the valleys'.[47] This, then, was the chief achievement of the Imperial Assemblage for the Dogra rulers: as recompense for their 'loyalty and attachment' not only were they confirmed in their power but their legitimacy was fully and publicly elaborated. And in this their Rajput–Hindu identity played a central and, conceptually speaking, a centralizing role.

As Eric Hobsbawm has pointed out, 'invented traditions', without necessarily breaking with the past, tapped into 'ancient materials' to establish new traditions for 'novel purposes'.[48] According to Hindu scriptural sources, the duties of the king, or *rajdharma*, included 'offering protection to prospective subjects; adjudicating disputes among social groups...patronising religious leaders and institutions; and distributing gifts...to other cultural activities and social groups claiming kingly support.'[49] Working in the imperial context of their state's formation, the Dogras reshaped rajdharma to limit their responsibility as rulers only to their Hindu subjects and, by the end of the nineteenth century, the Dogras began reinventing the Kashmiri political landscape itself as Hindu. Of course, an important distinction Eric Hobsbawm makes between 'old and invented practices' is that 'the latter tended to be quite unspecific and vague as to the nature of the values, rights and obligations of the group membership they inculcate.'[50] Indeed the Dogras were concerned with mining in rather general ways 'older' stores of Hindu symbolism. Thus, they became regular visitors to and patrons of worship at Haridwar and Benares, the great Hindu sacred centres of northern India.[51] The promotion of Sanskrit similarly provided access to a prestigious symbol, increasingly acquiring religio-political connotations. But while Maharaja Pratap Singh (*r.* 1885–1925) may have declared his intention of furthering the project begun by his father, Ranbir Singh, to establish 'once more the reputation Kashmir enjoyed in Sanskrit learning as in the days of old',[52] this link evidently had to be forged anew. As the noted Sanskritist G. Buhler remarked in 1875, excepting a very few Kashmiri Pandit families, for the most part 'the quality of the Sanskrit spoken or written' among them was mediocre.[53] Buhler's investigations explained the break in Sanskrit scholarship as a result of 'Mahommedan oppression' interrupting the rule of 'native kings'.[54] Concomitantly, renewed sponsorship of Sanskrit would also signal the revival of 'indigenous' Hindu rule.

Most pre-colonial aspirants to political power had been forced to acknowledge their inability to subjugate entirely the domain of religion and worship. The strength of the religious domain had drawn from the fact that any temple, mosque or religious order usually enjoyed the sponsorship of numerous political patrons in a world in which neither polities nor the benefits of legitimacy, gained from religious patronage, were bounded by territorial frontiers. While rulers might want to assert the primacy of their own patronage, this did not guarantee their hegemony. The Dogras were well aware of the significance of temples and Brahmins both in the political and the religious domain. They were also alert to the complications arising from the territorially perplexing nature of attempts to control this elusive religious domain. This explains the alacrity with which, at a time of political upheaval in 1846 when Sikh power was being dismantled by the East India Company, the Dogras intervened to cut off Sikh patronage and worship at Purmandal, a pre-eminent sacred centre in Jammu.[55] They insisted that Brahmans sent by their former Sikh overlords not return without the permission of the new Maharaja of Kashmir. Purmandal and other Jammu and Kashmir sacred centres were now perceived as 'belonging' to the newly defined Dogra territory and the merit of worship there would have to accrue solely to its own rulers. This incident marked a fundamental change in the relations between religious patronage, practice, and territory that would find full expression in Ranbir Singh's reign. Ranbir Singh sought to establish a fit between the sway of the Hindu religion over which he would preside as the chief patron and the borders of the political dominion that he would command as Maharaja.

This was both facilitated and necessitated by increasing British efforts at making the frontiers of princely states binding. In 1858 the right to wage war and make peace was removed from the domain of princely India, a prerogative of sovereignty appropriated in perpetuity by the colonial state. This meant that the Indian 'circle of kings' would remain forever frozen. Additionally, the colonial state inaugurated notions, new to India, of a subordinate 'native' sovereignty circumscribed by rigidly demarcated territorial frontiers. Sovereignty in pre-colonial India had operated in overlapping polities in which the primary political exercise had been one of winning over people rather than territory.[56] This had ensured fluidity both in the content and the boundaries of kingships. Colonial authorities, however, were concerned to tidy up the clutter left behind from such layered arrangements of power. Areas lying in British India but providing revenues that sustained the religio-political sovereignties of rulers located elsewhere presented one set of bewildering overlay that was steadily but inexorably sorted out.[57] While their sovereignty may have been territorially circumscribed and relegated to a subordinate level, the Dogra rulers turned aspects of this colonial transformation to their own advantage in order to increase their control over their subjects. From Ranbir Singh's perspective, as a recognized ruler of his state, he was given a territory whose frontiers could not err into British domains. At the same time, he was assured of his legitimacy, founded on his being a 'traditional' Rajput–Hindu ruler, to claim this territory and its populace. Within these parameters, Ranbir Singh's efforts were directed towards matching the political dominion allowed him and the religious identity assigned to him within the territories marked for him.

The chief instrument Ranbir Singh relied on was the Dharmarth Trust, or the trust for religious charity. In 1826 Gulab Singh had also invested funds for the Dharmarth,[58] yet his was a qualitatively different enterprise. It was not until Ranbir Singh's reign that a permanent and systematic arrangement was made for the administration of the Dharmarth funds. The Trust no longer remained a private fund bearing testimony to the piety of an individual ruler. Instead, Ranbir Singh proclaimed that the Dharmarth Trust was founded with the goal of providing 'his own spiritual redemption as well as that of his august family' and with 'a view solely to ensure the advancement of the sacred religion of the Hindus'.[59] Oblivious to any conflict between the goal of the personal spiritual redemption of the ruler and the greater good of the polity, Ranbir Singh conscripted the assistance of state officials in this endeavour.[60] The association of the Trust and by extension the officials of the state, and by further extension the state itself, with the Hindu religion was difficult to miss.

At one level, the goal of advancing the 'sacred religion of the Hindus' implied an unending project of building and repairing temples. At another, a principal purpose of the *Ain-i-Dharmarth* or regulations of the Trust was to structure this complex of Hindu shrines in the state within one common regulated framework of worship. Rules for the conduct of worship, the design of new shrines and the learning requisite for their priests were handed down to every state temple directly from Jammu, the Dogra political centre.[61] Fanning out from Jammu city, the Dharmarth included within its purview temples not only in Jammu province but also in Kashmir. Through the ceaseless construction of new temples in the interior, Ranbir Singh's control over the religious domain sought to extend to the farthest reaches of his territory. And headmen and villagers in the distant outposts of the state, many of whom would have been Muslim, were ordered to 'render proper help in the erection of temples'.[62]

Furthermore, Ranbir Singh also attempted to ensure that the Dogra maharajas would have no rivals to their authority as religious patrons. Brahmins were rendered subservient by being put on the payroll of the

Trust and potential competitors for the ruler's status as the chief patron of the Hindu religion within the state were also neutralized. Any person wishing to build a temple or have it named after him would have to apply for permission from the maharaja;[63] similarly with *prayog*, rituals of meditation and penance performed on behalf of others.[64] Essentially, any religious act involving a dedication within the state would have to be vetted by the Maharaja. In this context, a very significant decree in the *Ain-i-Dharmarth* prohibited any person disloyal to the state from performing particular rituals.[65] Tying in Hindu worship to the state, making loyalty to the latter a precondition for the former, Ranbir Singh worked to territorialize the domain of Hindu religious practice in an unprecedented manner. Interestingly, the duties of priests in remote districts included reporting, via the police, to the Dharmarth office at Jammu all occurrences in their villages.[66] The Dharmarth Trust made a religious centre in Jammu coincide with a political one, both expanding to fill up the territorial outlines of the state.

And the heart of this religious universe was the Raghunathji temple built in Jammu in 1857 and dedicated to Ram, the tutelary deity of the Dogras. Wall illustrations on the entrance to the chief temple made barely disguised associations between the god Hanuman and the Maharaja Ranbir Singh as the chief worshippers of Ram.[67] As the location of both Ram and Ranbir Singh's courts, Jammu was the centre of both the divine Thakur's[68] cosmic realm and the more earthly one's temporal domain. The extension of political control over the valley of Kashmir by the Dogras was matched by the extension to it also of the sway of Raghunathji's temple and forms of worship associated with it. Under the Dogras a political partnership was accompanied by significant moves towards religious accommodation and the approximation of different forms of Hindu worship: the Ram cult of the Dogras with the Shiva and Shakta worship of the Kashmiri Pandits. This was facilitated by the fact that it served the mutual interests of the parties involved. While the Pandits may have formed less than 5 per cent of the valley's population, their numerical weakness was trumped by the considerable influence they exerted, deriving from their unique tradition of literacy that made them indispensable to any regime's administration. The Dogras, who had assiduously cultivated them as political allies, could also substantiate their claim to legitimacy in Kashmir as Hindu rulers by associating with them its powerful Hindu minority. The Kashmiri Pandits, on the other hand, were concerned with retaining their privileged access to government employment by drawing on their religious association with their new Hindu rulers. Charles Girdlestone who had visited Kashmir in 1871, wrote that 'trading on the Maharaja's veneration of the Hindoo religion the Pundit employee rather affects long prayers and the narrating of stories from their mythology in the hope of worldly advantage.'[69]

Gradually Ranbir Singh began to embed aspects of the Rama cult in the valley. He erected temples dedicated to Rama and Hanuman worship on Kashmiri soil.[70] Along with the temples came religious festivals honouring Rama, such as Dussehra and Diwali, not celebrated in Kashmir before then.[71] Besides this, the Maharaja also extended patronage to Kashmiri Hindu forms of worship, making allowances for some of their specific customs. Both funding from and the regulations of the Dharmarth Trust were applied to the principal Pandit shrines such as Khir Bhawani, Shri Jawalaji, and Sharkaji. As a local concession, the *Ain* prescribed the serving of 'zarda and mutton' at Sharkaji.[72] Furthermore, in a clear attempt at appropriating the merit, political and religious, of the shrine its Brahmins were told that they 'should by turn perform *parkarma* (circumambulation) every day on behalf of His Highness.'[73] The domain of painting also witnessed efforts at affiliating Vaishnavite and Pandit practices, drawing together Jammu and Kashmir. An illustrated Kashmiri manuscript of a *Devi Mahatmya*,[74] probably compiled during Ranbir Singh's reign, demonstrated not only a fusion of artistic styles from the two regions but, given its subject, also the patronage increasingly extended by the Dogra rulers to the Shakta cult of Kashmir.[75]

By the time Ranbir Singh died in 1885, the religious boundaries of the Hindu faith united the provinces of Jammu and Kashmir in a state that not only had a Hindu ruler, but that also witnessed new degrees of control over a territorialized Hindu religious arena of patronage and worship. Indeed, the Dogra reinvention of their religio-political landscape as Hindu had registered so widely that the eminent civil servant Walter Lawrence could declare in 1931 that Kashmir was 'holy ground to *all* the Hindus of India'.[76] But such firm Dogra control also meant that the fluidity and competitive nature of pre-colonial patterns of patronage that had ensured a measure of deference to the Muslim religious domain in Kashmir had disappeared. And with this went the erasure of the vast proportion of Muslims in the state.[77] However, this is not to suggest that Kashmiri Muslims were left out of the power-sharing arrangements of the Dogra state simply because they were Muslims. The Dogras were neither particularly bigoted rulers nor did bigotry have anything to do with it. The marginalization of the Kashmiri Muslims became possible only because they became peripheral to the legitimating devices installed by the Dogras and their British overlords. The British guarantee of Dogra sovereignty vis-à-vis his subjects obviated the need for the ruler to seek legitimacy through the time-honoured practice of granting patronage to the religious and cultural sites of his diverse subject population. This meant that Muslim shrines and cultural symbols suffered the withering cold of neglect, while the Dogras in the later nineteenth century set about conjuring the ceremonial trappings of a specifically Hindu sovereignty derived from outside the territorial confines of their fiefdom and enacted within it. If the rulers could borrow symbols of sovereignty and legitimacy from elsewhere, there was nothing to prevent their subjects from welcoming extra-territorial bonds of solidarity such as those available from affiliation with Islam. Given the nature of this state, in which the religious affiliation of the ruler was explicitly tied to his legitimacy to govern, it is hardly surprising that an emerging political assertion by Kashmir's Muslims from the turn of the twentieth century should have also embodied a religious sensibility. This remains true of a largely popular insurgency in the valley of Kashmir begun in late 1989 and continuing to this day. Indeed, the stage was set more than a 100 years ago for a regional people to register their protest in a religious idiom against an equally religiously identified princely autocracy buttressed by colonial paramountcy. Ironically, while deriving the rulers' legitimacy from their Rajput–Hindu identity was intended to shift them from the periphery to an ideological and religious centre both in India and within their territories, when the Muslims of Kashmir weighed in, the Dogras' narrowly construed identity pushed them once more to the fringes of state legitimacy. By 1947, both Dogra sovereignty and that of their imperial underwriters were dismantled.

NOTES AND REFERENCES

1. Foreign (Secret), Governor General's Despatch to Secret Committee, No. 8 of 19 March 1846, National Archives of India, New Delhi (henceforth NAI).
2. Ibid.
3. Others included Hunza, Nagar, and Gilgit.
4. The Dogras, broadly stated, are a linguistic group from the region of Jammu. Their language, Dogri, shares many similarities with Punjabi. Although the Dogras counted Muslims among their numbers, this essay elaborates on the process, beginning in the mid-nineteenth century, of conceptually assigning them Hindu–Rajput status alone.
5. According to the 1931 Census of India, in the state as a whole, Muslims formed 77 per cent, Hindus over 20, Sikhs 1.4, Buddhists 1, and Zoroastrians, Christians,

and tribals conjointly contributed 0.5 per cent of the total population. *Census of India, 1931, Jammu and Kashmir State*, xxiv, part 1 (Jammu, 1933), p. 291.
6. C.U. Aitchison, 1876, *A Collection of Treaties, Engagements and Sunnuds*, Calcutta: Foreign Office Press, vol. VI, pp. 14–16.
7. C. Hardinge, 1891, *Viscount Hardinge*, Oxford: Oxford University Press, pp. 70, 123–4, 132–3. In 1846, the British continued Dalip Singh, a son of Ranjit Singh, as maharaja in Lahore under British protection. The 'independent' power of Lahore was finally dismantled in 1849, at the end of the second Anglo-Sikh war, when it was subsumed into directly administered British Indian territory.
8. Ibid., p. 134.
9. Ibid., pp. 134–5.
10. Letter from H.M. Lawrence, Agent Governor General, North West Frontier, to F.M. Currie, Foreign (Secret), Consultation Nos 1089–94, 26 December 1846, NAI; Demi-official letter from Captain Arthur Broome in Kashmir dated 13 August 1846, Foreign (Secret), Consultation Nos 1085–8, 26 December 1846, NAI.
11. A jagirdar was the holder of a jagir, or the right to the assessed land tax in an area assigned in lieu of salary or as a reward for service.
12. Aitchison, *A Collection of Treaties*, pp. 42–3.
13. *Political Diaries of the Agent to the Governor-General, North-West Frontier, and Resident at Lahore*. From 1 January 1847 to 4 March 1848, Allahabad: Pioneer Press, 1909, p. 267.
14. Ibid. *Dhurmurths* or *Dharmarths* were grants for religious purposes.
15. Letter from Arthur Broome, Artillery on Special Duty, to Henry Lawrence, Governor General's Agent, North Western Frontier, dated Jummoo, 23 July 1846, Mss.Eur.F.85, *Henry Lawrence Collection, Arthur Broome's Letters to and from Sir Henry Lawrence, dated 1846*, India Office Library, London (henceforth IOL).
16. Foreign (Secret), Governor General's Despatch to Secret Committee, No. 8 of 19 March 1846, NAI.
17. Ganeshdas Badehra, 1991, *Rajdarshini*, tr. Sukhdev Singh Charak, Jammu: Jay Kay Book House, p. 228.
18. Ibid.
19. Dirk H.A. Kolff, 1990, *Naukar, Rajput and Sepoy: The Ethnohistory of the Military Labour Market in Hindustan, 1450–1850*, Cambridge: Cambridge University Press, pp. 72–4.
20. Norbert Peabody, 2003, *Hindu Kingship and Polity in Precolonial India*, Cambridge: Cambridge University Press, pp. 39–40.
21. G.T. Vigne, 1843, *A Personal Narrative of a Visit to Ghuzni, Kabul, and Afghanistan*, 2nd edn, London: George, Routledge and Co., p. 254.
22. Thus, Thomas Machell had asserted that 'Golab Singh and his people [were] all Sikhs', while Hugh Rees James had described him as an 'oppressive Sikh ruler'. Mss.Eur.B.369, vol. 5, *Journals of T. Machell, Travels in Hindoostan, the Punjab, Scinde and Kashmir*, 1855–6, IOL, p. 189; Mss.Eur.D.974, Hugh Rees James Papers, IOL, pp. 18–19.
23. *Broadfoot Papers*, vol. III, B.L. MS 40, 129, Letter from Secretary to GoI to Lt

Col A.T. Richmond, Agent to GG, North West Frontier, dated 31 January 1844, British Library, London.
24. W.G. Archer, 1966, *Paintings of the Sikhs*, London: H.M's Stationery Office, pp. 53–6.
25. Victor Jacquemont, 1834, *Letters from India*, 2 vols, London: Edward Churton, vol. 2, pp. 1, 166.
26. *Calcutta Review*, vol. VI, 1846, pp. 297–301, reproduced as Appendix G in Badehra, *Rajdarshini*.
27. Letter from H.M. Lawrence, Agent Governor General, to F. Currie, dated 15 November, 1846, Foreign Dept (Secret), Consultation 26 December 1846, No. 1248, NAI.
28. L. Ganeshi Lal and V.S. Suri (ed.), 1955, *Siyahat-e-Kashmir*, Simla: Controller of Printing and Stationary, p. 196.
29. Major G. Carmichael Smyth, 1847, *A History of the Reigning Family of Lahore, with Some Account of the Jummoo Rajahs, the Seik Soldiers and their Sirdars*, Calcutta: W. Thacker & Co., reprinted 1961, Lahore: Government of West Pakistan, pp. 233–4.
30. Smyth, *A History*, p. 268.
31. J. Hutchison and J. Ph. Vogel, 1933, *History of the Punjab Hill States*, 2 vols, Simla: Dept. of Languages and Culture, reprinted 1982, vol.1, pp. 65–6.
32. Ibid., p. 96.
33. J.C French, 1931, *Himalayan Art*, Delhi: Neeraj Publishing House, 1931, reprinted 1981, pp. 1–2.
34. Lepel H. Griffin, 1892, *Rulers of India: Ranjit Singh*, Oxford: Clarendon Press, p. 13.
35. Foreign (Secret), Consultation Nos 1240–1, 26 December 1846, NAI (Emphasis mine).
36. Foreign (Secret), Consultation Nos 1243–7, 26 December 1846, NAI.
37. Ibid.
38. Examples of this include the greater support given to the application of Islamic law by Muslim rulers or the ban on cow slaughter and the establishment of firmer control over their holy places by Hindu and Sikh rulers.
39. C.A. Bayly, 1998, *Origins of Nationality in South Asia*, New Delhi: Oxford University Press, pp. 45, 214–21.
40. Thomas R. Metcalf, 2005, *Forging the Raj: Essays on British India in the Heyday of Empire*, New Delhi: Oxford University Press, p. 186.
41. Susanne Hoeber Rudolph and Lloyd I. Rudolph (edited with commentary), with Mohan Singh Kanota, 2002, *Reversing the Gaze: Amar Singh's Diary, A Colonial Subject's Narrative of Imperial India*, Cambridge, MA: Westview Press, p. 15.
42. Bernard S. Cohn, 1989, 'Representing Authority in Victorian India', in Eric Hobsbawm and Terence Ranger (eds), *The Invention of Tradition*, Cambridge: Cambridge University Press, p. 193.
43. James Talboys Wheeler, 1877, *The History of the Imperial Assemblage at Delhi*, London: Longmans, Green, Reader and Dyer.
44. Ibid., p. 68.

45. Ibid., p. 60.
46. Ibid., p. 64.
47. Ibid., p. 62.
48. Eric Hobsbawm, 1989, 'Introduction: Inventing Traditions', in Hobsbawm and Ranger (eds), *The Invention of Tradition*, pp. 4–6.
49. Barbara N. Ramusack, 2004, *The Indian Princes and Their States*, Cambridge: Cambridge University Press, pp. 4–5.
50. Hobsbawm, 'Introduction', p. 10.
51. The Dogras also bought property in these places to provide more permanent facilities for pilgrims and their own religious and charitable works. Foreign Dept (External B), May 1891, Pros. Nos 62–4, NAI; Foreign Dept (External B), March 1902, Pros. Nos 113–23, NAI; Foreign and Political Dept (Internal B), January 1921, Pros. Nos 128–9, NAI.
52. 'Memorandum by the Committee appointed by His Highness the Maharaja Sahib Bahadur to Report on the Archaeological and Research Department', 2 August 1911, OER, f. No. 293/E-8, 1909, Jammu and Kashmir State Archives, Jammu.
53. G. Buhler, 1877, 'Detailed Report of a Tour in Search of Sanskrit MSS Made in Kasmir, Rajputana and Central India', *Journal of the Bombay Branch of the Royal Asiatic Society* (Extra Number), xii (xxxiv), pp. 19–20 and 25–8.
54. Ibid., p. 25.
55. *Political Diaries of the Agent to the Governor General, North West Frontier and Resident at Lahore*, 1 January 1847–4 March 1848, pp. 124, 138–9.
56. See Andre Wink, 1986, *Land and Sovereignty in India: Agrarian Society and Politics under the Eighteenth Century Maratha Swarajya*, Cambridge: Cambridge University Press.
57. As a general rule, the British came to believe it an 'anomaly [that] the officials or in fact the Ministers of one State...[should hold] independent estates in the lands of a neighbouring power'. Foreign (Secret), Consultation Nos 116–17, 30 October 1847, NAI.
58. Sukhdev Singh Charak, 1985, *Life and Times of Maharaja Ranbir Singh*, Jammu: Jay Kay Book House, pp. 275–6.
59. *Ain-i-Dharmarth* (Regulation for the Dharmarth Trust Fund), 1884, Jammu: Ranbir Press, pp. 1–2.
60. Ibid.
61. Ibid., pp. 14, 115–16.
62. Ibid., p. 117.
63. Ibid., p. 97.
64. Ibid., p. 44.
65. Ibid.
66. Ibid., p. 116.
67. Madhu Bazaz Wangu, 1992, 'Hermeneutics of a Kashmiri Mahatmya', in Jeffrey R. Timm (ed.), *Texts in Context*, Albany: State University of New York Press, p. 153.
68. A term of honour used in address or reference to superior lords in both political and agrarian hierarchy, was used also in reference to deities.

69. Charles Girdlestone, 1874, *Memorandum on Cashmere and Some Adjacent Countries*, Calcutta: Foreign Department Press, pp. 25–6.
70. *Ain-i-Dharmarth*, pp. 129–34, 141–9.
71. Ibid., p. 130.
72. Ibid., p. 152.
73. Ibid.
74. *Mahatmyas* are Hindu sacred texts that narrate myths and legends of important deities, eulogize the deity's pilgrimage centre, and prescribe the rites to be observed by the pilgrims.
75. Karuna Goswamy, 1989, *The Glory of the Great Goddess*, Zurich: Museum Rietberg. It is also noteworthy that Ranbir Singh had also commissioned Pandit Sahebram, a respected Sanskritist of Kashmir, to 'prepare a trustworthy copy' of the great text of the Kashmiri Pandits, the *Nilamatapurana* 'for edition'. Buhler, 'Detailed Report', pp. 32–3.
76. Mss.Eur.F.143, Walter Lawrence Collection, copy of a letter from Walter Lawrence to Sir Samuel, 6 October 1931, IOL (Emphasis mine). Lawrence went further to suggest that should the colonial government permit cow slaughter in Kashmir, as individuals (he does not identify) had been suggesting, it 'would infuriate the Hindus throughout India, and it would, further alienate all the Hindu princes of India...'
77. Constraints of space prevent me from discussing fully this very important aspect of the history of Kashmir. For elaboration see Mridu Rai, *Hindu Rulers, Muslim Subjects: Islam, Rights and the History of Kashmir*, Princeton: Princeton University Press; London: C. Hurst; and Delhi: Permanent Black, 2004.

PART II

OUTSIDERS AND INSIDERS

Punishment on the Fringes
Maulana Thanesari in the Andaman Islands

Satadru Sen

Between the Revolt of 1857 and the Japanese victories of 1942, the British empire and its prisoners collaborated in the development of an elaborate society of convicts in the Andaman Islands, 800 miles off the east coast of India. To create a semblance of order in this settlement of 12,000 rebels, murderers, thieves, infanticidal mothers, members of so-called 'criminal tribes',[1] and thousands of indigenous Andamanese, colonial administrators devised a complex system of punishment and reward, control and patronage, utilizing systems of labour, segregation, surveillance, medical supervision, and family-based rehabilitation.[2] As these systems emerged, the prisoners themselves became partially and inconsistently self-policing, trying to access the advantages of cooperation with the colonial regime, even as they resisted or remained indifferent towards British authority.

Scholarship on the first 50 years of the Andaman Island's penal colony is marked by an acute paucity of first-hand narratives by the convicts themselves. Such narratives are relatively abundant in studies of Australia, and to a lesser extent French Guiana.[3] Researchers such as Yang and Anderson, who study the overwhelmingly non-literate British–Indian convict diaspora, must necessarily glean most of their information from government documents, and from the private writings of British administrators and visitors to the penal colony.[4] A rare Indian convict autobiography from the Andamans in the nineteenth century is an Urdu narrative by the Maulana Muhammad Jafar Thanesari, a 'Wahhabi' arrested in 1863 for conspiring to smuggle funds to anti-British mujahideen in Afghanistan. He was initially sentenced to death, but his punishment was commuted to life in penal transportation, which meant exile in the Andaman Islands.[5] Beginning in 1866, he spent nearly 18 years in the penal colony, and then returned to Punjab with a new wife, new children, and considerable wealth and social status. If punishment is defined as the correction of a flawed political relationship, the colonial regime's treatment of Thanesari was quite successful, because it resulted in the conversion of a trouble-maker into a moderately satisfied and law-abiding subject of the crown. It did not, however, eradicate all inclinations and opportunities for dissent—rather, it produced, reproduced, and gave new form to dissident gestures.[6]

We must be careful not to ascribe to Thanesari the voice of the 'typical' or 'subaltern' convict. The very fact that he wrote his memoirs marks him as a member of the convict elite.[7] His status in the penal colony, and his status in mainland society upon return, both derived ultimately from his literacy in multiple languages: Urdu, Persian, Hindi, and eventually English. The voice that emerges from the manuscript is that of the incarcerated intermediary: by turns colonized and colonizer, a subject who recognizes the authority of his British superiors but who disregards that authority whenever he can get away with it, a man who is both resentful and grateful, a convict who feels his humiliation but who is nevertheless conscious of his high status in the society of the humiliated.

It is also an unreliable voice that must be heard with caution. This essay is, among other things, an experiment in reading a document of doubtful veracity, in which what is true and productive is unreliability itself. Thanesari wrote his memoirs after his return to the mainland, and the narrative is very much an attempt on the part of the author to represent himself in a particular light, or multiple lights, before an audience of his peers in northern India: fellow-Wahhabis, the Muslim elite in provincial cities, and more broadly, an Urdu-literate post-1857 readership that shared with him the experience of being simultaneously traumatized and rewarded by the colonial encounter. This audience had evolved significantly in the two decades following Thanesari's departure for the penal colony. In the 1880s, the political milieu of Islam in India was informed not only by numerous 'little traditions' of regionally structured Muslim communities, but also by a cosmopolitan intellectual tradition which lent itself to pan-Islamic identities and activism, and by partially state-sponsored formulations of an Indian–Muslim community that might be deployed in opposition to Hindus or, perversely, in opposition to the colonial regime.[8] In this context, Thanesari found it necessary to represent his participation in the improvised (and aberrant) bureaucratic, intellectual, communal, and familial world of a penal settlement as an apologia, and as an experience of martyrdom. While this agenda leads him to deviate constantly from what might be considered the 'archival truth' of documented episodes and policies, it is nevertheless an exercise in colonial world-construction, in which the incarcerated/colonized subject attempts to reorder his surroundings by transforming the ambiguously rewarding experience of the modern into unambiguous affirmations of fundamental truths and identities. Fundamentalism, Harjot Oberoi has pointed out, is nothing if not a modern enterprise.[9] Thanesari's narrative is thus at once a kind of adventure-travel literature calculated to attract readers curious about life in a notorious penal colony, and an attempt to put forward his personal tragedies and ultimate triumph over the adversities of a banishment that is political, spiritual, and social.

The nature of the triumph and the adversity are both rooted in the author's self-conscious religious and political identity as a Wahhabi. The Wahhabi movement, which was rooted in the teachings of Sayyid Ahmed of Rae Bareli and sought to rescue Islam from a moral and political corruption implicitly linked to colonialism,[10] had by the 1840s acquired a limited following among insurgent groups in the Northwest Frontier. Alex Padamsee has pointed out that while there is little evidence of Wahhabi involvement in the events of 1857, Anglo-Indian and official opinion in the 1860s retrospectively implicated the movement in the Mutiny on the basis of several converging factors: W.W. Hunter's writings about Indian Muslims, the trial of Maulvi Ahmadullah of Patna in 1863, and a post-1857 obsession with grand conspiracies in native society.[11] Thanesari and other Wahhabis in the Andamans, like many of their 'secular' fellow-prisoners, had been swept up in a broad legal and discursive net generated by the 'Mutiny', which not only produced them as rebels but also produced a dubious ideological and political affiliation with the war.[12]

Exile gave Thanesari the material with which to reinforce his Wahhabi credentials and to locate those credentials in colonial history. He agreed that he was a Wahhabi, did not deny that Wahhabis were engaged in a jihad, but rejected the allegations of rebel activity and tried to retrieve Wahhabis from Hunter's imputations. Exile, in fact, generated the need for reinforcement, not only because it immersed Thanesari in experiences, knowledges, and perspectives that destabilized his Wahhabi identity, but also because the claim of innocence was itself a difficult negotiation between assertion (of an identity) and denial (of a specific act associated with that identity). Thanesari uses his memoirs to represent his punishment as a series of religio-political trials, which test his faith and present him with opportunities to prevail over his personal weaknesses and communal adversaries. Regarding Thanesari's explicit self-location within the Wahhabi ideology of jihad, that is, struggle that is personal/spiritual as well as communal/political, Ayesha Jalal has emphasized that the construction of such struggles must be understood in their temporal context.[13] Thanesari's struggles must be examined, therefore, in the context of his punishment in two colonies: the penal colony and the colonial mainland. There can be little doubt that the Maulana translated his imprisonment in ways that might promote his status as a heroic spiritual and political figure in concentric circles of the colonized faithful: Wahhabis and Muslims, convicts and the 'free'.

Given its investment in the response of the reader, the published narrative lacks the 'honesty' of a diary. As the Rudolphs have noted in their study of the memoirs of another colonial subject, even diaries are written with potential readers in mind.[14] There are two overlapping levels of unreliability in Thanesari's memoirs, which correspond to the 'lived' context of the penal colony and the 'represented' context of the mainland. Not only does he have many opportunities to misrepresent (or reinvent) himself in the society of convicts, he has the chance to misrepresent the original misrepresentation upon returning to the mainland as an author. As far as possible, I have attempted to check Thanesari's story against other sources of information about convict society in the Andamans, so that we might utilize the emphases, distortions, and silences within his narrative.

What I intend to do is search Thanesari's narrative of penal transportation for insights into the nature of the penal colony, the nature of the penal experience, and the nature of a convict self-representation. I shall focus first on the issue of convict labour, and the benefits that this conferred upon the 'labourer'. The work that Thanesari did in the penal colony demonstrates that punishment in the Andamans operated on a market principle of sorts. Because the British needed loyal intermediaries at every level of the prison administration, they were obliged to bargain with convicts who might serve in such positions, and to reduce the punitive content of punishment. For convicts who possessed certain qualifications, such as literacy, the penal experience could generate unparalleled opportunities for professional and social advancement, and dramatically altered relationships with the punishing colonial state. At the same time, the nature and circumstances of the work could severely destabilize the identity of the worker, compelling him to make compensatory gestures that might reassure his audience about his social and political location.

I shall then examine Thanesari's perceptions of the politics of religion and race in the Andamans. The nineteenth century, Francis Robinson has observed, was marked by sharply increased levels of status-anxiety, ideological ferment, and self-assertion among Muslims who belonged to the intertwined landowning, administrative, and clerical classes of late-Mughal India.[15] After 1858, especially, these Muslims sought to reposition themselves in a colonial state which was not interested in their religio-political priorities, and which forced them to compete professionally and politically against better-equipped outsiders and unbelievers. The tension manifested itself in diverse Islamic-revivalist and modernizing movements on the mainland (such as the Deoband madrasa, Aligarh College, the Dars-i-Nizamiyya, and the Wahhabi insurgency that Thanesari was connected with),[16] and it was very much present in the contested society of the penal colony. We find a high degree of communal self-consciousness in segments of the convict population, and intense competition between Hindu and Muslim convicts for access to the colonial state. We find, also, that under certain circumstances, this animosity was submerged under an Indian convict identity that was defined in opposition to the colonizer, and defined also by the experience of punishment. This political and penal context determined the Maulana's ability to choose between the identities of a Wahhabi, a Muslim, and a colonized and punished Indian.

Finally, I examine Thanesari's acquisition of a family in the islands. Women and families in the Andamans were central to the British effort to control and rehabilitate male convicts by domesticating disorderly men.[17] Thanesari's narrative allows us to see how male convicts themselves may have viewed these rehabilitative mechanisms. It indicates that the right to marry and have children in the penal colony was not simply an incentive to good behaviour and a disincentive to homosexuality, but also a marker of wealth and success, an opportunity for religious proselytization, and a source of relief from the loneliness of life in the Andamans. It casts light, also, on the problems that developed when convicts who already had families on the mainland married again in the islands, and tried to choose between two places, families, and societies.

PRIVILEGED/WORKER

In the nineteenth century discourse of crime, criminality was very substantially defined as the reluctance to work.[18] Much of punishment in Victorian Britain and its colonies was geared towards putting the idle to work, within and without the prison.[19] The labour regime in the Andaman Islands was divided very broadly into two phases: a painful phase of closely supervised forced labour, which lasted up to 10 years, followed by a period of rehabilitative labour, when the convict worked under conditions of greater autonomy, and was given a tangible share of the fruits of his or her exertions.[20] Whereas the first phase underlined the political supremacy of the colonial state over the individual criminal, the second phase was a process by which offenders could be rewarded for their obedience, and integrated into the legitimate structures and hierarchies of the penal colony.

There is, however, no doubt that at least some convicts were allowed to bypass the initial stage of punitive labour. This was due in no small measure to the colonial state's perpetual search for reliable prison employees. Arnold has argued that colonial prison regimes encountered serious disciplinary problems with their employees, including convict workers.[21] There can be little doubt, however, that British prison administrators in India in the second half of the nineteenth century preferred convict workers over free employees when it came to appointing guards, overseers, and clerks.[22] Free workers were almost uniformly seen as corrupt, sullen, lazy, and disorderly, and as agents of disorder among the convict population.[23] Convict employees, on the other hand, tended to be the 'better sort' of prisoners, who had acquired their positions of responsibility by demonstrating their obedience. Also, the prison regime could—in theory—punish them if they misbehaved. In the Andamans, free employees were almost completely eschewed by the British authorities.[24] This was substantially due to the great ideological significance of labour in a penal colony where prisoners stayed for long periods, and where it was possible to train convicts to perform hierarchically organized tasks.[25] Colonial administrators were fond of reiterating that the Andaman Islands were not simply a prison, but a colony in the full sense of the term: men and women were brought here not so much to be punished, as to be redeemed and resocialized through the discipline of labour.[26]

There can be little doubt that the regime's reliance on convict labour gave prisoners the power to bargain for status, comfort, and, ironically, freedom from labour.[27] The settlement's need for qualified clerical staff created an instant elite among literate convicts. The privileged status of clerical workers was, in fact, part of the folk knowledge of the penal colony. When Thanesari arrived in the Andamans, he was apparently told by another prisoner: 'The clerks are the rulers and the masters here. They can do anything they want.'[28] This rumour of privilege was then visually confirmed: even before he had disembarked from the convict ship *Jamuna*, Thanesari saw a long line of men, dressed immaculately in white, waiting at the quay. These, he writes, were 'Maulvis and clerks.'[29] Upon landing, Thanesari seems to have escaped the long lines, the humiliating interrogations, the classificatory procedures, the close confinement, the bar fetters (a prime cause of gangrene and death), and the chain gangs that awaited most newly arrived convicts in the Andamans. He escaped, also, the convict uniforms and the meagre rations. It is possible that he exaggerates his good fortune to keep his post-carceral reputation as 'respectable' as possible. Given Thanesari's investment in the Wahhabi ideology of martyrdom, however, this seems unlikely. Thanesari does not shrink from providing details of the torture and forced marches he endured before embarking for Port Blair.[30] It is credible, therefore, that he was welcomed at the dock by prisoners who had apparently known he was coming. He was taken to the home of a clerk in the marine department. There, his shackles were removed. He was given good clothes to wear and introduced to various 'respected persons' (all convicts).

Thanesari was appointed Deputy Chief Clerk at the court of the superintendent of the penal colony. He moved into a comfortable house, and not the barracks in which convicts usually lived in the initial phase of their stay in the Andamans. The Maulana was given full freedom within the confines of the penal colony, and, to make life even easier, he was assigned a servant, whose wages were paid by the settlement authorities. For a 27-year-old who had been convicted of sedition and almost hanged, this was a remarkable social and professional recovery. Such a turnaround of fortune would have been impossible on the Indian mainland. In the Andamans, however, frontier conditions and the agenda of rehabilitation combined to create precisely such opportunities.

It is worth asking how the Port Blair authorities came to the conclusion that Thanesari was worthy of privileged treatment. Although the British made energetic efforts to generate and transmit information about convicts who were transported to the Andamans, the systems of record-keeping and surveillance were less than fail-safe. It was not unknown for prisoners to step off the transport ship into a void of official knowledge.[31] In Thanesari's case, it seems that the British gathered their information about the prisoner not from official sources such as Thanesari's 'history sheet', but from convicts who were already present in the settlement. These included men who had been a part of Thanesari's social circle in Punjab, and who had slipped into clerical jobs in the Andamans. They had known in advance that Thanesari was coming, demonstrating, again, that far from being utterly isolated from mainland society, the Andamans were in fact a part of the mundane universe of colonial India, connected to the mainland through letters, rumours, and the constant back and forth of convicts. Thanesari thus had a familiar social niche waiting for him when he arrived in the islands. Within this niche, he had a reputation that was substantially independent of the punishing colonial state. Allowing for his interest in exaggerating his own importance, it is likely that his fellow convicts recognized him as a member of the respectable classes, with a certain status as a learned man. The colonial state borrowed this reputation from the society of convicts, and used it to determine Thanesari's status in the official hierarchy of the penal colony.

In a circular process, official privilege boosted Thanesari's standing in the society of convicts, and even in the society of the free. He understood this process and did his best to help it along. Not long after his arrival in the islands, he began to write letters to old acquaintances in Punjab, filled with glowing descriptions of his comfortable life and his 'independent government job'. In fact, Thanesari admits, he 'exaggerated' his comforts, in order to 'make those people jealous who had given false testimony against innocent Muslims and were living a shameful life.'[32] This is a curious confession, simultaneously undermining and reinforcing the credibility of the confessor. It is, however, entirely consistent with Thanesari's self-representation as a flawed saint and politician: a man whose credentials as a Wahhabi are communicated through his frequent criticism of his own weaknesses, which are then legitimized by his unimpeachable political intentions.

The effort at projecting a good life in the penal colony was more successful than Thanesari had intended. His letters came to the attention of the Government of India and the Punjab administration, and became the subject of consternation. John Lawrence, the Governor of Punjab, demanded that Thanesari be subjected to hard labour for the duration of his sentence, and H. Man—the superintendent of the Andamans settlement—was asked to explain why a convict in a penal colony was living an apparently painless life. In spite of this embarrassment, Man's administration did not retaliate against Thanesari. He did not find himself working in a chain gang. His house, job, and servant were not touched.

Thanesari attributed this reprieve to the bureaucratic difficulty of retracting official privileges. He added that the Port Blair authorities were unfamiliar with the Rebellion of 1857, and thus not prejudiced against Wahhabis.[33] The explanation is quite implausible. The Andamans settlement, while overdetermined, was established as part of the larger British reaction to the crisis of 1857, and the memory of 1857 had a long life in the penal colony.[34] Moreover, even as administration in the Andamans became increasingly bureaucratized, superintendents had a great deal of discretion in dealing with convicts, especially in situations that could be interpreted as problems of order or discipline. The only circumstances in which superintendents were required to seek the authorization of the Government of India involved the death penalty and the deportation of convicts from the settlement.[35] Man's regime was thus unlikely to be hampered by an exaggerated sense of bureaucratic propriety, and Thanesari's odd observation is almost certainly related to his desire to imagine the penal colony as a geography where the political baggage of the mainland could sometimes be made to disappear.

What is most likely is that the regime treated Thanesari leniently because it needed his services. To ensure his cooperation, it was willing to forgive his local trespasses, even if it meant crossing the colonial government on the mainland. The tension between administrators in Calcutta who wanted predictable punishment, and administrators in Port Blair who wanted to maximize their own flexibility, was a persistent feature in the history of the penal settlement.[36] The two conflicting approaches to prison administration represent a transition in the ideology of punishment that was more or less complete in England by the nineteenth century, but that was still unfinished in colonial India. As, Linebaugh and Thompson have noted about eighteenth century English criminal justice, provisions for discretion in the enforcement of the law allowed judges, police officers, and administrators to be unpredictably merciful.[37] The Benthamite contention that justice must be consistent and precise—and as such, neither vicious nor merciful—was, in the early 1800s, relatively alien to English thought. Mercy as an instrument of authority was imprecise, irrational and pre-modern, but it was well suited to a political environment that privileged personalized ties of deference, gratitude, loyalty, and obedience. Thus, even as the British on the mainland sought to standardize colonial punitive practices, the British in the Andamans operated on the understanding that their control over the convict population depended upon the power to intervene personally and unpredictably in local society. This meant not only the power to be unpredictably punitive, but also the power to be unexpectedly lenient, as Man was with Thanesari.

The Maulana would benefit repeatedly from the Port Blair regime's inclination to protect him. When he was forced to appear in court on charges of theft, Man swallowed his anger and exonerated him. Thanesari is vague about the accuracy of the allegations, but he admits that he violated regulations when, in 1870, he tried illegally to purchase 'some essential items for my marriage' from the mainland. He was found out, but once again, shielded from punishment by Man and his deputy, M. Protheroe.[38] The latter, especially, was an invaluable source of support to Thanesari. In the final years of the Maulana's stay in the penal colony, he was Chief Clerk in Protheroe's office in Aberdeen. Protheroe was not simply Thanesari's superior; he was also his student. Educated convicts like Thanesari were sometimes employed as language instructors to British administrators in the Andamans, and it is reasonable to speculate that the dynamics of the teacher-student relationship subverted and altered the convict–jailor relationship, and modified the relationship between the colonized Indian and the colonizing European.

Thanesari's privileged status also shaped the circumstances under which he returned to the mainland. (For most convicts in the Andamans, 'life in penal transportation' actually meant a period of 20 years. Since Thanesari had been arrested in 1863, his sentence expired in 1883.) He showed a strategic reluctance to return to Punjab, pointing out to the authorities in Port Blair and Lahore that it made no sense for him to give up his 'excellent house and a good job which gives me 100 rupees', for a life of uncertainty, unemployment, and harassment by the local police. With the support of Protheroe, who wrote him glowing letters of recommendation, he was actually able to negotiate the terms of his release and repatriation: the Government of Punjab promised him a job commensurate with his status in the penal colony.[39]

Thanesari's return to the mainland reflects just how penal transportation could affect the social status of privileged convict employees. After nearly two decades overseas, he was able to claim that he had returned not in disgrace or in obscurity, but in triumph. Crowds of well-wishers greeted him in Delhi, Thanesar, and Ambala. Once again, information had travelled between the penal colony and the 'free' colony independently of the colonizer: Thanesari's letters and reputation had preceded him to the mainland. He was also able to take with him the knowledge that he had negotiated with the punishing state. In Ambala, he was given a job as a language trainer for colonial civil servants, a position that indicated a successful reintegration into the political universe of British India. At the same time, ambiguities crept into this heroic homecoming. Thanesari's salary in Port Blair had been twice as high as his wages on the mainland. Also, consistent with a chronic complication in colonial projects for the rehabilitation of released prisoners, police surveillance over his activities appears to have continued in Ambala, even as he worked closely with British officials.[40] In a sense, Thanesari had been more privileged as a prisoner in the penal colony than he was after his release.

It is clear that immunity from punishment was not the only perquisite of Maulana Thanesari's life as a clerk in the Andamans. The job allowed him to develop independent sources of wealth and prestige, and to cultivate skills that further boosted his social and professional status. He was entrusted with large amounts of government funds, and there is no doubt that he engaged in illegal trade with his contacts on the mainland by exploiting his ability to manipulate official records. Beginning in 1872, he learned English, which expanded the scope of his clerical responsibilities, and enhanced his status with administrators as well as with convicts who had need for his services. He taught Persian, Hindi, and Urdu to other upwardly mobile convicts, and drafted appeals and applications for prisoners who wanted to approach the local administration.[41] Convicts in a complex penal settlement such the Andamans frequently needed access to the local government, not only to defend themselves against the threat of punishment, but also to safeguard property acquired in the islands. This work earned Thanesari more than 100 additional rupees each month, and it allowed him to represent himself as an effective defender of Muslim convicts in their disputes with non-Muslims. He notes that he was instrumental in saving several men from the executioner's noose, and that such men were eternally grateful.[42] This gratitude became part of a political standing that was autonomous of the colonial administration, even as it was enabled by the Maulana's position within the administration.

INDIAN/MUSLIM

It is evident from Thanesari's writing that employment in the prison administration, and the maintenance of the political status of communities defined in terms of religion and race, were closely connected in the Andamans. This connection was by no means universal in nineteenth century penal colonies; Anderson's study of Mauritius in the first half of the nineteenth century does not reveal any persistent Hindu–Muslim rivalry.[43] In the Andamans, race and religion were both officially recognized as principles of social organization. European and Eurasian convicts lived separately from other prisoners, and were subject to different codes of discipline and punishment.[44] Muslims and Hindus were classified, transported, and fed separately, as were 'up-country men' and prisoners from the south and the east of India. There were regulations in place that recognized, restructured, and regulated the boundaries of caste.[45] In the twentieth century, the British routinely used subaltern Muslim convicts as overseers with authority over elite Hindu political prisoners. It is evident from the outraged rants of V.D. Savarkar that this double deployment of religion and class was resented by at least some of the Hindus, and relished by the overseers.[46]

As a representative of a mid-nineteenth century social and political milieu that was marginal to the English literate core of colonial India, Thanesari provides a perspective on intercommunal relations in the penal colony that is different from that of either the British administrator, or the twentieth century Hindu nationalist. Nevertheless, Thanesari's writing indicates that some of the tensions of Savarkar's time had their parallels in the Andamans in the 1860s and 1870s. His recollections highlight, especially, an intense competition between self-aware ethnic groups, and a willingness on the part of convicts to use the state as an instrument of competition. They also indicate that this competition could provide a forum for articulate prisoners in search of local political careers and subsequent reputations as heroic leaders of contextually defined communities.

Antagonism between Muslims and Hindus is the most prominent example of this competition. Thanesari recognized the court—or rather, the court bureaucracy—as an offensive and defensive weapon in this antagonism, as well as a vital battleground that both communities sought to capture and control. His own use of English language clerical skills to defend Muslims against non-Muslims is only one example of this contest. When Thanesari's illegal trading activities were discovered, it was because Hindu clerks had intercepted his correspondence and taken the evidence to the superintendent. Thanesari's defence included references to these religious tensions in convict society, and when Protheroe and Man decided to overlook his offence, they apparently did so with a warning: 'Hindus are your enemies. Be careful.'[47]

The specifics of the tension that Thanesari referred to in his own defence concerned cattle slaughter in the penal colony. John McLane has dated the modern cow protection movement on the Indian mainland to Kuka revivalism in Punjab in 1870, and located it within a larger context of Islamic revivalism as well as a Hindu nationalist mobilization.[48] It appears that convicts in the Andamans anticipated the Kukas by a year. The specifics of bovine politics in the islands reinforce Sandria Freitag's contention that cattle riots in British India functioned to create new public spaces, agendas, and organizations in partial autonomy from the state,[49] but they also show how political affiliations could be asserted, negotiated, qualified, and represented within such semi-autonomous forums. In the April of 1869, Muslim convicts in the settlement decided to sacrifice a bull during the Id festival. Hindu prisoners objected vehemently, but the bull was killed anyway. Thanesari writes: 'The Hindus, as is their nature, became very agitated. When the sacrificial blood flowed in front of the Hindus, there were riots and much uproar. Had the police overseer not arrived in time, a great deal of bloodshed would have occurred and many would have lost their lives.'[50]

After police intervention had prevented a wider riot, the cow protection battle moved into the local courts, and into the domain of convict clerks. As a Wahhabi, a court clerk, and an autobiographical author, Thanesari occupies a strategic location within and without the story. Not surprisingly, it appears that he played a central role in the controversy; he writes that the Hindus (again, 'as is their nature') went to court in order 'to get me severely punished'. When the court—presided over by Protheroe—disappointed the defenders of the local cattle, the enraged Hindus apparently retaliated against Thanesari by framing him on charges of embezzlement.[51] The assumption by Thanesari of his own centrality in the matter is not simply a failure of modesty. Thanesari was in fact central, not only because he had asserted (and subsequently advertised) his leadership in the society of Muslim convicts by leading the effort to sacrifice the bull, but also because as a court clerk, he had his hand on the legitimizing apparatus of the colonial state. The convicts recognized that the court in Port Blair was not simply the voice of British administrators like Protheroe, but the voice, also, of the convict intermediaries who influenced Protheroe's opinion.

Thanesari alleges that when he was charged with embezzlement, a Hindu clerk named Monga Lal tampered with the official records to furnish the accusers with supporting evidence. Other Hindu bureaucrats apparently connived to bribe witnesses, and confiscated Thanesari's account books. Thanesari, however, was able to conspire with a Muslim clerk to recover his account books, and to 'correct' the 'tampered' records. The embezzlement charges were dismissed by Protheroe, who also ordered that Monga Lal be imprisoned for six months (presumably on Viper Island, where local offenders were sent), and that another Hindu clerk be flogged. Before proceeding to Viper Island, however, Monga Lal sprang another unpleasant surprise on Thanesari: he told Protheroe that the Maulana had diverted government timber to build furniture for his own house. He even offered to escort Protheroe to Thanesari's house, so that Protheroe might see for himself. Thanesari concedes that this accusation, at least, was true.[52] This time, he was saved by Protheroe's reluctance to send his favourite clerk to Viper. Protheroe told Monga Lal that the timber was a gift, warned him to stop spying on Thanesari, and sent him on his way.[53]

Thanesari arrived in the Andamans with a highly developed sense of his Wahhabi identity, and an acute perception that Hindus were likely to be a hostile group. At least partially, he blamed his criminal conviction on Hindus.[54] In the penal colony, he seems to have slipped into a social milieu that was largely, if not exclusively, Muslim. Hindus, however, were not the only 'enemy' that he recognized in the Andamans; nor did he consistently view Hindus as a menace. He reserved his longest and most articulate diatribes for Europeans, Eurasians, Indian Christians, and the English language itself. Here, also, the context for the hostility was the Port Blair bureaucracy.

Thanesari was conscious, and intensely resentful, of the privileged status of European, Eurasian, and Christian convicts in the Andamans. He pointed out that while Indians from the highest ranks of mainland society were subjected to humiliating and painful labour in the penal colony ('because of their black skin and Indian birth'), other prisoners ('white-skinned Europeans and many black-skinned Anglo-Indians, who had embraced Christianity and used to wear European dress') were assigned lighter work, residential bungalows, better food, and servants. A special target of Thanesari's ire was an Indian Christian prisoner named Thastier, who had been arrested in Awadh and given a job in the court of the Deputy Commissioner of the Andamans, along with a furnished house and a paid servant.[55]

Thastier thus had essentially the same privileges in the penal colony that Thanesari himself took for granted. This provides at least a partial explanation of why Thanesari took such exception to him. Thanesari's privileged life in the Andamans was a social resource to him, in the sense that it reinforced his credentials as a leading member of convict society. Nevertheless, it is likely that such privilege was simultaneously a source of marginalization and resentment: it conveyed an insider status in the penal regime that cut him off from less privileged convicts. Thanesari's attacks on Thastier and others like him can be seen as an attempt to counteract this alienation. When Thanesari wrote that 'the discrimination [by the settlement authorities] in favour of European dress...made *all of us* sad and angry,'[56] (italics mine) he was trying to insert himself into a very specific convict 'us', based on black skin, non-Christian religion, non-European dress, and distance from the white/Christian colonial Other.

This vision is evident in Thanesari's admiration for Sher Ali, the convict who assassinated the Viceroy, Lord Mayo, in 1872.[57] It is manifest also in the inclusive and sympathetic language which he uses, periodically, to describe Hindu convicts. He compares Thastier's privileged life not with the hardships of the 'innocent Muslims' whom he mentions elsewhere, but with the humiliation of the Hindu raja of Jagannath Puri, who came to the Andamans as a political prisoner. The raja, Thanesari noted with anger, was compelled to do hard labour alongside low caste convicts, and flogged when he was physically unable to work.[58] The raja died not long after his arrival in the penal colony. This treatment of the raja anticipates the British handling of middle class political prisoners in the islands in the twentieth century; in each case, the reversal of status was a major part of the punishment.

Thanesari could be inclusive towards Hindus and Sikhs in contexts other than that of life in the Andamans: reflecting on the recent history of the subcontinent, he expressed admiration for 'the dignity and honor' with which the Sikhs had ruled in Punjab, and the Marathas in the Deccan.[59] Because the Sikh and Maratha regimes were among the last major pre-colonial powers in South Asia,[60] such celebratory references are rich in coded meaning, especially when they come from a Muslim writer who is also prone to waxing nostalgic about Mughal power. Thanesari emerges as a proto-nationalist of sorts: a man who shares the nostalgic and defensive world view of elite Muslims in mid-nineteenth century India, but who is also groping for the language and symbols that might fashion a broader Indian identity defined in opposition to white/Christian identity and privilege.

The allegation of nationalist inclinations is necessarily tenuous in the case of a man who locates himself within a transnational religious ideology. Nevertheless, two points might be made that give weight to the suggestion. One is that nineteenth century penal colonies relied, for their punitive effect, in the inducement of what Alice Bullard has called 'fatal nostalgia': a traumatic, disorienting, and quite specific condition of longing that, when it did not literally kill the transported individual, could leave him or her open to radical reformulations of political identity.[61] Thanesari's pre-transportation political identity was not cut from the same ideological cloth of the Paris Communards that Bullard writes about, but 'nostalgia' is undeniably central to his experience of punishment, and it is quite plausible that his resocialization and reeducation in the Andamans would cause him to imagine his relationship with 'India' differently than he had in the past.

The second point is that the separation between the transnational anti-colonial politician and his nationalist counterpart is rarely 'clean' in India after the Mutiny.[62] Moreover, I would argue that the nature of the colonial penal settlement, with its reliance on modern bureaucratic categories of nationhood, race, geography, and power concentrated within the confines of a community that was both lived and imagined,[63] made it almost inevitable that the politics of resistance would be articulated occasionally in national terms by those who had already learned to imagine large and historically charged political communities. A penal colony which British jailors could imagine as a model colony[64] could also be imagined by convicts as a model India, in which nationhood manifested itself as extraordinary socio-political reconfigurations. Expressing his wonderment at the convergence of identities bound by not only by a pre-existing notion of 'India' but also by subjection to a common punishing agent, Thanesari wrote:

What an interesting place this is! I think there is no other place in the world where people from so many different ethnic backgrounds live together. Just try to imagine that a Bengali man is married to a Madrasi woman, or a Bhutia man is married to a Punjabi woman. The spouses don't understand each other's language, and when they fight, each uses his or her language which is incomprehensible to the other. When there is a wedding, and women from different regions, each wearing the clothes of her homeland, gather to sing songs in their own languages and dance in their own way, it is a wonderful scene to watch. Restrictions of caste and region, from which all of India suffers, are totally absent here. You will find a Pasi woman in a Brahmin's house, and a Brahmin woman in a Jat's house.[65]

The penal colony is, as such, a transforming place, and Thanesari cannot react to it simply as a militant Muslim. Significantly, he expressed regret for his part in the bull sacrifice, writing: 'If I had had the vision that I have today, I would have sacrificed a goat in place of the bull, and not hurt the feelings of hundreds of people.'[66] Historicizing the convict experience requires conceding the likelihood that a long-term resident of the penal colony—which, more than a jail, is a complex social and political environment—will evolve ideologically, although not necessarily in the state-approved direction of 'reform'. The Wahhabi who lands in Port Blair cannot be expected to remain 'simply' or 'essentially' a Wahhabi ten years into his stay, or when he is released 20 years after leaving the mainland. A double process of negotiation is likely to become necessary to reconcile what is acquired and unexpected with what was expected and already there: not only an 'internal' ideological adjustment, but also an 'external' rearticulation of the political self, such as Thanesari's narrative. This negotiation is most effective when conducted on familiar ground: the Maulana, the militant killer of bulls and battler of Hindus, justified the subsequent broadening of his circle of political inclusion by citing Islamic scripture.

Given this unstable self-image, participation in the colonial courts and avid pursuit of colonial knowledge posed serious dilemmas for Thanesari. He devoted several pages to this conflict within and around him. On the one hand, he pointed out:

The English language is a treasure of knowledge and the arts. A person who does not know English cannot be well-informed about world affairs. Unless one learns English, one cannot be active and business-minded. Nor can one earn a living without English these days.[67]

This is more than a simple appeal to pragmatism. It reflects a genuine fascination with the intellectual universe of an alien language, a recognition that English was the language of 'world affairs', and a desire to become actively engaged in this wider world of politics and ideas. This is strikingly apparent in Thanesari's response to the indigenous Andamanese, who he imagined not only as racially and culturally distinct from his Indian-convict self, but in quasi-ethnological terms, writing:

These people are from four feet to five-feet-four inches tall and like Negroes, they are black, have round heads, bulging eyes and woolly hair on the head, and are very strong and healthy. In all there are twelve aboriginal tribes. The language of one tribe has very little similarity with that of another tribe. They cannot count beyond two. They tattoo their bodies with pieces of broken bottles and the tattoos look like beehives or clothing.[68]

He went on to describe Andamanese religious beliefs, marital customs, and political relations with the Port Blair regime, producing a narrative that is clearly informed by the anthropological-governmental project that gained momentum in the Andamans during Thanesari's stay in the islands.[69] While it would be a stretch to claim that Thanesari fully shared the scientific-historical vision of civilizations, savages, Selves, and Others that was produced and promoted by his contemporaries E.H. Man and M.V. Portman, it is tantalizingly apparent that the energetic work of colonizer-anthropologists[70] had overflowed the 'civil lines' of Ross Island and Port Blair and infiltrated the world view of a section of convict society. As the influenced/contaminated native, Thanesari did not simply see English as a necessary bridge to a powerful but alien world; from his location on the edge of the modern colony, he desired what lay across the bridge.

At the same time, he was frightened by what awaited him on the other side, and by the contamination that was facilitated by his desire. He was, it might be surmised, also concerned about how his foray would be interpreted by untransported Muslims on the mainland, whose identities had not been destabilized in quite the same ways. Even as he learned and praised English, he warned:

This language is so closely connected with the materialistic life that it is dangerous and harmful to the spirit. If a young man, who has not yet learned the Koran and the traditions of the holy Prophet in detail, learns English and reads English books of various types as I used to do, he will become an irreligious, uncultured person with excessively free ideas, to the extent that it would be...impossible to reform him.[71]

He was careful to differentiate between the English language itself (which is 'not so harmful') and specific types of English literature ('that are against the teachings of the Prophets'). Whereas knowledge of the language is an asset in the colonial world, the literature is a virtual minefield:

Such knowledge will certainly make a person irreligious and atheistic if he is not well-acquainted with Islam. It will create doubts in his mind which will last a lifetime. And although he may claim to be a Muslim, he will not be a true believer.[72]

It is not difficult to see, in such warnings, a profound anxiety about how to interpret and represent his exploration of new cultural territory. Thanesari went on to describe his own brush with self-destruction, noting that his faith had weakened, that his ritual observations had become irregular, and that he had all but forgotten the Hadees.

Eventually, the Maulana writes, he underwent a physical test of faith: he became seriously ill. When, after much repentance, he finally recovered his health, he resumed his neglected religious rituals. He did not, however, abandon the English language and his dangerous books. Unwilling and unable to turn away from the guilty pleasures of colonialism, he learned to make the gestures of compromise that made it possible to live with seemingly irreconcilable cultural and moral identities. This compromise was not simply the resolution of a private existential dilemma. It was also the answer to a vitally important political question, which had to do with his ability to retain his status in the society of the punished/colonized even as he penetrated more deeply into the society of the punisher/colonizer.

In many ways, Thanesari's dilemmas and contortions reflect those of his better-known contemporary, Syed Ahmad Khan. Both men operated in a climate of intense anxiety about the divide between colonial India on the one hand, and the world of the Muslim elite on the other. Both men were drawn to the possibilities of the former world, and both were conscious that this exploration could cost them their place in the latter.[73] The solutions that they held up—one in the penal colony, the other in an experimental college—were quite similar. Like Syed Ahmad in Aligarh, Thanesari came to the conclusion that English language training could be combined with Islamic education, and that the products of this mixing would be culturally and politically viable. Like Syed Ahmad—who, Gail Minault recounts, was outraged by Mumtaz Ali's heresy on the subject of women's rights even as he himself outraged religious conservatives[74]— Thanesari found it necessary to emphasize his religiosity in order to make his 'westernization' palatable to himself and to others.

FAMILY/MAN

Thanesari's conflicted views of Hindus and Muslims, religious Selves and Others, spilled over into his relations with women in the penal colony and free society. There are two generalizations that I would like to extract from the Maulana's family life in the context of his punishment. The first is that for transported convicts, families in the penal colony became vital social, economic, and emotional resources; prisoners sought to acquire them as quickly as possible. At the same time, these convicts often had families on the mainland. In the extraordinary circumstances of penal transportation, each family served its purpose. The 'new' family both supplanted and supplemented the 'old'. Second, for male convicts, marriage was not simply a response to loneliness and sexual deprivation. It was also an exercise in social networking between communities within the incarcerated population. This function took on special importance when convict marriages crossed the lines of caste and religion. Intercaste marriage was common in the Andamans; the British—after a prolonged debate—adopted a 'don't ask, don't tell' policy on the issue.[75] Thanesari's writing indicates that inter-religious marriages were not unknown. It is evident, also, that such a marriage could be represented as a victory for the husband's community over that of the wife: a significant accomplishment in the context of the political rivalries between semi-organized Muslim and Hindu convicts, and between Wahhabis and other Muslims, being narrated by a Wahhabi man.

Convict families served multiple masters. For British administrators who supervised the Indian Ocean colonies in which men significantly outnumbered women, and where the colonial power controlled women's entry into local society, the family was a device within which individual criminals and their disorder might be contained.[76] This strategic deployment of the family was not limited to convicts; Carter has noted the phenomenon among indentured workers in Mauritius in the mid-nineteenth century.[77] It is certainly tempting to view the convict family exclusively in terms of power relations and control. Foucault called the family 'the privileged locus of emergence for the disciplinary question of the moral and the abnormal.'[78] This formulation, which has informed some otherwise very insightful work, such as McClintock's analysis of gender and empire[79]—has drawn criticism from even those scholars who have generally been receptive to Foucault. Ignatieff has noted that the Foucauldian view of the family over-emphasizes relations of domination and is simplistic to the point of self-parody.[80] It is a mistake to view convict marriage and the convict family in the Andamans solely as systems for the domination of women convicts by male prisoners, and prisoners of both sexes by the incarcerating state. Ignatieff is right to draw attention to 'the collaborative and sacrificial elements of family attachment',[81] and these elements were undoubtedly present in the families that formed in the society of transported convicts.

When Thanesari was taken to the Andamans, he left his wife and two children behind. Not long after his arrival in Port Blair, he asked that his wife be allowed to join him in the islands. This petition was rejected, he writes, because 'the law did not permit that'.[82] This statement is puzzling, because the Port Blair authorities had long been eager to import the wives of convicts. It was hoped that wives and families would mitigate a wide array of problems—ranging from violence and political disloyalty to homosexuality—that might be expected in a predominantly male world.[83] The effort to import wives failed because women were generally unwilling to join convict husbands in the Andamans, and not because of reluctance on the part of the British.[84] It seems likely that Thanesari's wife refused to follow her man to the penal colony, and he protected his masculine honour by deflecting the responsibility on to the regime. He writes that his wife was willing 'to some extent', which indicates a lack of enthusiasm on her part.[85]

In 1866, Thanesari married a young Kashmiri Muslim in the Andamans. He writes that she had been brought to the penal colony because of 'an unexpected tragedy', and he emphasizes her youth.[86] This is almost certainly an euphemism for unwed pregnancy followed by infanticide, which was the crime that most often brought women to the Andamans.[87] In a convict settlement where every woman was 'fallen' to some degree, Thanesari was pragmatic about his wife's past, and did not see it as an obstacle in the way of his own social advancement. Nevertheless, he was aware that this marriage might reflect badly upon him in life after the Andamans. This explains the pains he took to underline his second wife's religiosity—after she married him and due to his influence, of course. He writes that she became a devoted follower of the Maulvi Yahya Khan, an elderly Wahhabi convict who befriended Thanesari in the islands.[88] Thanesari's narrative thus represents the marriage as a masculine/Wahhabi triumph over a wayward woman from the Sufi geography of Kashmir.

The Kashmiri woman—we are not told her name—died within a year of her marriage to Thanesari. The Maulana immediately sold her jewellery, and sent the proceeds (some Rs 300) to his first wife in Panipat. He asked that she use the money to buy shoes and send them to him in Port Blair. Thanesari calculated that he could sell the shoes locally at three or four times the cost of purchase.[89] What is most significant about this exchange is not that individual convict women in the Andamans possessed Rs 300 worth of jewellery, or that Thanesari was an alert and well-connected businessman even in the penal colony. These simply indicate the existence of a lively local economy which was both isolated from and connected to the mainland economy. This incomplete isolation generated trading opportunities as well as high prices for everything from gold to shoes, and created the conditions in which enterprising convicts—women as well as men—could acquire and invest wealth. Thanesari's trading venture is more significant because it shows a pragmatic approach to families. Not only did the Maulana immediately and unsentimentally convert his dead wife into capital, he also involved his living wife in his business venture. Wives and families on both sides of the Bay of Bengal functioned as vital points of contact, both social and economic, for convicts in the Andamans. Families served as conduits of money, news and reputations, enabled trade, and allowed transported convicts to maintain (and even expand) their presence in the memory of mainland communities. In other words, families in the penal colony and on the mainland made sure that the Andamans did not become a terrifying black hole in the collective imagination of Indian criminals and their associates, which is precisely what the British had intended the penal colony to be.[90]

After the death of his Kashmiri wife, Thanesari became an eligible bachelor once again. He was young (barely 28), well-off by convict standards, well-connected, and well-employed. He developed a fear that numerous women were trying to 'lure' him into marriage by coming to his house under official pretences. 'Women here behave in such a shameless manner that even prostitutes would be ashamed', he wrote defensively, not unlike other conservative Indian men who have lived overseas among 'disorderly' women.[91] The perception that local women found him irresistible may have been accurate, however, since marriage was one of the few avenues of upward mobility open to convict women in the Andamans.[92] Thanesari fully intended to marry again, and his friends initiated negotiations with two Punjabi Muslim women. Such peer groups of prisoners, which played a leading role in organizing marriages in the Andamans, functioned as surrogate families for individual convicts. There were, apparently, certain misgivings about the women under review: since both were confined to their barracks much of the time, nobody could vouch for their 'character'. The society of convicts did not exist in perfect moral isolation from the society of the free, and concepts like reputation and character played a role in determining women's eligibility as wives. The crimes that brought women to the penal colony could be overlooked in the construction of this character, but local behaviour mattered, not least when the groom had to re-enact his wedding and his own moral credentials for a mainland readership. In this particular case, prenuptial negotiations broke down not because of the groom's misgivings, but because both women unexpectedly married other men. 'They turned out to be loose women,' Thanesari wrote sadly. 'I was looking for a young and virtuous woman.'[93]

This model of youth and virtue turned out to be a Hindu from Almora in northern India, who was transported to the Andamans in 1868. She had been convicted of trying to murder another woman by pushing her down a well, but Thanesari insisted that his wife was framed by jealous neighbours. While such protestations of innocence are hardly surprising, the fact that the Maulana went out of his way to marry a Brahmin is revealing of some of the most critical dynamics of convict society. The revelation begins with the language in which the woman (who, like the Kashmiri, is never named) is described. 'She was extremely prejudiced in her Hinduism,' Thanesari writes. 'She could not tolerate standing near a Muslim woman or even a touch of her clothes.' Nevertheless, 'although she was born in a Brahmin family in a hilly area where there are no Muslims at all, she did not indulge in polytheism or idolatry and never worshipped.'[94] Thus, even as the future wife is portrayed as being very Hindu, that is, sufficiently non-Muslim to make conversion meaningful, she retains redeeming qualities that qualify her otherness, and create a sympathetic cultural and moral space within which courtship can proceed.

As Thanesari describes it, his wooing of this woman is inseparable from a simultaneous process of religious conquest.

I said: 'If you embrace Islam, it will be good for you in this world as well as on the Day of Judgment, and you will be saved from going to hell.' She was surprised to hear this, but destiny had already decided that she would become a Muslim and give birth to my children. On the very first night after her arrest she saw the beaming face of an old Muslim man in an early morning dream. The man kicked her and said: 'Get up and say Namaz, because it is for your good that you have been arrested.' She woke up frightened, narrated the dream to a Muslim guard, and asked him what it might mean. He said: 'You will certainly become a Muslim as a result of your imprisonment.' Because of destiny and the prophecy in the dream, she accepted my proposal and agreed to embrace Islam and become my wife.[95]

Once the courtship is complete, the wedding comes as the celebration of a successful conquest. It is, however, an accommodating conquest, in which tenderness coexists with communal triumph. Thanesari writes:

On the twenty-seventh night of Ramadan I organized a great feast and converted her to Islam. After she had learned the Muslim rituals and Namaz, I informed the authorities and married her on the fifteenth of April, 1868. Hundreds of people were present at my wedding and the marriage was solemnized by Maulvi Ahmedullah Sahab. On the next day a grand reception was arranged. This wife gave birth to ten of my children, of whom eight are still alive. And this was the wife who accompanied me from Port Blair to India. She spent twenty-two faithful and devoted years with me. She is a pious and adaptable woman.[96]

We do not know why the woman in question agreed to marry Thanesari. It is best to reject romantic passion as a motive, since nothing in the Maulana's writing indicates that either was besotted. It is likely that Thanesari exaggerated her initial Hindu rigidity; he was probably more accurate when he referred to her as adaptable. For her, marriage and religious conversion opened doors that would otherwise have remained closed. Her status in her original society on the mainland—especially her marital prospects—had already been disrupted by criminal conviction, arrest, and penal transportation.[97] This made converting to Islam and marrying a Muslim relatively painless. On the contrary, these gave her access to the social and economic resources of a privileged husband.

Thus, 'inter-religious' marriage in the Andamans could serve multiple purposes: it boosted Thanesari's status among Muslim convicts, and repaired his wife's damaged social status by allowing her to reinvent herself. For both husband and wife, children provided additional status in local society; Thanesari recounts the feasts, attended by large numbers of elite convicts, that surrounded the birth of sons and daughters. Also, for the Maulana, his new family in the penal colony provided a way of remembering the family he had left behind on the mainland. In one of the more poignant instances in the history of displacement and migration, Thanesari named his new children after his old. When he was told that his oldest son, Mohammad Sadiq, had died in Panipat, he writes, 'I consoled myself with the fact that I had with me his namesake. I informed my wife in India about the replacement of the dead son with a namesake.'[98]

It seems clear that the two families—the old and the new—became partially integrated as the time of Thanesari's release approached. His financial contacts with his first wife continued; in 1882, he sent her money, jewellery, and clothes to meet the expenses of his oldest daughter's wedding. He could not play the dominant role in arranging the marriage—that responsibility passed to the bride's mother—but he tried, nevertheless, to preserve some authority as a man and a Muslim, telling his readers that he had instructed his wife to 'marry our daughter to some religious-minded boy.'[99] He continued to hope that he would be released in time to be present at the wedding, and he bought presents and souvenirs in anticipation.

Thanesari did not, however, lose sight of his local family. After his release was announced in January of 1883, he stayed on in the Andamans until November. He was waiting for his wife's release, and for the birth of another child: his wife in the Andamans was pregnant at this time. Convicts in the penal colony sometimes went back to the mainland leaving their local spouses and children behind in the Andamans;[100] Thanesari was not one of them. He used the extra time in the penal colony to negotiate with the colonial authorities over an acceptable job on the mainland, and to sell his possessions at the best possible prices. He campaigned, also, to have his home converted into a mosque. This last project was almost certainly intended for mainland consumers of his martyred Self: he writes that it made him more popular than ever among Muslim convicts, and that the plan fell through because the Port Blair regime feared that the mosque would become a centre of Wahhabi political activity.[101]

In the autumn of 1883, Thanesari left the penal colony on board the *SS Maharani*, accompanied by his wife, eight children, and Rs 8,000 worth of valuables. When he reached the mainland, he moved quickly to determine the relationship between his two families. He was clear that he wanted to retain his ties with his first family, which had survived 20 years of physical separation and intermittent communication. He visited his first wife in Panipat, and wondered at the sheer familiarity of this rediscovered world: 'I felt as though I had left my family this morning, and returned later in the day.'[102]

Nevertheless, he understood that things had, in fact, changed: he notes, with a sense of shock, that the son who was less than a year old at the time of the Maulana's arrest was now an intimate stranger of 20. We are not told how his first wife's social relationships had evolved over the two decades of her husband's absence, yet they must have changed. Under the circumstances, Thanesari was clear that his primary family was the one he had acquired in the penal colony. After five days in Panipat, he returned to Ambala. He distributed his accumulated wealth between his two wives, and adopted a somewhat disingenuous posture as a renouncer of material comforts ('now my personal property consists of only a few books and some clothes').[103]

Jafar Thanesari's account of his years in the Andamans indicates how convicts who possessed certain cultural and professional assets were able to utilize the experience of penal transportation to reinvent themselves, or at least to adjust their identities, not only in the penal colony but also in the 'free' society of the mainland. For all its unreliability, the narrative confirms that some prisoners were able to negotiate a mutually beneficial arrangement with the British authorities in the Andamans. For literate convicts, the experience of penal transportation generated opportunities for positive social mobility that probably surpassed opportunities that existed in free society.

Thanesari's narrative also adds to our understanding of the political community and the family in a nineteenth century Indian penal colony, complicated as these were by the circumstances of dislocation, distance, and an intensely cosmopolitan prison. In spite of the mixing of ethnicities and religions, communal identities remained intact, and in some contexts, became more sharply defined. But in other contexts, the boundaries of community could be suspended, or reimagined to delineate an Indian convict identity determined by the interrelated forces of colonialism and punishment. The exploration of new languages and ideas was profitable and irresistible, but it also generated intense anxieties about the perforation of cultural boundaries. This made religious self-assertion that much more important. Marriage, families, and the convict experience itself could be utilized rhetorically to raise the status of the 'conqueror' in the eyes of his community.

NOTES AND REFERENCES

Primary sources listed below refer to the records of the Home Department (HD) of the Government of India (GOI), Port Blair, Public and Judicial Branches. All GOI records are located in the National Archives of India (NAI), New Delhi.

1. Sandra Freitag and Anand Yang, 1985, 'Collective Crime and Authority in North India', in Anand Yang (ed.), *Crime and Criminality in British India*, Tucson: University of Arizona Press, pp. 108–27, 140–63.

2. Satadru Sen, 2000, *Disciplining Punishment: Colonialism and Convict Society in the Andaman Islands*, New Delhi: Oxford University Press, pp. 1–30.

3. Lucy Frost and Hamish Maxwell-Stewart (eds), 2001, *Chain Letters: Narrating Convict Lives*, Melbourne: Melbourne University Press, p. 15; Cassandra Pybus and Hamish Maxwell-Stewart, 2002, *American Citizens, British Slaves: Yankee Political Prisoners in an Australian Penal Colony*, East Lansing: Michigan State University Press, p. 6; Peter Redfield, 2000, *Space in the Tropics: From Convicts to Rockets in French Guiana*, Berkeley: University of California Press, pp. 86–92.

4. Clare Anderson, 2000, *Convicts in the Indian Ocean*, London: Macmillan, chapter 1; Anand Yang, 2004, 'The Lotah Emeutes of 1855: Caste, Religion and Prisons in North India in the Early Nineteenth Century', in James Mill and Satadru Sen (eds), *Confronting the Body: The Politics of Physicality in Colonial and Postcolonial South Asia*, London: Anthem, pp. 102–17.

5. Muhammad Jafar Thanesari, *Kalapani*, Delhi: Urdu Markaz, 1964, pp. 4–54. The published work is in Urdu; the page numbers cited here are from an unpublished English translation in my possession.

6. A distinction must be made here between Mutiny-era political prisoners like Thanesari, and those who were imprisoned explicitly in connection with nationalist agitation in the twentieth century. The latter, Ujjwal Singh has noted, were ideologically distinct from the 'common' convicts, and not intended for any kind of rehabilitation. Ujjwal Singh, 1998, *Political Prisoners in India*, New Delhi: Oxford University Press, pp. 23–69. The earlier generation of rebels, however, were seen by the British as relatively amenable to reincorporation

into the political order of the colonial state, provided they could be attached to the 'right' leadership. Sen, *Disciplining Punishment*, pp. 61–75.

7. The term 'convict elite' may sound like an oxymoron, but prisoners who had been in the islands for some years, those who possessed special talents, and those who demonstrated particular political loyalty were all rewarded with various degrees of freedom, power, money, and sexual opportunity. Sen, *Disciplining Punishment*, pp. 100–19.

8. Mushirul Hasan, 1996, 'The Myth of Unity', in David Ludden (ed.), *Contesting the Nation: Religion, Community, and the Politics of Democracy in India*, Philadelphia: University of Pennsylvania Press, pp. 185–208.

9. Harjot Oberoi, 1999, 'Sikh Fundamentalism', in Sudipta Kaviraj (ed.), *Politics in India*, New Delhi: Oxford University Press, p. 328.

10. Barbara Daly Metcalf, 1982, *Islamic Revival in British India: Deoband, 1860–1900*, Princeton: Princeton University Press, pp. 299–309.

11. Alex Padamsee, 2005, *Representation of Indian Muslims in British Colonial Discourse*, Houndmills: Palgrave, pp. 150–3.

12. Sen, *Disciplining Punishment*, p. 63.

13. Ayesha Jalal, 2003, 'Partisans of Allah: Jihad in Theory and History', paper presented at the South Asia Speaker Series, Washington University, 3 October.

14. Lloyd Rudolph, Susanne Hoeber Rudolph, and Mohan Singh Kanota, 2000, *Reversing the Gaze*, New Delhi: Oxford University Press, pp. 27–38.

15. Francis Robinson, 2001, *The 'Ulama of Farangi Mahall and Islamic Culture*, New Delhi: Permanent Black, pp. 177–210.

16. Gail Minault, 1982, *The Khilafat Movement: Religious Symbolism and Political Mobilization in India*, New York: Columbia University Press; David Lelyveld, 1978, *Aligarh's First Generation: Muslim Solidarity in British India*, Princeton: Princeton University Press, pp. 3–34

17. Satadru Sen, 'Domesticated Convicts: Producing Families in the Andaman Islands', in Indrani Chatterjee (ed.), *Unfamiliar Relations: Family and History in South Asia*, New Brunswick: Rutgers University Press, 2004, p. 261.

18. Martin Wiener, 1990, *Reconstructing the Criminal: Culture, Law and Policy in England, 1830–1914*, Cambridge: Cambridge University Press, p. 47.

19. Janet Semple, 1993, *Bentham's Prison*, Oxford: Clarendon Press, pp. 161–5.

20. GOI Home, Judiciary, 30 December 1871, pp. 94–8.

21. David Arnold, 1994, 'The Colonial Prison', in David Arnold and David Hardiman (eds), *Selected Subaltern Studies VIII*, New Delhi: Oxford University Press, pp. 148–87.

22. GOI HD, Judiciary, 9 January 1869, pp. 55–72, 75–435.

23. GOI HD, F.J. Mouat to Rivers Thompson, 6 January 1860.

24. GOI HD, Port Blair, October 1873, pp. 60–2.

25. Sen, *Disciplining Punishment*, pp. 86–92.

26. GOI HD, Judiciary, April 1872, pp. 81–2.

27. Ibid., 7 October 1871, pp. 30–2.

28. Thanesari, *Kalapani*, p. 57.

29. Ibid.

30. Ibid., pp. 13–15.
31. Sen, *Disciplining Punishment*, pp. 175–82.
32. Thanesari, *Kalapani*, p. 78.
33. Ibid.
34. Even in 1871, administrators in Port Blair muttered darkly about what they might do if 'a time of danger like 1857 should again visit India'. GOI Home, Public Branch, 7 January 1871, pp. 128–35; 22 April 1871, pp. 53–4.
35. GOI HD, Judiciary, 24 September 1870, p. 6.
36. Sen, *Disciplining Punishment*, p. 96.
37. Douglas Hay, Peter Linebaugh, and E.P. Thompson, 1975, *Albion's Fatal Tree: Crime and Society in Eighteenth-Century England*, New York: Pantheon, pp. 39–41.
38. Thanesari, *Kalapani*, pp. 79, 83.
39. Ibid., p. 105.
40. Ibid., pp. 116–17. Colonial jailors frequently complained that over-zealous police surveillance ruined the rehabilitation of released prisoners. See Administration Report of the Hazaribagh Reformatory School, 1883, NAI.
41. Thanesari, *Kalapani*, pp. 83, 90.
42. Ibid., p. 90.
43. Anderson, *Convicts in the Indian Ocean*, pp. 91–4.
44. GOI HD, Judiciary, 15 July 1871, 47A.
45. Sen, *Disciplining Punishment*, pp. 105–6, 221–3.
46. V.D. Savarkar, 1984, *My Transportation for Life*, Bombay: Veer Savarkar Prakashan, pp. 125, 198. Savarkar is widely regarded as the pre-eminent ideologue of Hindu nationalism in twentieth century Indian politics. He was imprisoned in the Andamans between 1911–21.
47. Thanesari, *Kalapani*, p. 83.
48. John McLane, 1977, *Indian Nationalism and the Early Congress*, Princeton: Princeton University Press, pp. 271–331.
49. Sandria Freitag, 1996, 'Contesting in Public: Colonial Legacies and Contemporary Communalism', in Ludden (ed.), *Contesting the Nation*, pp. 211–23.
50. Thanesari, *Kalapani*, pp. 79–80.
51. Ibid., p. 81.
52. It is entirely possible that the previous charge of embezzlement also had some basis in truth. Thanesari is less than energetic in denying it.
53. Thanesari, *Kalapani*, p. 82.
54. Ibid., pp. 17, 86–7.
55. Ibid., p. 68.
56. Ibid., p. 70.
57. H.W. Hunter, 1892, *Rulers of India: The Earl of Mayo*, Oxford: Clarendon Press, pp. 192–5; Thanesari, *Kalapani*, pp. 86–9. Thanesari himself developed his ideas about colonial politics by reading Hunter's histories, and by reacting angrily at what he saw as Hunter's prejudice against Wahhabis.
58. Thanesari, *Kalapani*, pp. 68–9.
59. Ibid., p. 97.

60. J.S. Grewal, 1990, *The Sikhs of the Punjab*, Cambridge: Cambridge University Press; Stewart Gordon, 1993, *The Marathas, 1600–1818*, Cambridge: Cambridge University Press.

61. Alice Bullard, 2000, *Exile to Paradise: Savagery and Civilization in Paris and the South Pacific, 1790–1900*, Stanford: Stanford University Press, pp. 182–209.

62. Cases in point are Abdul Bari and Maulana Azad, who found themselves drawn into Indian nationalist politics in the aftermath of the First World War, albeit with different priorities, levels of enthusiasm, and interpretations of the political problem at hand. Minault, *The Khilafat Movement*, pp. 25–43.

63. Benedict Anderson, 1983, *Imagined Communities*, New York: Verso, pp. 12–19.

64. Sen, *Disciplining Punishment*, pp. 100–9.

65. Thanesari, *Kalapani*, pp. 109–10.

66. Ibid., p. 81.

67. Ibid., p. 91.

68. Ibid., p. 64.

69. Satadru Sen, forthcoming, *Savagery and Colonialism in the Indian Ocean: Power, Pleasure and the Andaman Islanders*, Edinburgh: Routledge, chapter 1.

70. Ibid. See also M.V. Portman, 1899, *A History of Our Relations with the Andamanese*, Calcutta: Office of the Superintendent of Government Printing.

71. Thanesari, *Kalapani*, p. 91.

72. Ibid., p. 92.

73. Lelyveld, *Aligarh's First Generation*, pp. 102–46.

74. Gail Minault, 1992, 'Women's Rights in Islam and Women's Journalism in Urdu', in Kenneth Jones (ed.), *Religious Controversy in British India*, New York: SUNY Press, p. 182.

75. GOI HD, Port Blair, October 1884, pp. 81–2.

76. Sen, 'Domesticated Convicts'.

77. Marina Carter, 1995, *Servants, Sirdars and Settlers: Indians in Mauritius, 1834–1874*, Oxford: Oxford University Press, p. 237; and 1994, *Lakshmi's Legacy: the Testimonies of Indian Women in Nineteenth-century Mauritius*, Mauritius: Editions de l'Ocean Indien, pp. 113–46.

78. Michel Foucault, 1978, *Discipline and Punish: The Birth of the Prison*, New York: Vintage, p. 215.

79. Anne McClintock, 1995, *Imperial Leather: Race, Gender and Sexuality in the Colonial Contest*, New York: Routledge, pp. 132–72.

80. Michael Ignatieff, 1983, 'State, Civil Society and Total Institutions', in Stanley Cohen and Andrew Scull (eds), *Social Control and the State*, New York: St Martin's Press, p. 98.

81. Ibid.

82. Thanesari, *Kalapani*, p. 70.

83. Sen, 'Domesticated Convicts'.

84. For convicts' families to join them in the Andamans, clearance was required from the Port Blair authorities as well as from the provincial administration on the mainland. Usually, the mainland authorities did not object, provided there was no significant financial cost. Sometimes cost was not a deterrent: Thanesari

notes that the Government of Bengal arranged for the family of Mian Abdul Ghaffar, a convict who had been transported in connection with the Rebellion of 1857, to travel to the Andamans at government expense. Thanesari, *Kalapani*, p. 96.

85. Ibid., p. 75.
86. Ibid., p. 70.
87. GOI HD, Port Blair, June 1890, pp. 74–8.
88. Thanesari, *Kalapani*, p. 74.
89. Ibid.
90. GOI HD, Judiciary, 19 June 1869, 14–15 A.
91. Thanesari, *Kalapani*, pp. 75, 110.
92. Sen, 'Domesticated Convicts'.
93. Thanesari, *Kalapani*, p. 75.
94. Ibid., p. 76.
95. Ibid., p. 77.
96. Ibid.
97. It was not uncommon for women sentenced to long terms of imprisonment in mainland Indian jails to petition the authorities to be transported to the Andamans, where they might find husbands, a measure of freedom, and economic opportunities. Mary Carpenter, touring Indian prisons in the 1860s, encountered several such petitioners in Calcutta's Alipore Jail; 1868, *Six Months in India*, London: Longman and Green, pp. 202–3.
98. Thanesari, *Kalapani*, p. 98.
99. Ibid., p. 103.
100. GOI HD, Port Blair, April 1877, pp. 5–6, 71–2.
101. Thanesari, *Kalapani*, pp. 105–6.
102. Ibid., p. 117.
103. Ibid., p. 113.

'Weel about and turn about and do jis so, Eb'ry time I weel about and jump Jim Crow'

Dancing on the Margins of the Indian Ocean

Clare Anderson

THE THEFT OF A MUSICAL SNUFFBOX

On 17 April 1838 two men, George Lloyd and George Morgan, appeared before the Supreme Court of Calcutta. The Court found them guilty as charged: of having assaulted a man named William Tipping on the public street and of stealing his musical snuffbox valued at Rs 14. The judge sentenced both men to seven years' transportation, but while Lloyd was ordered to Van Diemen's Land, one of Britain's penal settlements in Australia, Morgan's destination was to be the East India Company's Indian penal settlement in the Tenasserim Provinces of Burma. The newspaper, *The Calcutta Courier*, reporting the trial, noted that Morgan's 'demeanour had all along been very contemptuous'. On leaving the courtroom he had, apparently, 'thanked his lordship'.[1]

The reason for the discrepancy in sentencing was that George Lloyd was white British—he came from Hackney in east London[2]—and George Morgan was African. As was usual practice for white transportation convicts sentenced by the criminal and military courts of India, Lloyd was ordered to one of the Australian penal settlements, which during the nineteenth century included New South Wales (1788–1840), Van

Diemen's Land (1803–53), and Western Australia (1850–68). George Morgan's place of birth is not altogether clear, and his name gives us no clues. Morgan himself represented it as a place 'within the tropics'.[3] His contemporaries described him variously as a 'native of Africa', an 'African' or 'Caffree', 'a black', an 'American black', and a 'Yankee'.[4] His convict conduct register is of little assistance, for it mistakenly recorded his 'native place' as Calcutta.[5] Morgan's body carried its own social markers and the records speak of 'marks of African descent'—a reference to tattoos and/or cicatrization—around his mouth and nose. However, in an interesting allusion to his prior experience of African inmates, the keeper of Calcutta jail John King noted that they were not as prominent as on 'the generality of his Country men'.[6] In the face of this rather vague set of descriptions I think we can assume that Morgan was African, though we do not know precisely where he was born. Whatever the case, as was the norm for Indian, black or mixed race prisoners transported from India, his destination was not Australia but one of the East India Company's penal settlements in the Indian Ocean, which at the time comprised Bencoolen (1787–1825), Penang (1790–1860), Mauritius (1815–53), Malacca and Singapore (1825–60), and the Burmese provinces of Arakan and Tenasserim (1828–62).[7]

Australia refused Indian convicts on the basis that its climate was 'unsuitable' for their 'race'. In 1815, government passed legislation ordering that Indians should not be transported more than 30 degrees north or 25 degrees south of the equator. This injunction was bound up with ideas about the complex and yet mutually constitutive relationship between race and climate, for it did not include white Europeans born in India.[8] At the same time, white convicts were not sent to the Straits Settlements (as Penang, Malacca, and Singapore were known after 1826) or Burma, though this had more to do with the presentation of a socially cohesive colonial society than climatic determinism. One visitor to Singapore wrote in 1837 that respect for the British would be lessened if such convicts were seen working outdoors. He noted that the Chinese community called New South Wales 'theifo country'.[9] In 1848, a white Scotsman named Thomas Hutton was transported to Malacca in error. Governor W.J. Butterworth wrote of 'serious objections' to employing European and Indian prisoners together on public works projects, especially as the Straits were surrounded by hostile territory.[10] Such arguments were repeated in 1855 when it was rumoured—falsely—that European convicts in future would be sent from India to Singapore. This belief had its origins in the transportation of a white convict called David Thom, after which the Singapore authorities petitioned the Government of India over their fears that the port would become a British penal colony. They claimed that this would 'lower and degrade the European character in the eyes of the natives'.[11] The government did its best to reassure them that they were not planning to set up a penal settlement for Europeans in the Straits.[12] The racialization of convict transportation from India is part of a broader argument about the unevenness of colonial rule, for the Australian penal settlements were the destination for perhaps as many as 1,000 African, Indian, and Chinese convicts sentenced to transportation in Britain, the West Indies, the Cape of Good Hope, Hong Kong, and Mauritius during the first half of the nineteenth century.[13] Though the Australian authorities on occasion raised climatic objections to their transportation,[14] these held little sway in the Caribbean and Indian Ocean colonial contexts that, unlike India, lacked alternative convict destinations.

I will not go into the ambivalent social position of Eurasians—people of mixed Indian and British parentage—during the early colonial period here; other historians have covered this ground skilfully.[15] However, I would like to note that Eurasian prisoners embodied a sort of 'double ambivalence', for in India despite their criminal conviction the colonial authorities viewed them primarily through their 'racial' connection to the British and not their offence. Indeed, they enjoyed the same privileges as white prisoners with regard to rations, separate accommodation, and the prohibition of hard outdoor labour—the common fate of most Indian prisoners in the early nineteenth century presidencies. Eurasian convict women inhabited a similar discursive terrain. The transportation of Maria Davis to Mauritius in 1828 was the cause of considerable annoyance to the government, for example, because it felt it necessary to confine her entirely apart from the Indian convict settlement on the island. In 1855, the Bengal government transported another young Eurasian woman named Victoria Hassey to the Straits Settlements. The social and religious anxieties her transportation caused were revealed by Governor Butterworth when he wrote that there was 'much sympathy and compassion here especially among the ladies of the community—this person is young, educated, and a Christian, yet she is mixed with heathen females, and no instructions have been sent to me to treat her otherwise than an ordinary native female criminal.'[16]

During the 1830s, dozens of white convicts were transported overseas from India. Most of them were military offenders who had been court martialled. However, a few—like George Lloyd and George

Morgan—were sentenced by the Supreme Courts of Calcutta, Bombay, and Madras. They were part of the mobile and transient population of the early nineteenth century Indian Ocean, the flotsam and jetsam of port cities home to a community of poor Europeans. There are few statistics available on their numbers during this period. P.J. Marshall puts the 1837 census figure at 3,138 'English', rising to 7,534 'Europeans' in 1850.[17] This relatively small community created considerable colonial anxiety, for the poor were a social embarrassment within the framework of a morally superior 'civilizing mission'. The chief magistrate of the city described Morgan as 'one of the worst London thieves we ever had here'; it was certainly not the first time the men had appeared in court.[18] Yet despite the presence of vagrants and loafers, theirs was no idle underclass. Like their compatriots both Lloyd and Morgan were multiskilled and could turn their hand to a range of trades. Lloyd claimed experience as a servant and groom.[19] Morgan described himself variously as a sailor, a cook, a servant, a waiter, a carpenter, and a cooper.[20]

I have written elsewhere of the escape of British convicts from Australia to Calcutta in the late eighteenth and early nineteenth centuries, and what absconding reveals about both subaltern mobility in the Indian Ocean and British society in early nineteenth century Calcutta.[21] In this essay I want to focus attention once again on such issues, this time reflecting upon George Morgan's transportation to Burma—and as we will see his retransportation to Van Diemen's Land—to think about questions of colonial identity. As we will see, in the 1830s 'race' was not simply a matter of 'birth', 'blood', or 'colour', but embodied a more complex set of social meanings. There were multiple connections within and between both the geographical and social fringes of empire, which were places of discursive and social instability and contingency.

George Morgan's Escape

As soon as a transportation ship—the *Amherst*—was ready to leave with its cargo of convicts, George Morgan was put on board for the month-long voyage to Burma. The ship left on 21 July, with 68 Indian convicts, including 59 so-called thugs, also on board.[22] It was bound for Rangoon, the dropping off point for convicts destined for the Tenasserim Provinces. When it had crossed the Bay of Bengal the ship moored for a night on the Rangoon River. Morgan took the chance to escape. The ship's master—the aptly named Captain Jump—claimed later that Morgan had told him that he had been a servant to the keeper of the Calcutta jail. Assuming that he was of 'good character', Jump had removed his iron fetters. When he was interviewed later on, keeper John King denied this practice in the strongest terms, adding that Morgan was wearing double irons when he was escorted on board the transport ship, and that he had given a letter to the captain detailing the nature of his crime and sentence. It seems likely, as King implied, that Morgan had used what we might describe as his social capital to great effect, to win relative shipboard freedom and the opportunity to abscond. And so, on the evening of 21 August, a month after the ship's departure, a sentry let Morgan up from below decks to answer a call of nature. Morgan's influence clearly extended to the sentry, for even though Morgan did not come back he did not report him missing until the next day.[23]

The authorities placed a warrant for Morgan's arrest in one of the Calcutta newspapers, but nothing was heard of him for three months. He was then spotted in Coringa (in the Madras Presidency), coming off the ship *Hammond Shaw*. The master attendant of the port had seen Morgan's description in the press and recognized him. Morgan protested that he was the victim of mistaken identity, and maintained that he was not the wanted man, but the African-born Peter Halygar. When brought before the assistant magistrate of the district, he said that had left his 'native country' 11 years ago, when he was 15 years old, to go to sea. Since then he had worked the oceans, travelling to Brazil, America, Batavia, and Singapore. He had gone to Rangoon, he said, eight months before his arrest to join his wife and child. He added that he was a Roman Catholic.[24]

The ship's commander, William Gibson, was at a loss to confirm that his passenger was George Morgan, reporting only that he had seen him several times previously in Rangoon and knew he was African from his hair style: 'most Africans wear their hair plaited in the same manner, they take pride in it.' The man had done some coopering work for him on a previous occasion, he said, and had approached him to ask if he could work his passage to India. Gibson agreed, and took him on board.[25] According to John King, Morgan had served time in prison with a man named Peter Halygar and they were great friends. Halygar was also 'of African descent', which perhaps explained Morgan's choice of new identity. However, Halygar was so fair skinned that until he took his hat off to reveal his hair he looked European, while Morgan was 'very dark'.[26] The authorities assumed correctly that they had got their man, and arrested him.

Morgan promptly tried to escape from jail—not once, but twice. District Magistrate G.A. Smith reported that his language and conduct were so 'gross', 'indecent', and 'outrageous' that he had no doubt that he would try again.[27] He was keen to get rid of his troublesome prisoner, and to send him on to Calcutta as soon as his superiors granted permission. There, Morgan would stand trial on the charge of escaping from transportation, which was a capital offence.[28] His behaviour was so violent that Smith even recommended he be shipped on an armed vessel, though it was eventually agreed that he could go on any ship if he was properly secured.[29] Escape seemed hopeless, and Morgan turned to one of the few strategies of resistance still available to him: silence. In a particular irony for a man who as we will see was renowned for his singing, Morgan refused to say another word until his case went to trial.[30]

JUMP JIM CROW

Several of the surviving documents on George Morgan note that he had a fine voice, and that he was well known in Calcutta for his rendition of the song 'Jump Jim Crow'.[31] Jim Crow is now understood as a colloquial reference to America's segregation laws. However, this belies its origins as an old slave plantation song, sung in the coastal Carolinas and in the West Indies. In the 1830s Jump Jim Crow was popularized by the actor Thomas Dartmouth Rice (1808–60). Rice was a blackface performer who won fame on both sides of the Atlantic. Dressed as a slave runaway, with a blacked-up face and wearing worn out clothes and shoes, an imitation of enslavement was at the core of his act. As W.T. Lhamon Jr argues convincingly in a study of the cultural meanings of Jump Jim Crow, at this time blackface performance was different from the later racial parodying of minstrel shows. Rice would sing and dance, and then pretend to stop. The audience would cry out for him to continue, thus determining within an accepted script the shape of the performance as well as to some extent the lyrics.[32] Nevertheless, the chorus was always half the song and went something like this: 'Weel about and turn about and do jis so, Eb'ry time I weel about and jump Jim Crow.'[33]

Jumping Jim Crow was a slippery sort of fellow, and in Rice's theatrical performances he constantly evaded the police with what Lhamon describes as a 'melting instability'.[34] Jim Crow took every opportunity to run rings around white authority figures, in an act that mimicked and mocked the social identities of African slaves *and* their masters. The post-colonial theorist Homi Bhaba represents mimicry and mockery as a subaltern transformation of the familiar. He is worth quoting on this point: 'imitation subverts the identity of that which is being represented, and the relation of power, if not altogether reversed, certainly begins to vacillate.'³⁵ As Parama Roy puts it in her consideration of identities in colonial and post-colonial India: 'The ambivalence that undergirds the procedure of colonial mimicry produces simultaneous and incommensurable effects, destabilizing English and Indian identities as part of the same operation.'³⁶ This was a time, as Lhamon writes, when 'Jim Crow encouraged blacks *and* his disaffected white followers.'³⁷ In other words, Jim Crow songs and skits inverted the social order of things, drawing attention to the misfortune of 'whites' who longed to be 'gentlemen of colour':

Now my brodder niggars,
I do not think it right,
Dat you should laugh at dem
Who happen to be white.
Weel about and turn about and do jis so,
Eb'ry time I weel about and jump Jim Crow.

Kase it dar misfortune,
And dey'd spend ebery dollar,
If dey only could be
Gentlemen ob colour.

Weel about and turn about ...

It almost break my heart,
To see dem envy me,
An from my soul I wish dem,
Full as black as we.³⁸

It was this social inversion that assured the popularity of Jim Crow. Rice embodied a character that was characterized by interracial mobility. He 'organized and represented...a working class integration'³⁹ that cut across colour. And yet Jim Crow had a more radical edge also, for the lyrics of the songs conveyed dreams of liberation from slavery.

Should dey get to fighting,
Perhaps de blacks will rise,
For deir wish for freedom,
Is shining in deir eyes.

Weel about and turn about ...

An if de blacks should get free,
I guess dey'll fee some bigger,
An I shall concider it,
A bold stroke for de niggar.⁴⁰

This emancipation was based on the brotherhood of all, black and white, once again presenting a world of unity across colour lines. As Jim Crow sings:

I'm for freedom,
An for Union altogether,
Aldough I'm a black man,
De white is call'd my broder.[41]

In the days before minstrel shows took up the mantle to produce scurrilously racist performances, Rice's audiences were multiracial, and ordinary men and women from *all* communities used Jim Crow to poke fun at the pretensions of their social betters. Rice's routine was astonishingly successful. He performed Jim Crow across America, and in 1836 he took his show to London where it completely sold out. Jim Crow became the first great icon of international popular culture.[42]

According to *The Calcutta Courier*, not only did George Morgan know and perform regularly the song 'Jump Jim Crow', but he was singing it at the very moment of his arrest in Madras. The newspaper represented his capture into a blackface skit, with Morgan transformed into Jim Crow. That the readers of the *Courier* would have understood this as a literary device—likening his arrest with that of an enslaved trickster—shows just how far across the oceans knowledge of the act had spread. The newspaper reported:

He entered the Police with heavy fetters strongly riveted to his feet, and seemed withal to be in good humour, though when spoken to on the confinement which he might now expect for fourteen years, he appeared much affected: With a sigh, said he, 'I can't be sulky or devil a bit would they pin me. I have too much good natur[e]—good natur[e] has been my ruination.'[43]

Escaping from enslavement was one of the key themes of the Jim Crow performances, and the irony of Morgan's predicament would have been obvious to the *Courier*'s readers. Yet Jim Crow/George Morgan was not a man to let the authorities get the better of him. The newspaper report ended with the words: '[H]owever', added [Morgan], 'doubling these irons will help me to go quicker to the bottom, and then I shan't do no mischief no more.'[44]

It is possible that Morgan had seen Rice perform in London, for we know he had spent time in the metropolitan capital before he went to Calcutta. Even if he had not, by the late 1830s clearly Jim Crow had moved beyond the Atlantic or British metropolitan world, across the Indian Ocean to South Asia, Burma, and with George Morgan's eventual retransportation to Van Diemen's Land, to the Australian colonies. I would argue that the appeal of Jim Crow in the colonial context lay in the social uncertainties and instabilities that characterized early British expansion. We do not know the lyrics adopted by George Morgan, or other Jim Crow performers, of whom there were surely many. Yet the widespread performance of the act destabilizes any simplistic reading of subaltern identity by revealing its transformative appeal within a socially and economically divided and multiracial colonial context. Most especially, African-born Morgan was not alienated by the genre of blackface performance but became its cultural advocate. As will become clear, this renders even more complex his own 'racial' identity. Jim Crow/George Morgan danced a complex dance. He did not so much challenge the boundaries of empire as express just how ill-defined their social fringes could be.

The Retrial of George Morgan

It was not unusual for the Indian press to report on Supreme Court trials, especially when the defendants were colourful characters or the offence was somewhat unusual. After his escape from transportation to Burma, Morgan's case qualified on both counts, and his case duly appeared in *The Calcutta Courier*. As we have seen, in April 1838 the court sentenced African-born Morgan to transportation to Burma, and his white co-defendant George Lloyd to Van Diemen's Land. A year later in April 1839, Morgan stood before the bar once again, this time on the charge of escaping from the vessel in which he was bound for transportation. He pleaded 'not guilty'. The trial of a real runaway Jim Crow presented a curious colonial allure, and through it social boundaries were collapsed and remade, for Morgan was successful in persuading trial judge J.P. Grant to rethink his 'racial' identity.

According to the *Courier*, Morgan appeared before the judge and jury smartly and respectably dressed, and showing 'the greatest composure'. He wore a black band around his head, presumably to cover his braided hair. Morgan's 'clear voice' and 'good English' were noted, as they had been by the keeper of Calcutta jail, John King.[45] Morgan was allowed to question witnesses and he showed great skill in the courtroom. His main defence strategy was to trip up those who testified against him. Take the report of this exchange with George Gardner, for instance. Gardner was chief mate of the *Emily*, the ship that had taken Morgan from Coringa to Calcutta: 'Prisoner was delivered to his charge by Mr Smith, the collector of Coringa...He had never seen prisoner at Coringa. Questioned by Morgan. You say you brought me from Coringa, and you say you never saw me in Coringa ...' Even more striking was the appearance of John Balcolm, second mate of the *Emily*, who caused 'some mirth' in the courtroom by the 'unsophisticated way in which he volunteered his testimony'. In other words, unlike Morgan, he did not understand the conventions of the court. The *Courier* reported that he 'occasionally apostrophized the prisoner, when not quite certain of the correctness of his own memory.' Morgan did not need to expose Balcolm to ridicule, for as an ordinary plebeian man he was already ill at ease. 'Never knowed nothing of Morgan,' he apparently said, 'afore he see'd him aboard the sloop.' The ineloquence of this working man was a stark contrast to Morgan's fluency and poise.[46]

Much of the case hinged around how Morgan had been treated on the ship. Morgan questioned closely H.V. Weston, the second officer of the *Amherst*, asking him about shipboard rations. From his testimony we learn that as was usual practice the convicts' rations had been supplied by the East India Company, with their substance dependent on how many Hindus and Muslims there were on board. It was quite normal for Muslim convicts—who ate cooked food at sea—to receive a larger allowance than non-cooking Hindus. Morgan had been entered on the ship register as a Christian, but the Company had failed to issue him with separate rations. Morgan claimed that when he asked him for an increased allowance, Weston had told him that he had been entered on the roll as a Muslim and so could not be issued more than other convicts of that class. Rations were an explosive issue in colonial jails and penal settlements, and changes to them frequently met with fierce resistance on the part of prisoners and convicts.[47] Special rations were supposed to be issued to Europeans and Eurasians, and they were not shy about demanding their rightful allowance. In 1832, for instance, Eurasian convicts in the Tenasserim Provinces refused to take the same rations as Indians, and went on a hunger strike.[48] On the whole, the colonial authorities were reasonably sympathetic to them. During the period Morgan spent in the Calcutta jail he was not issued with rations but with a money allowance with which to buy his food directly from prison vendors. Europeans received 4 *annas* per day, 'native Christians' 3, and Indians 1.[49]

Yet there is no doubt that European and Eurasian prisoners thrown into jail in culturally unfamiliar surroundings suffered real hardships. One Joaquim Marks, a Portuguese-born sailor who was kept in prison for a year-and-a-half waiting to have his sentence of transportation— from Bombay to Van Diemen's Land—petitioned the government for enough money to buy 'European' provisions. He wrote that 'native food' made him sick, and that the jail warders cheated him when they shopped for him at the bazaars.[50] There is further evidence to suggest that Eurasian prisoners viewed Indian convicts with contempt.

Convict petitioners in the 1840s described Indians as the 'scum of society', with questionable morals.[51] This was part of a general social distancing between Europeans and Eurasians and Indians which gained momentum after questions of loyalty were brought into sharp relief through the 1857 Revolt.

A few years after Morgan's case, in 1843 the new commissioner of the Tenasserim Provinces, George Broadfoot, tried to render Eurasians' experiences of transportation akin to that of Indians. His equalization of their work, rations, and clothing resulted in a near riot, and a speedy reversal of policy. Whilst Broadfoot viewed Eurasians first as convicts, the authorities in Calcutta—as, it has to be said, did usually penal administrators on the ground—saw them first as a distinct social category.[52] Those Eurasians who petitioned against the measures were well aware of this, and framed their claims against them in familiar terms. One man, Thomas Leonard, wrote of his 'sudden relapse into the Society of Heathens of every degree in guilt of monsters in villainy and barbarity', and claimed that his character might never be retrieved if he were made to eat and work with them.[53] The new commissioner of the provinces, J.R. Colvin, later wrote of the inappropriateness of working or housing Eurasians with Indians: 'in whose society any cases of better feeling, which may exist in their minds, might be liable to be blunted or effaced.'[54] This was at least partly a question of education, for the colonial authorities relied on Eurasians as clerks. Their vernacular language skills also meant that they could be employed as overseers to Indian convicts.

In addition to his alleged mistreatment over rationing, Morgan had also been lodged below decks with the other convicts, which breached usual practice on transportation ships carrying Christians. It is possible that Morgan's treatment in this respect hinged on his falling outside the normal penal categories; indeed, it seems that only one other African was transported overseas from India during this period.[55] Whatever the case, Morgan used his retrial to protest against his shipboard treatment in the strongest terms, and in court continued to question second officer Weston thus:

The Prisoner. Do you know whether a man would choose to be treated as a Mussulman or a Christian?
Witness [Weston]. I don't say it was your choice.
Prisoner. It was not.[56]

When the judge asked Morgan if he had anything further to say in his defence he said that had he been transported to Australia with

George Lloyd after his original trial, he would never have tried to escape. 'Gentlemen of the Jury,' he said, 'I believe I am a Christian. I was born and brought up as such. I was born within the tropics, but received the education of an European...On board the ship I was treated as a native, though I am a Christian...If I had been treated as a Christian, I should not have attempted to escape.' He reminded the court that he had not used violence during his flight. He then asked the keeper of Calcutta jail to testify for him. John King confirmed that he had treated Morgan like a European while in prison because his 'habits and manners' were entirely European. Judge Grant summed up the case and after a short deliberation the jury found Morgan guilty, but recommended him to the mercy of the court.[57] In effect this was a plea against capital punishment, a penal option for convicts who had escaped from transportation.

The judge surmised that although he was African Morgan had shown himself to be of 'European habits'. This, he said, had not been proved at Morgan's first trial, hence the predicament in which he found himself on board the ship to Burma. Nevertheless, because escaping from transportation was a capital offence, although he would not sentence him to death he had no choice but to increase his sentence from seven to 14 years. He then ordered that Morgan be transported to the Australian penal settlement in Van Diemen's Land, the usual destination for white Europeans convicted in India at this time.[58] Morgan was embarked on the *Guillardon* a few weeks later,[59] by chance the same ship that had transported his partner in crime, George Lloyd, a year before.[60] As the judge's decision shows, what constituted 'Europeaness' was clearly a question of religion, education, association, 'habits', and 'manners', and not simply birthplace or colour. Administrators in the penal settlements had the same approach to the treatment of such prisoners. Commissioner of the Tenasserim Provinces, J.R. Colvin, later referred to convicts like Morgan as 'Europeans in association and training'.[61]

AFTERWORD: VANISHING IN VAN DIEMEN'S LAND

George Morgan arrived in Van Diemen's Land on 26 September 1839. He underwent the usual period of probation and was assigned to various work stations. Between 20 April 1840, when he was first sent out to labour, and 6 May 1841, he was disciplined no less than four times—for misconduct, refusing to work, absenting himself without leave, and neglecting his duty. His punishments were a mix of increased hard labour and solitary confinement on bread and water. Convict management in penal colonies across the Indian Ocean relied on a mixture of negative and positive incentives. Morgan was almost certainly aware of this, and in August 1841 perhaps somewhat cleverly intervened when a fellow convict assaulted an overseer. The authorities remitted half his sentence straight away. Sensibly, Morgan managed to stay out of trouble and was not disciplined again. He received his ticket-of-leave in October 1845, and was recommended for a conditional pardon in September 1846. This was approved in November 1847, just eight years after his arrival.[62] This was perhaps Morgan's ultimate triumph, and his release from convictism—albeit conditional on continued good conduct—might be read as the moment when 'gentleman of colour' Jim Crow mocked those who 'happened to be white' in order to take imaginative, if not actual, flight from enslavement and domination.

George Lloyd—Morgan's original codefendant—had a somewhat different fate which also ended in escape. By 1842 he had been put to work on the boats, a relatively easy option for a convict with maritime skills. Nevertheless, his conduct register catalogues repeated drunkenness, misconduct, and illegal absence. In September 1845 he was found guilty of stealing seven chests of tea, and was sent to Port Arthur for seven years, the most dreaded penal station (for secondary punishment) on Van Diemen's Land. Not surprisingly, the authorities refused his subsequent applications for a ticket-of-leave. In January 1850, however, he absconded and was never seen again.[63]

As I mentioned at the beginning of this essay, the British and colonial authorities shipped hundreds of African, Indian, Chinese, and Mauritian convicts to the Australian penal colonies during the first half of the nineteenth century. Recent scholarly work has presented a challenge to established methodologies in thinking about how some such convicts represented their penal fate as well as the unacknowledged social impact black convicts had on these early colonies. Yet with few exceptions most accounts have focused on the social context in which non-Anglo-Celtic convicts were transported, for beyond ship indents or conduct registers they more or less vanish from sight as soon as they arrive in Australia. As Ian Duffield puts it, there are silences even within the boundaries of meticulous colonial record keeping. Searching for black convicts can be like looking for 'the proverbial needle in a haystack'.[64] And so it proves with our jumping Jim Crow, about whom we know almost nothing once he escaped from the grip of convict record keeping.

I think Duffield's methodological honesty is important because it forces us to acknowledge that there will always be historiographical gaps at the fringes of empire. Duffield hints at this when he writes movingly of our need to question who we are and how we relate to those we consider our social (and historical) 'others'—for in fact 'they' are often 'us'.[65] Nevertheless, I am interested in the process of identity formation among convicts like George Morgan—and what it might add to our understanding of social negotiations in the early colonial Indian Ocean more generally. Teasing such material from colonial archives that in their local focus suggest immobility not mobility, piecing that material together, and using it imaginatively is no easy task. Working with literary ideas about social performance might prove a fruitful way forward.

As Richard Waterhouse shows in his study of the Australian popular stage, blackface theatre spread beyond the United States and Britain to Australia and New Zealand during the early colonial period.[66] Theatres became forums in which the manners of the upper classes could be ridiculed, and their authority challenged. Audiences were a microcosm of society, and disorder and rioting were widespread. In the Antipodes, blackface performance held enormous appeal, and actors adapted it to meet the needs of their audience. The first staged performance of Jim Crow took place in Sydney's Theatre Royal in 1838 and by the 1840s the act was performed every night.[67] We do not know what lyrics were used, though there is a reference to an 1844 performance containing asides to 'local, political and other interesting subjects'.[68] It surely included allusion to relations of power in a convict society.

I like to think of George Morgan taking his Jim Crow act to Van Diemen's Land, of embodying this cultural symbol of interracial mobility in a new society where all sorts of social identities were up for grabs. As we have seen, the politics of social difference in the early nineteenth century Indian Ocean were constituted in ways that did not necessarily embrace the politics of what we might term racial difference. Embodied expressions of class and culture also constituted 'otherness'. Nowhere was this more apparent than in early colonial Van Diemen's Land, a place where marginalized communities of convicts both allied themselves with and displaced indigenous peoples, in both cases to devastating effect. It is perhaps no surprise that Jim Crow images attracted a further meaning in the colony, becoming a device through which indigenous peoples could be mocked. Jim Crow thus became what Waterhouse describes as a prism through which Europeans viewed 'the last Tasmanians'.[69] George Morgan might have danced on the margins of Indian Ocean penal settlements, but not solely as an African, a gentleman, or as a convict. Race and status at the fringes of empire were fluid and culturally contingent identities. Moreover, they could be performed in imaginative ways.

ACKNOWLEDGEMENT

This essay is part of a broader project on subaltern mobility in the Indian Ocean funded through the National Maritime Museum Sackler-Caird Fellowship. I thank the Museum for its generous support of my research, and the staff in the India Office Records (IOR), Tamil Nadu State Archives (TNSA), and Archives Office of Tasmania (AOT) for their help and assistance.

NOTES AND REFERENCES

1. *The Calcutta Courier*, 17–20 April 1838. The original Supreme Court records of the case no longer survive.
2. AOT Con35/1 1179 George Loyd [Lloyd] *per Guillardon*, arr. 13 December 1838.
3. *The Calcutta Courier*, 25 April 1839.
4. AOT Con35/1 1802 George Morgan *per Guillardon*, arr. 26 September 1839; IOR P/141/28 (9 October 1838): R. Jump, Commander *Amherst*, to E.A. Blundell, Commissioner Tenasserim Provinces, 1 September 1838; P/141/32 (8 January 1839): G. Smith, Magistrate Rajahmundry, to D. McFarlan, Chief Magistrate Calcutta, Smith to H. Chamier, Chief Sec. to Govt of Madras, 24 November 1838; IOR P/141/36 (7 May 1839): Deposition of Henry Weston, 4 April 1839; *The Calcutta Courier*, 5 April 1839.
5. AOT Con35/1 1802 George Morgan *per Guillardon*, arr. 26 September 1839.
6. IOR P/141/32 (8 January 1839) Memo. John King, Keeper of Calcutta Jail, n.d. (November 1838); P/141/37 (11 June 1839): Warrant of five European convicts, 4 June 1839.
7. Clare Anderson, 2007, 'Sepoys, Servants and Settlers: Convict Transportation in the Indian Ocean, 1787–1945', in Ian Brown and Frank Dikotter (eds), *Cultures of Confinement: A History of the Prison in Africa, Asia and Latin America*, London: Hurst, pp. 185–220.
8. IOR F/4/534: Extract judicial letter Bengal, enc. Act 53 George 3rd Cap. 155—Sec. 121, 7 October 1815.
9. George Windsor Earl, 1837, *The Eastern Seas, or Voyages and Adventures in the Indian Archipelago, in 1832-33-34,Ccomprising a tour of the Island of Java—Visits to Borneo, the Malay Peninsula, Siam, &c.; Also an account of the present State of Singapore, with observations on the commercial resources of the archipelago*, London: W.H. Allen and Co., pp. 443–7 (quote 446).
10. IOR P/143/25 (8 November 1848): W.J. Butterworth, Governor Straits Settlements, to J.W. Dalrymple, Off. Under Sec. to Govt of Bengal, 13 September 1848.
11. IOR P/145/10 (10 May 1855): R.S. Palmer, Sheriff of Calcutta, to A.W. Russell,

Under Sec. to Govt of Bengal, 5 April 1855; IOR P/145/15 (9 August 1855): E.A. Blundell, Governor Straits Settlements, to C. Beadon, Sec. to Govt of India, 1 June 1855, enc. The Magistrates of Singapore to Blundell, 1 June 1855. Turnbull also discusses this case: 'Convicts in the Straits Settlements', p. 91.

12. IOR P/145/15 (9 August 1855): Beadon to Blundell, 27 July 1855.

13. Lesley C. Duly, 1979, '"Hottentots to Hobart and Sydney": The Cape Supreme Court's Use of Transportation, 1828–38', *Australian Journal of Politics and History*, vol. 25, pp. 39–50; James Hugh Donohoe, 1991, *The Forgotten Australians: The Non Anglo or Celtic Convicts and Exiles*, Sydney: published by the author; Ian Duffield, 1986, 'From Slave Colonies to Penal Colonies: The West Indians Transported to Australia', *Slavery and Abolition*, 7 (1), pp. 25–45; 1987, 'The Life and Death of "Black" John Goff: Aspects of the Black Convict Contribution to Resistance Patterns During the Transportation Era in Eastern Australia', *Australian Journal of Politics and History*, 33 (1), pp. 30–44; 2001, '"Stated This Offence": High-Density Convict Micro-Narratives', in Lucy Frost and Hamish Maxwell-Stewart (eds), *Chain Letters: Narrating Convict Lives*, Melbourne: Melbourne University Press, pp. 119–35; 2002, 'A Storm in a Teapot? Five Stories About the Trials of Priscilla's Life and their Household Remedy, Arsenic Trioxide', in *To The Islands: Australia and the Caribbean*, special edition of *Australian Cultural History*, vol. 21, pp. 19–31; V.C. Malherbe, 1985, 'Khoikhoi and the Question of Convict Transportation from the Cape Colony, 1820–1842', *South African Historical Journal*, vol. 17, pp. 19–39; Cassandra Pybus, 2006, *Black Founders: The Unknown History of Australia's First Black Settlers*, Sydney: University of New South Wales Press.

14. See, for example, correspondence enclosed in AOT CSO 5/56/1222.

15. Durba Ghosh, 2006, *Sex and the Family in Colonial India: The Making of Empire*, Cambridge: Cambridge University Press; C.J. Hawes, 1996, *Poor Relations: The Making of a Eurasian Community in British India 1773–1833*, London: Routledge Curzon; P.J. Marshall, 1997, 'British Society in India under the East India Company', *Modern Asian Studies*, 31 (1), pp. 89–108. On marriage and children in the army, see Douglas M. Peers, 1998, 'Privates off Parade: Regimenting Sexuality in the Nineteenth-century Indian Empire', *International History Review*, 20 (4), pp. 844–53.

16. IOR P/145/22 (8 November 1855): Extract letter from Butterworth, 12 July 1855. On both women, see Clare Anderson, 2007, 'Gender, Subalternity and Silence: Recovering Convict Women's Experiences from Histories of Transportation, c. 1780–1857', in Anindita Ghosh (ed.), *Behind the Veil: Resistance, Women, and the Everyday in Colonial South Asia*, New Delhi: Permanent Black, pp. 146–9.

17. P.J. Marshall, 2000, 'The White Town of Calcutta Under the Rule of the East India Company', *Modern Asian Studies*, 34 (2), p. 309. On poor Europeans, see also, David Arnold, 1979, 'European Orphans and Vagrants in India in the Nineteenth Century', *Journal of Imperial and Commonwealth History*, 7 (2), pp. 104–27; Sarmistha De, 1995–6, 'Marginal Europeans and the White Underworld in Colonial Bombay', *Jadavpur University Journal of History*, vol. 16, pp. 32–56; S. Chandra Ghosh, 1970, *The Social Condition of the British*

Community in Bengal, 1757–1800, Leiden: Brill; Harald Tiné-Fischer, 2003, '"White Women Degrading Themselves to the Lowest Depths"—European Networks of Prostitution and Colonial Anxieties in British India ca. 1870–1914', *Indian Economic and Social History Review*, vol. 2, pp. 163–90; 2005, 'Britain's Other Civilising Mission: Class-prejudice, European "Loaferism" and the Workhouse System in Colonial India', *Indian Economic and Social History Review*, 42 (3), pp. 295–338; 2008, *Low and Licentious Europeans: Race, Class and 'White Subalternity' in Colonial India*, New Delhi: Orient Longman; Aravind Ganachari, 2002, '"White Man's Embarrassment"—European Vagrancy in Nineteenth-Century Bombay', *Economic and Political Weekly*, 37 (2), pp. 2477–85; Peter Stanley, 1998, *White Mutiny: British Military Culture in India, 1825–1875*, London: Christopher Hurst; R.K. Renford, 1987, *The Non-Official British in India to 1920*, New Delhi: Oxford University Press.

18. IOR P/141/25 (25 November 1838): McFarlan to F.J. Halliday, Sec. to Govt of Bengal, 24 October 1838; *The Calcutta Courier*, 20 April 1838.

19. AOT Con35/1 1179 George Loyd *per Guillardon*, arr. 13 December 1838; Con16/1 1179 George Loyde.

20. IOR P/141/32 (8 January 1839): Smith to Chamier, 24 November 1838; Memo. of King, n.d.; *The Calcutta Courier*, 5 April 1839; IOR P/141/37 (11 June 1839): Warrant of five European convicts, 4 June 1839.

21. Clare Anderson, 2008, 'Discourses of Exclusion and the "Convict Stain" in the Indian Ocean (c. 1800–1850)', in Ashwini Tambe and Harald Fischer-Tiné (eds), *The Limits of British Control in South Asia: Spaces of Disorder in the Indian Ocean Region*, London: Routledge, pp. 105–20.

22. IOR P/141/26 (24 July 1838): J.H. Patton, Superintendent Alipur Jail, to Halliday, 21 July 1838.

23. IOL P/141/28 (9 October 1838): Jump to Blundell, 1 September 1838; IOL P/141/25 (6 November 1838): McFarlan to Halliday, 24 October 1838, King to B. Finie, Second Clerk to McFarlan, 23 October 1838.

24. IOR P/141/32 (8 January 1839): Statement given before the Assistant Magistrate by Peter Halygar an African by birth, about 26 years of age, a Mariner by profession, of the Roman Catholic Religion, 3 November 1838.

25. Ibid.: Statement given before the Assistant Magistrate by William Gibson, a native of Scotland, aged 26 years, a Master Mariner a Presbyterian, 4 November 1838. According to Jump, Morgan's hair was plaited in front and tied across the forehead: IOR P/141/28 (9 October 1838): Jump to Blundell, 1 September 1838.

26. IOR P/141/32 (8 January 1839): Memo by King, n.d.

27. TNSA Judicial Proceedings (JP) vol. 356B: G.A. Smith, District Magistrate Rajahmundry, to Chamier, 8 December 1838.

28. IOL P/141/32 (8 January 1839): Chamier to Halliday, 11 December 1838.

29. TNSA JP vol. 359A: Smith to Chamier, 27 December 1838, Chamier to Smith, 15 January 1839.

30. IOL P/141/36 (7 May 1839): The information of George Morgan, 2 April 1839.

31. IOR P/141/32 (8 January 1839): Smith to McFarlan, 5 November 1838; McFarlan to Smith, 15 November 1838; Memo by King, n.d.

32. W.T. Lhamon, Jr, 2003, *Jump Jim Crow: Lost Plays, Lyrics, and Street Prose of*

the First Atlantic Popular Culture, Cambridge, Mass: Harvard University Press, p. 93.

33. Ibid., pp. 95–102.
34. Ibid., p. 3.
35. Homi Bhabha, 1984, 'Of Mimicry and Man: The Ambivalence of Colonial Discourse', October, vol. 28, pp. 125–33, reprinted in Frederick Cooper and Ann Laura Stoler (eds), 1997, *Tensions of Empire: Colonial Cultures in a Bourgeois World*, Berkeley: University of California Press, pp. 152–60.
36. Parama Roy, 1998, *Indian Traffic: Identities in Question in Colonial and Postcolonial India*, Berkeley: University of California Press, p. 1.
37. Lhamon, *Jump Jim Crow*, p. x (my emphasis).
38. Ibid., pp. 98–9.
39. Ibid.
40. Ibid.
41. Ibid.
42. Ibid., p. viii.
43. *The Calcutta Courier*, 5 April 1839.
44. Ibid.
45. Ibid.
46. Ibid., 25 April 1839.
47. Clare Anderson, 2007, *The Indian Uprising of 1857–8: Prisons, Prisoners and Rebellion*, London: Anthem, pp. 27–54; David Arnold, 1994, 'The Colonial Prison: Power, Knowledge, and Penology in 19th-Century India', in David Arnold and David Hardiman (eds), *Subaltern Studies VIII; Essays in Honour of Ranajit Guha*, New Delhi: Oxford University Press, pp. 148–87.
48. IOR P/140/10 (24 July 1832): A.D. Maingy, Commissioner Tenasserim Provinces, to J. Thomason, Dep. Sec. to Govt of Bengal, 1 May 1832.
49. IOR P/140/10 (24 July 1832): Thomason to Maingy, 24 July 1832.
50. IOR P/403.26 (24 January 1844): Petition of Joaquim Marks, 1 December 1843. See also AOT Con 35/1 357 Joachim Marks *per Waterlily* and *Sarah*, arr. 2 September 1844.
51. IOR P/142/5 (28 August 1843): J.H. Quigley and other East Indian convicts to G.A. Bushby, Sec. to Govt of India, 15 July 1843; Petition of Thomas Leonard, 8 July 1843; IOR P/142/33 (12 June 1845): Petition of John Henry Quigley, convict Moulmein, 28 April 1845.
52. IOR P/142/5 (8 August 1843): Turnbull to G. Broadfoot, Commissioner Tenasserim Provinces, 8 August 1843.
53. IOR P/142/5 (28 August 1843): Petition of Thomas Leonard, 8 July 1843.
54. IOR P/143/8 (27 October 1847): J.R. Colvin, Commissioner Tenasserim Provinces, to Halliday, 22 September 1847.
55. IOR P/140.4 (6 March 1832): J. Thomason, Dep. Sec. to Govt of Bengal, to A.D. Maingy, Commissioner Tenasserim Provinces, 23 February 1832.
56. *The Calcutta Courier*, 25 April 1839.
57. Ibid.
58. Ibid., 30 April 1839.
59. IOR P/141/37 (11 June 1839): Warrant of five European convicts, 4 June 1839.

60. AOT Con35/1 1179 George Loyd *per Guillardon*, arr. 13 December 1838.
61. IOR P/143/8 (27 October 1847): Colvin to Halliday, 22 September 1847.
62. AOT Con35/1 1804 George Morgan *per Guillardon*, arr. 26 September 1839.
63. AOT Con35/1 1179 George Loyd *per Guillardon*, arr. 13 December 1838.
64. Duffield, 'A Storm in a Teapot?', p. 30.
65. Ibid., p. 31.
66. Richard Waterhouse, 1990, *From Minstrel Show to Vaudeville: The Australian Popular Stage 1788–1914*, Kensington: New South Wales University Press, p. 15.
67. Ibid., pp. x–xii, 23, 27–8.
68. Ibid., p. 30.
69. Ibid., p. 100.

Psychiatry on the Edge?

Vagrants, Families, and Colonial Asylums in India, 1857–1900

James H. Mills

ROUTES INTO THE ASYLUM

There were various routes by which an Indian could be admitted to a lunatic asylum in the period 1857–1900. The *Rules for the Management and Control of the Lunatic Asylum at Lucknow*, included in the published responses to Sir James Clark's enquiry into the treatment of lunatics in India give a fair summary of these routes.[1]

The authorities empowered to order the admission of lunatics are:

First—Officers exercising the powers of a Magistrate, in respect of wandering or dangerous lunatics, or lunatics who are neglected or maltreated (Sections 4+5 of Act XXXVI of 1858).

Second—Judges of the principal Civil Courts of Districts, in respect of all other lunatics except the two classes hereafter mentioned (Section 8 of Act XXXVI of 1858).

Third—The Local Government as regards criminal lunatics (Sections 390, 394, 396 of the Criminal Procedure Code).

Fourth—Military Officers commanding Divisions, in respect of native non-commissioned officers and soldiers afflicted with insanity (Section 41, page 291 Bengal Military Regulations).

Fifth—The Inspector of Jails, as regards the removal of any lunatic from one public asylum to any other within the circle of his inspection (Section 11, Act XXXVI of 1858).

Elsewhere in the *Rules* there are further details provided about criminal lunatics.

Persons confined under the provisions of Chapter XXVII of the Criminal Procedure Code, whether unsentenced but found guilty of the act charged (Section 394) or already sentenced (Section 396) or found unsound of mind on trial by the Court of Sessions (Section 389) or deemed of unsound mind by the Magistrate after recording the examination of the Civil Surgeon of the district or some other Medical Officer (Section 388) shall be admitted into the asylum under the order of the Local Government to which the case shall be reported through the usual channel by the Magistrate or Court of Sessions, or other officer, as the case may be (Sections 390 and 394).[2]

The distinction between the criminal lunatic and the lunatic admitted as neglected, dangerous or wandering is one that was central in asylum administration. This essay will focus on the latter group rather than the former.[3] Criminal admissions were from contexts, such as the prison or the court room, where individuals were already under the eye of the authorities and as such odd behaviour was likely to be noticed. Non-criminals, that is those picked up while at liberty, needed to have come to the attention of officers of the colonial state and in turn needed to have been judged of sufficient concern by those officers to have warranted detention in a hospital. It is argued therefore that by tracing the route into the asylum for those non-criminal admissions, the historian can get a glimpse of the concerns and anxieties of the colonial state in this period.

Act XXXVI of 1858 governed the admission of non-criminal lunatics into the asylums of British India.[4] It stated in Clause IV that:

it shall be the duty of every Darogah or District Police Officer to apprehend and send to the Magistrate all persons found wandering at large within his district who are deemed to be Lunatics and all persons believed to be dangerous by reasons of Lunacy. Whenever any such person as aforesaid is brought before a Magistrate, the Magistrate, with the assistance of a Medical Officer, shall examine such person, and if the Medical Officer shall sign a certificate in the Form A in the schedule to this Act, and the Magistrate shall be satisfied on personal examination or other proof that such person is a Lunatic and a proper person to be detained under care and treatment, he shall make an order for such Lunatic to be received into the Asylum established for that Division...[5]

In Clause V, it established that:

if it shall appear to the Magistrate, on the report of a Police Officer or the information of any other person, that any person within the limits of his jurisdiction deemed to be a Lunatic is not under proper care and control, or is cruelly treated or neglected by any relative or other person having the charge of him, the Magistrate may send for the supposed Lunatic and summon such relative or other person as has or ought to have the charge of him...If there be no person legally bound to maintain the supposed Lunatic, or if the Magistrate thinks fit so to do, he may proceed as prescribed in the last preceding Section...[6]

Wanderers, the dangerous, and the neglected were the targets of this legislation although there is evidence that the asylums and the authorities subsequently refined this. It is doubtful if the police regularly concerned themselves with the treatment of the insane in Indian homes, as Dr Simpson of the Dacca asylum wrote in 1862: 'With Native Police this section becomes null and void'.[7] Indeed, some 10 years after the Act the opinion of the superintendent of Moydapore in Bengal was being reproduced in official correspondence:

It is I think, allowed by all who have any intimate knowledge of the village population of this country that the number of lunatics in our asylums represents a very small proportion of that unfortunate class to be found in every district; and that the vastly larger proportion is kept at home and supposed to be taken care of by their relatives; but this care consists of a degree of severity towards them, especially if they have the least tendency to be obstreperous.[8]

The filtering into asylums of those insanes neglected in their homes envisaged by the 1858 Act seems largely to have been forgotten or sidelined in the admission of non-criminal lunatics. By far the largest proportion of this group was made up by what can be termed public order offenders: the dangerous wanderers.

THE VAGRANT

Take for example the first admissions in the second volume of case notes. Of the seven patients admitted at the beginning of 1863 (8 January–12 February), five had been admitted because they had been found in the act of 'wandering'. So, for example:

Gosalee. Maniah. 28. Hindoo. Beggar. 8th Jan'63.

Sent in by City Mag. of Lucknow found knocking about the city calls himself 'Moonshie Ram Dyal'. Is very wild and displays much excitement and general incoherence in making replies to questions.

June 1863. Died of chronic diarrhoea.[9]

A month later there is:

Ram Deen. Mania. 35. Hindoo. Kapoor. 12th Feby/63.

Sent in by Cantonment Magistrate—was found wandering about Suddur Bazar at night. He talks + mutters very great nonsense, is apparently harmless.

1864. This man was never in the enjoyment of good health. Always looked sickly + did not improve in his mental condition about 6 weeks ago he began to suffer from Diarrhoea—it gradually reduced him + became intractable. Died on 14th July 1864.[10]

Such admissions are typical throughout the period for which case notes are available. A year before in 1862 there is the case of Allee Jaim.

Allee Jaim. Mania. Mussl. Beggar. 40. 19 Feby 1862.

Feb 1812. This man was sent in by City Magistrate of Lucknow—he had been taken up by Police as a beggar—whether from want or dissipation he appears to be weak in intellect and is so reduced in flesh + natural vigour that it is evident he has not long to live. Suffered from diarrhoea ever since admission—gradually got weaker + died 25th March 1862.[11]

Indeed, entries still read like this in the following decade:

Mosst.Khunnia. Chronic Mania. 23. Hindoo. Labour. 29th April 1870.

Certified by the magistrate 'not violent'.

1870 April 29. Sent in from Roy Bareilly—has been wandering about that district for years picking up her living how she could, she appears a harmless, quiet individual.[12]

The asylum as a receptacle for the vagrant was part of a wider set of social policies in British India aimed at controlling and policing the Indian population. These policies sprang from two sets of anxieties, those of modern government systems in general and those born of the colonial experience of governing.

European forms of government had identified vagrants and vagrant groups as a threat from the fifteenth century onwards and had occupied themselves with disciplining them. Jütte points out that:

vagrancy was a socially defined offence which reflects the dual problem of geographical and social mobility in early modern Europe. Offenders were arrested and punished not because of their actions, but because of their marginal position in society. The implication was that vagrants were no ordinary criminals; they were regarded as a major threat to society, and therefore pursued by all authorities and stigmatized as deviants.[13]

In England the vagrant had a central place in the demonology of popular culture[14] and became a focus of early governmental social legislation. As early as 1383 there was a law enabling local justices and sheriffs to detain and deal with vagabonds in their areas, and the series of Poor Laws established in the reign of Elizabeth I set about going beyond the notion of simply punishing the vagrant and established a principle of settlement and compulsory employment.[15]

By the nineteenth century, the vagrant in Britain was viewed as an incontrovertible 'social danger' for whom special severity was reserved by the penal system.[16] Nikolas Rose suggests that this was because, to the authorities of the period,

pauperism was a rejection of regular employment which meant also an existence outside the benign self-regulating mechanisms of the economy…a refusal of all those relations which were so essential to a healthy, wealthy and well-ordered polity.[17]

If the vagrant-as-customary-concern-of-western-forms-of-government idea partially explains why the British should focus on the Indian itinerant when they exported those forms of government to Asia, it does do only that. As suggested earlier there were anxieties peculiar to the Europeans in India which need to be taken into consideration when explaining the direct action taken against vagrants.

Veena Oldenburg focuses on the British perceptions of Indian cities in *The Making of Colonial Lucknow* and shows how they were behind the spatial reorganization of the urban centre in the 1860s and 1870s. She quotes Europeans during the 1850s describing 'vast multitudes of people parading backwards and forwards, on horseback, in palkies and on foot',[18] and deciding that in its 'narrow but picturesque street bazaars…the population was literally "teeming" so that it was impossible to ride or even drive in the streets save at a walk.'[19] It is important to note the emphasis in these impressions, as what the Europeans conjure up is an image of unfathomable mobility and their perceptions of restlessness and insect-like 'teeming'. Such a volume of people, constantly moving around through narrow and unplanned alleyways and streets, was experienced as a threat by the numerically tiny European population. This fear was reflected, says Oldenburg, in the overestimation of the population by the British. From the 1850s it was held in the colonial imagination that the city must be at least a million strong, a figure which was still present in newspaper reports in 1867 despite an official estimate of the population at about 300,000.[20] These perceptions of the Indian population as a teeming, threatening swarm were only heightened by the experiences of the 'Mutiny' of 1857–8, when 'hordes of unemployed and desperate men roamed the city for food or treasure, and bands of soldiers plundered and terrorised those inhabitants who had not fled into the countryside for safety.'[21]

The city, and indeed much of northern India, had proven beyond the command of the British because they had been unable to monitor and check the movements of the Indian population. Once power was regained then a number of measures were taken to remedy this lack of control. The most dramatic was probably the large-scale reconstruction projects. The British undertook to alter the physical environments of the cities so as to render the movements of the Indian population subject to their scrutiny. Oldenburg shows how before the reconstruction,

> streets served principally as areas where people milled, mingled, and socialised, where itinerant hawkers lined the curbs, where goods and services were bought and sold...The street was a public space with social and recreational functions. In Lucknow the custom was often to go to the street not to get anywhere; the street itself was a destination and an event.[22]

This situation produced crowds and constant movement and meeting, a situation which put the streets and the population beyond the control of the colonials. So much of the old system of winding alleys, dead-end lanes, and cramped bazaars was demolished and replaced by broad, straight boulevards, flanked by uniform rows of shops and punctuated with police posts and barracks. This was an attempt to 'reduce the seeming chaos',[23] which the British felt around them, it was all part of a strategy to render the movements of the Indian population the subject of colonial surveillance and control. This was a pattern that dominated many of the cities under British dominion after 1858: 'the dynamics that transformed Lucknow were also at work in other pre-colonial cities...the era of reconstruction in Lucknow therefore serves as a paradigm for the understanding of urbanisation in the mid-nineteenth century colonial setting'.[24]

Another approach to the colonial anxiety about mobile Indian populations was to attempt to fix groups and communities identified as particularly prone to movement. The strategy is most obvious in the Criminal Tribes Act of 1871 which was originally applied just in the Northwestern Provinces, the Punjab, and Oudh.[25] Provisions included having suspect tribes register themselves in fixed places and necessitated their possessing a license before moving. The emphasis was on surveillance and restriction of movement to render these groups visible and predictable. Such measures, however, could not deal with individual vagrants though, part of the 'riff-raff'[26] perceived to move through Indian society and who were considered 'dangerous as well as criminal'.[27] One response to this problem was Section 295 of the Criminal Procedure Code:

> Whenever it shall appear to the Magistrate of the District or to an officer exercising the powers of a Magistrate that any person is lurking within his jurisdiction not having any ostensible means of subsistence, or who cannot give a satisfactory account of himself, it shall be competent to such Magistrate or other officers as aforesaid to require security for the good behaviour of such person for a period not exceeding six months.[28]

Failure to provide security would result in imprisonment, although from the criminal statistics available it is difficult to work out exactly how often imprisonment for vagrancy occurred under this section.[29] Examples like that of the Barwars in Oudh do show, however, that imprisonment was used as a solution to the mobility of the Indian population. The Chief Commissioner noted that he had

received a petition from some Barwars complaining of the persecution they are subjected to, and asserting that two hundred of their caste-men, being a very large proportion of the males of the tribe, are undergoing imprisonment without having been convicted of any special offence under the Penal Code.[30]

He explained that this group, 'by tradition worship a deity of theft' and 'that they are of roving habits',[31] although he did admit that the system of illegal detention seemed like 'a mode of indiscriminate terrorism'[32] on the part of the district authorities. These people were not members of a British-classified wandering tribe, rather they had become linked in the colonial imagination with a deity of theft and so even if they were 'industrious and have business at fairs and such places',[33] they were regarded with suspicion and so members were picked up and incarcerated while travelling with very little legal justification.

It is in this context then that the non-criminal lunatic admission should be understood. Admission into a lunatic asylum was one of the strategies devised by the colonial authorities for containing what they perceived as the wanton and dangerous mobility of elements of Indian society. The asylum and the prison in conjunction with laws like Section 295 of the Criminal Procedure Code and Act XXXVI of 1858 and indeed with non-legal detention were all in the range of institutional solutions to individual vagrancy. Apart from the asylum or the prison, vagrants could end up in the idiot ward, the hospitals, and dispensaries or local poor houses.[34]

Indeed, such was the concern to have wanderers tucked away safely that it is often difficult to distinguish between the different institutions. In other words a vagrant would not necessarily need to be an idiot to end up in an idiot ward, a criminal to end up in a prison or a lunatic to end up in an asylum. It was enough to be an itinerant to qualify for eligibility for admission into whatever local institution had spaces available. There are examples like that of Maharanee where, despite a number of crimes having been committed, the vagrant is just bundled into the asylum out of harm's way rather than dragged through the legal system and sentenced to prison.

Maharanee (f). Mania. Mussl. Beggar. 35. 25 Novr.1861.

1861 Novr. This woman was sent into the Asylum by the Dy. Commr. of Nawabgunge, Barabunkee—no history of her case is obtainable, her antecedents are quite unknown. She was picked up on the road, after having entered a house, abused the inmates + smashed sundry articles of pottery—her name even was unknown: till after her admission + whether she gave a correct one is impossible to say. She is very weak, suffers from diarrhoea + talks with great volubility. She never gave indications of much intelligence, gradually became weaker, lost her appetite—diarrhoea became intractable + on March 30th 1862 she died.[35]

Similarly there are examples of vagrants who are detained by the police and who then become entangled in the system with no one accepting responsibility for them or knowing what to do with them as they are passed on by various authorities.

Angnoo. Dementia. Hindoo. Barber. 25. 14 October 1861

1861. Sent in by police. His papers were irregular and returned to City Magistrate for correction, but they were never received.

He had been picked up in the district + forwarded from thannah to thannah until brought to the asylum. He was in very low state of health, scarcely ate any food + could with difficulty be managed. He had diarrhoea or fever which improved by good food. During the cold weather however, it returned + became quite intractable. Died 26th March 1862.[36]

There are even instances which show detainees being juggled between institutions unwilling to accept individuals forced upon them by the policy of incarcerating wanderers.

Punchum. Mania. Hindoo. Faqueer. 60. 27th Novr.

1861 Nov. This man was admitted from City Hospital. He was brought there by the Police and no history of his case was procurable. Was in a very weakly state. Was quite unable to take food + died 2nd Dec.1860.[37]

These are full reproductions of the individual records. What they show is that little consideration is given to whether the people admitted are insane or not, there is no evidence of the process of diagnosis, and no record of symptoms supposed to demonstrate insanity. Indeed what they do show is less the admission of lunatics and more the incarceration of people physiologically weakened by the harsh experiences of living rough. These examples provide a glimpse of a system which primarily concerned itself with arresting population movements considered unjustified or undesirable in the context of the overriding goal of preserving order, and which then dealt with the problem of what to do with the individuals detained by shuffling them between the available institutions. This process was justified by reference to the legal excuses provided in legislation like the Code of Criminal Procedure and Act XXXVI of 1858. With the lunatic asylums, this would suggest that vagrancy was very often sufficient to qualify an individual to be classified as insane. Section 295 of the Criminal Procedure Code stated that its object was the individual who had no obvious means of subsistence and he/she 'who cannot give a satisfactory account of himself'. Consider examples such as that of Kirmuhia:

Kirmuhia. Dementia. Koree. Labour. 30. 1st November 1860

Novr. Sent by Mr Bicken AC, had been for several days hanging about the Treasury without being able to give any account of himself. He appeared to derive immense pleasure at the sight of glittering rupees + appeared annoyed at the crowd of people who resorted to the Treasury. On admission is quiet + taciturn, can give no satisfactory account of himself.

1861 Jany. Is quiet + well conducted. Obedient to orders + makes himself useful in the garden. Nothing has transpired regarding his previous history.

June. Has been suffering from diarrhoea for a long time past, got gradually weaker + on 29th June died.[38]

The significance of this case note is the reproduction of the language of Section 295. This mirroring of the requirement phrased in the Section as the need to 'give a satisfactory account of himself' is intriguing and suggests that the circumstances of the admission are closely related to the concern of Section 295 to give the authorities the power to detain vagrants. Indeed this use of the phrase recurs throughout the case notes in examples like Jookeea:

Jookeea (f). Mania. 20. Hindoo. Beggar. 10th Sept/62.

1862. Sent in by City Magistrate of Lucknow was found wandering about the streets, could give no account of herself, is young and good-looking. Appears to be suffering from weakness of intellect, gives very brief + often incoherent and absurd replies to questions—is very tractable.

1865 March. Somewhat improved since admission. Looks happier + talks sensibly, occupies herself a little in spinning.[39]

Look at the details in this case. A frightened young woman who has ended up without a home and family for whatever reason is challenged by the police. In her anxiety and confusion she clams up and her answers therefore seem brief and incoherent to the white male of whom she is naturally fearful. With the knowledge that, as a vagrant, she will have to be detained somewhere and as her reluctance to answer vaguely qualifies her for one of the diagnoses of which he is aware, the British doctor decides she is weak of intellect and agrees to have her admitted.

If this is rather filling in the gaps in the notes it is undeniable that very little in her record, or indeed in others like Kirmuhia above who share the pointed entry on their notes of being unable to account for themselves, suggests obvious eccentricity or 'insanity' in the patients. It would seem that the criteria which these individuals have fulfilled are not those of insanity but those of Section 295, that is by refusing to disclose what they were doing and where they were from, they became classified as an object of concern to the authorities as vagrants. The language of the case notes reflects this. In these instances they were found lodging in the asylum to keep them off the streets. It appears then that the state of vagrancy often led to an individual being accused of the state of insanity.

FAMILY AND COMMUNITY ADMISSIONS

While the concern of the colonial authorities seems to be with those wanderers and itinerants on the fringes of India's communities, there were some admissions from the heart of Indian families. Those admitted by their families or communities can roughly be divided in terms of their fate as there were those who were subjected to a short period in the institution by those around them while some were abandoned to it altogether. Those who were reclaimed will be considered first:

Mooloowa. Mania ch. 22. Hindoo. Labour. 28 Sept/65

29th Septr 1865
Sent to the asylum at the request of his Uncle Seeun Village Samgunpoor as they had no means of keeping him under control—is very violent and abusive.

1st Feby 1866
As bad as ever.

7th May 1866
Made over to his mother by order of the Visiting Committee.[40]

In Mooloowa's example, it seems that the 'control' sought by his family is not simply physical restraint. Various accounts show how Indians devised ways of restricting the physical freedom of those within their community without involving the British authorities. The Lucknow case notes have a couple of examples such as Deerumeere who was 'found wandering about the district with irons on his legs, put on by his relatives to keep him fast',[41] or Nundia who appears to have 'escaped from his home in chains where he had evidently confined for years.'[42] Other devices are mentioned in other sources. A witness in a murder case described the proceedings once the member of a neighbouring family started having fits of violent behaviour. 'Zalim was then put into the stocks by his brother. I never saw him out of them. He had his food whilst in the stocks, and answered the calls of nature in the same place.'[43] The District Superintendent of Police for the area described the stocks. 'They consisted of a piece of wood roughly fashioned by the relations themselves and did not belong to any outpost or station. The latter stocks have been entirely done away with for some time back.'[44]

In Mooloowa's case then, physical restraint was not the object of the committal. He was being punished. The idea of committing family members as a means of disciplining them is familiar from studies done of the place of the asylum in other societies.

A young slater's assistant, apparently living with his parents, was committed for threatening to cut his father's throat, having a razor, and 'delusions'. On admission he smelled of whiskey, seemed to be recovering from a drunken bout but was quite rational and coherent. A few days before, he said, he tried to separate his father and mother in a family quarrel; both were drunk. They subsequently swore informations against him, and in his words 'had him sent here to teach him a lesson'. A week after admission his father came to take him out on bail; questioned by the doctor, he corroborated the son's story. He 'moreover assured me that at no time did he consider his son insane, but that he thought it would do him (the son) good to get a few days here'.[45]

Using such archival examples, Mark Finnane constructs the argument that in Ireland, during the same period as is being discussed here, 'the use of the asylum, or the threat of it, as an instrument of control in the family could be quite blatant.'[46]

This conclusion would seem applicable to the example of Radha, aged 25, who appears in the Lucknow case notes.

Radha. Mania. 25. Brahmin. Cult. 1 Feby/65

1st Feby 1865
Sent in by City Magistrate of Lucknow.

22nd April 1865
This man was brought by his brother for confinement, he was found very difficult to manage at home—constantly running about his village abusing the women. No improvement since admission

Septr 1865
Made over to his friends at their request.[47]

Obviously embarrassing his relatives with his behaviour towards the womenfolk where he lived, and evidently refusing to obey his family's wish that he refrain from such behaviour, they, or certain of them, had decided to punish him by severing him from his community and admitting him into the strange institution. It was only meant to be a punishment though as he was not abandoned, being collected from the asylum again a few months later.

Since the step of committing to an asylum was not done simply to have the person restrained then, the Indian community could do this without involving the British. To remove the errant member from his kin group into an unfamiliar institution where he was exposed to an alien regime was indeed a punishment, it denied the person access to the group for whom his behaviour was meant to have significance and isolated him from the people his actions were meant to influence. For the family, or the member of the family who had taken the responsibility for the step, it was a way of asserting the authority of the status quo to which the disruptive behaviour had been a challenge.

It is interesting to note that most of the examples of Indians admitted by Indians for a short term are junior members of the family being committed by senior ones. Mooloowa quoted above is 22 years old and admitted by his uncle. Shew Dial is 28 years old and 'brought to the Asylum by his father who is a chowkidar in Lucknow.'[48] Kandhya is only 20 and was 'said to have attempted to fire his village and to have been so violent as to be uncontrollable by his brother.'[49] Clearly then, those within the family with power were exercising it to discipline those over whom their authority was held. However, this was a punitive rather than a purgative exercise, the family or community was asserting its authority over a member who was considered to be transgressing its correct functioning but who as a young man was valuable enough as a source of labour not to abandon.

If committal could be a disciplinary procedure, the admission of young women for 'puerperal mania' is intriguing. This was the name given in the nineteenth century to erratic behaviour in new mothers in the immediate post-partum period. In Victorian Britain, motherhood was constructed as the 'pure and almost sacred state'[50] of femininity, and so women who behaved in ways viewed as unfeminine in the post-partum period, be it flaunting their sexuality, threatening violence, or expressing extreme emotion, were deemed to be acting in a deviant manner and were treated as lunatics.

In India childbirth is similarly given cultural meaning, although the text varies somewhat from the British example. Studies of contemporary India show that 'a new mother is unclean for five weeks. For all that time no one should eat food which she has cooked.'[51] She is considered embarrassing, 'her physiological processes are shameful, distasteful and striking evidence of her sexuality.'[52] It seems that the culture chastises her for her behaviour in childbirth by denying her access to her natal family for a specified period after the birth.

If this was the case in the 1860s then there appears to be an interesting convergence of cultures between the British medical officers at the asylum and the Indian men of the local communities. These groups would have considered female behaviour in the period immediately after child birth potentially problematic. As such, cases like that of Mosst. Goolaba are especially intriguing.

Mosst. Goolaba. Puerperal Mania. 25. Hindoo. Labour. 15th June 1870
Certified by the Magistrate. Talks nonsense.

15th June 1870
Sent in by the Magistrate of Lucknow it is evidently a case of puerperal mania the woman has become mad after the birth of each child.

11th July
Admitted for treatment by order of the Committee.

5th Decr 1870
Discharged much improved and made over to her mother.[53]

There is very strong evidence here that her family were involved in her admission. It seems unlikely that she has been admitted to the asylum before, as a previous admission is usually traced and remarked upon in the case notes.[54] The information that she has on other occasions behaved in a similar manner to that which she was exhibiting on admission is likely therefore to have come from someone who the superintendent would accept such information from, that is a member of her family who he would find credible as a witness to her other births. That such a family exists for her is proven by the fact that her mother comes to collect her. She is not noted as violent, which other records suggest would have been the case if she had been,[55] so it seems unlikely that she has been noticed by the police. If her only misdemeanour is to express herself in unfamiliar verbal formulations, that is to talk nonsense, it is probable that the only people in a position to notice and inform the medical officer writing the case note would have been her family as it would not have been likely, especially in the post-partum period, that anyone else would have had access to her.

The only clue that the case note offers as to why she has been considered insane, that she 'talks nonsense', could be less a symptom of illness and more the key to explaining her admission. A refusal to talk in the prescribed manner, which is likely to have entailed, or been interpreted as entailing, a lack of respect for senior members of her family has been linked with the local understanding of childbirth as a time when the female is most in defiance of the norms established for her by the patriarchal culture and it has been decided that hers is a challenge to the established order of the family. She has therefore been banished from that unit until such time as she again recognizes the authority of that order. She is not abandoned though as she is valuable, being young enough to be productive and having proven to be reproductive. So she is taken back when 'Much improved', that is, once more quiet and respectful, and after a lengthy enough time for her to have become dissociated from her sexualized period.

There are then reasons to believe that the involvement of families in the admission of junior members of the family to the alien space that was the British asylum seems in certain cases to have been a disciplinary measure. There is no evidence that these families and communities were admitting their members out of a desire for access to western methods of treatment for mental health, or in the belief that they were mentally ill and were in need of therapy. There is evidence that those admitted by their families or community members had been exhibiting behaviour which would have embarrassed their families or been interpreted as disobedience or improper behaviour. No doubt, after a number of attempts to get the errant member to toe the line the unfamiliar environment of the British institution and estrangement from the family were decided upon as a means of silencing the challenge of the junior member to the established order of the family. The member was banished but not abandoned as the youngster was valuable to the family, at the very least as a source of productive and/or reproductive labour.

There were those, however, that did suffer the fate of being left in the asylum until death.

Bhugia. Mania. 40. caste. Service. 15th Jany/63

1863. Sent in by City Magistrate at the request of her husband who is a sweeper at the Martinière College She has been insane for years but has recently become wholly unmanageable She roams about picking up all sorts of filth and rubs herself over with excrement—at home she is entirely intolerable.

June 1864. This woman is much the same, I see no reasonable hope of her ultimate recovery.

Jany 1870. No better is likely to remain and die an inmate of the Asylum.[56]

The idea that admission to the asylum is being used by the Indian community as a disciplinary measure is difficult to sustain for those cases where the patient is left to die in the institution. Another explanation is needed for those abandoned.

The work of Nancy Waxler, who has studied mental illness in modern day Sri Lanka, contains a number of insights which offer an explanation as to why Indians were abandoning members of their families to the alien institution. She concludes that 'deviance and the sanctions society uses serve integrating functions in small societies',[57] going on to state that, 'the peasant family that provides treatment for its mentally ill member is, at the same time, effectively strengthening its own family structure by creating obligations between the patient and family, obligations that must be fulfilled later... In this sense the family group is further integrated by the fact of the child's illness.'[58]

While a mental illness incident in the family can actually be the occasion of the group bonding itself as a unit, long-term disorder tended to have other consequences:

Both beliefs and practices press the mentally ill person toward return to normality... In Sri Lanka for example the costs of remaining sick for long periods after appropriate treatment are much greater than the costs of return to normality; those who do remain chronically ill are threatened not only with barren lives, but also, ultimately, by lack of food and shelter and, most significant, loss of family ties.[59]

While it would obviously be very difficult to compare modern Sri Lankan villages with mid-nineteenth century north Indian ones, the model she derives from her study seems useful in explaining the patients abandoned to the asylum in the Lucknow case notes. The latter of those who are abandoned to the asylum seem to show that they were suffering from long-term disorders. This was the case with Bhugia who was committed by her husband when her behaviour worsened after years of problems and also appears to be the case with Bhoondoo:

Bhoondoo. Dementia. 35. caste. service. 16 June/63

Sent in from Cantonment Joint Magistrate. His mother states he has been getting worse for the last two years, and is now unsafe. Cannot be trusted for one moment alone, and is sometimes violent.

20th August. Died of chronic dysentery.[60]

Using these patients then it is possible to suggest that in north India, as in the Sri Lanka of Waxler's study, those suffering with long-term mental disorders were viewed as a burden to be removed permanently from the family. It must be remembered that the minority of such evictions from the family would have been into the asylum. The majority would have been onto the street, which accounts for the number of wandering lunatics for which the British built the asylum in the first place.

It could be then that these are examples of Indians sending their mentally ill into the British asylum. But they are not sent in because the Indians have any faith in the western modes of therapy. They are being sent in not for treatment but for care, in other words there is no expectation of cure on the part of the families when these patients are consigned to the asylum of the British, rather there is the expectation that the cast-off relatives or friends will at least be fed and given a bed, something the family is unwilling to supply any longer.

CONCLUSION

The British attempted the legitimation of their non-criminal lunatic admission policies by claiming humanitarian motives. 'It is refreshing to think that the condition of insanes of this country attracts so much attention; for there is no doubt that their condition was very miserable, and that they were much neglected,'[61] opined J. Penny, the superintendent of the asylum at Delhi. This tactic is familiar. What Foucault calls the image of 'the confrontation of the wise, firm philanthropist and the paralytic monster,'[62] is dismissed as a powerful myth in his revision of the role of Tuke and Pinel, those pioneers of asylum administration, and he points out that 'beneath the myths themselves, there was an operation, or rather a series of operations, which silently organised the world of the asylum.'[63]

In the context of India the asylum was caught up in a series of operations by the colonial state that sought to organize the wider world of India. Individual wanderers and vagrants were routinely admitted to and incarcerated in lunatic asylums as acts of social control rather than as acts of medicine or psychiatry. The objective was simply to keep them off the streets rather than to accurately diagnose and cure them. As such the lunatic asylum needs to be viewed alongside such mechanisms as the Criminal Tribes Act as a tool of the post-1857 efforts to impose a new social order on India. The former is evidence that the colonial state sought to discipline the Indian population through interaction with and control of corporate groups. The asylum system is a reminder, however, that that state also possessed an awareness of the need to monitor and to curb the movements of individuals on the fringes and margins of those groups.

However, a more complex picture of the asylum emerges when the activities of the family are considered. It seems that families were using the asylum in a similar way to the colonial state. Those that had marginalized themselves in the family through challenging behaviour, age or infirmity were dispatched to the hospital by senior members of the social unit. Those young enough to remain of use to the community were reclaimed in the hope that they had calmed down enough to be reintegrated with the other members. Those who were unlikely or unable to serve a further purpose were removed from the fringes of the family and permanently isolated in the asylum.

From this perspective the colonial asylum begins to look less Foucauldian. The hospital is certainly implicated in the operations of the state but it is also clearly located in the strategies of the family and community. Although founded by the colonial state the hospitals were themselves increasingly colonized by locals. In short, the hospital becomes a site that is used by two competing sources of power in the social history of modern India. However, the colonial state and the Indian family both had similar objectives in using the resources of the asylum; the management and control of those whose behaviour had earned them the precarious status of fringe-members.

NOTES AND REFERENCES

1. Home (Public) 19 December 1868, 46–59A. These references are drawn from the collections of the National Archives of India, New Delhi.
2. Home (Public) 19 December 1868, 51A.
3. For an analysis of criminal admissions to Indian asylums see J. Mills, 2000, *Madness, Cannabis and Colonialism: The 'Native-Only' Lunatic Asylums of British India, 1857–1900*, Basingstoke: Palgrave Macmillan, pp. 80–102.
4. Ibid., Appendix II.
5. W. Theobald, 1868, *The Legislative Acts of the Governor-General of India in Council*, Calcutta: Thacker and Spink.
6. Ibid.
7. *Annual Report of the Insane Asylums in Bengal for the Year 1862*, p. 34. The annual reports were consulted at the National Library of Scotland.
8. Govt of Bengal to Govt of India (henceforth GOI) 21 July 1868 in Home (Public) 8 August 1868, 56–59A.
9. Case Book II, patient no.1, admitted 8 January 1863. These references are drawn from the three case books of the Lucknow Asylum between 1859 and 1872 available courtesy of Dr Aditya Kumar at the Agra Mental Hospital.
10. Case Book II, patient no. 7, admitted 12 February 1863.
11. Case Book IA, patient no.168, admitted 19 February 1862.
12. Case Book IV, patient no.186, admitted 29 April 1870.
13. R. Jütte, 1994, *Poverty and Deviance in Early Modern Europe*, Cambridge: Cambridge University Press, p. 147.
14. See G. Salgado, 1977, *The Elizabethan Underworld*, J. Dent: London, chapters 6, pp. 117–34; 7, pp. 135–50; and 10, pp. 183–200.
15. P. Slack, 1988, *Poverty and Policy in Tudor and Stuart England*, London: Longman, pp. 113–31.

16. D. Garland, 1985, *Punishment and Welfare: A History of Penal Strategies*, Aldershot: Gower, p. 64.

17. N. Rose, 1979, 'The Psychological Complex: Mental Measurement and Social Administration', *Ideology and Consciousness*, vol. 5, p. 45.

18. Meer Hasan Ali in V. Oldenburg, 1989, *The Making of Colonial Lucknow 1856–1877*, New Delhi: Oxford University Press, p. 18.

19. G.H. Rouse in V. Oldenburg, 1989, *The Making of Colonial Lucknow*.

20. Ibid., pp. 18–19.

21. Ibid., p. 64.

22. Ibid., p. 39.

23. Ibid., p. 40.

24. Ibid., preface, pp. xvii–xviii. See also A. King, 1976, *Colonial Urban Development: Culture, Social Power and Environment*, London: Routledge, p. 214.

25. M. Radhakrishna, 1989, 'The Criminal Tribes Act in Madras Presidency: Implications for Itinerant Trading Communities', *Indian Economic and Social History Review*, XXVI(3), p. 271.

26. D. Arnold, 1985, 'Crime and Crime Control in Madras, 1858–1947', in Yang (ed.), *Crime and Criminality in British India*, p. 85.

27. Ibid.

28. *The Code of Criminal Procedure: An Act passed by the Legislative Council of India on the 5th September 1861*, 1862, London: W.H. Allen: London, Section 295.

29. Security could be taken for other offences as well such as 'bad livelihood' and the total defaulters imprisoned is recorded in the various Judicial (Criminal) statistical tables rather than by section under which committed.

30. *Report on the Administration of Criminal Justice in Oudh for the year 1880*, p. 7.

31. Ibid., p. 6.

32. Ibid.

33. Ibid.

34. There appears to have been one such in Lucknow. Various case notes refer to the transfer of inmates to and from this institution to and from the Asylum. See, for example, Lum Boor (Case Book IV, patient no. 6, admitted 17 October 1868) 'transferred by order of visitors to the poor house' or Buslee (Case Book IA, patient no. 25, admitted 29 May 1860) 'admitted from almshouse, is perfectly idiotic but happy'.

35. Case Book IA, patient no. 153, admitted 25 November 1861.

36. Case Book IA, patient no. 140, admitted 14 October 1861.

37. Case Book IA, patient no. 95, admitted 27 November 1861 (in the original volume this case note was not numbered and appeared in the pages relating to admissions of April 1861).

38. Case Book IA, patient no. 66, admitted 1 November 1860.

39. Case Book IA, patient no. 226, admitted 10 September 1962.

40. Case Book II, patient no. 222, admitted 28 September 1865.

41. Case Book IA, patient no.128, admitted 24 August 1861.

42. Case Book II, patient no.158, admitted 28th February 1865: case note transcribed as on original.

43. Deposition of Seetul Sonar in NWP Judicial (Criminal) March 1864, 14A. The NWP sources were drawn from the Uttar Pradesh State Archives in Lucknow.

44. Super. Police Goruckpore to I.G. Police Benares, 22 October 1863 in NWP Judicial (Criminal) March 1864, 26A.
45. M. Finnane, 1981, *Insanity and the Insane in Post-Famine Ireland*, London: Croom Helm, p. 163.
46. Ibid.
47. Case Book II, patient no. 149, admitted 1 February 1865.
48. Case Book IA, patient no. 202, admitted 10 June 1862.
49. Case Book II, patient no. 70, admitted 8 December 1863.
50. E. Showalter, 1987, *The Female Malady: Women, Madness and English Culture, 1830–1980*, London: Virago, p. 58.
51. A village midwife quoted in R. Jeffery and P. Jeffery, 1994, 'A Woman Belongs to Her Husband: Female Autonomy, Women's Work and Childbearing in Bijnor', in A. Clark (ed.), *Gender and Political Economy: An Exploration of South Asian Systems*, New Delhi: Oxford University Press, p. 99.
52. Ibid., p. 100.
53. Case Book IV, patient no. 202, admitted 15 June 1870.
54. For example, Hanooman's notes (Case Book IA, patient no. 222, admitted 20 August 1862) record that he 'had previously been an inmate in the Asylum and was discharged in July 1861'. The tracing of previous admissions seems to have been so efficient that those treated in the Jail Hospital for insanity before the establishment of the Asylum have it noted when admitted into the Asylum. Kurreem Buy (Case Book IA, patient no. 40, admitted 20 July 1860) was 'once in the Asylum in the Jail'.
55. For example, another puerperal maniac is admitted three months after Mosst. Goolaba. Mosst.Rhuman (Case Book IV, patient no. 220, admitted 15 September 1870) was 'Certified by the Magistrate Violent'. She was handed over to her husband eight months later.
56. Case Book II, patient no. 3, admitted 15 January 1863.
57. N. Waxler, 1979, 'Is Mental Illness Cured in Traditional Societies? A Theoretical Analysis', *Culture, Medicine and Psychiatry*, vol. 1, p. 239.
58. Ibid., p. 243.
59. Ibid., p. 248.
60. Case Book II, patient no. 38, admitted 16 June 1863.
61. *Annual Report of the Lunatic Asylums of the Punjab for the year 1871–2*, p. 6.
62. M. Foucault, 1988, *Madness and Civilization: A History of Insanity in the Age of Reason*, New York: Vintage, p. 242.
63. Ibid., p. 243.

'The more this foul case is stirred, the more offensive it becomes'[1]
Imperial Authority, Victorian Sentimentality, and the Court Martial of Colonel Crawley, 1862–4

Douglas M. Peers

Historians have customarily sought out big events and large processes on the understanding that these would in turn have big effects. Chaos theory, on the other hand, has argued that little influences could have cataclysmic effects as illustrated by the so-called butterfly effect which has popularized the notion by suggesting that a butterfly flapping its wings in one continent could trigger a hurricane in another. What I wish to present is a historical variant of the butterfly effect, not out of a wish to add chaos theory to our already over-burdened arsenal of theories and models, but rather to explore how the reverberations of seemingly inconsequential events on the margins of the British empire, in this case a trial that came to be known as the Mhow Court Martial, not only can be made intelligible, but how it can consequently be used to illuminate the interplay between social practices, cultural idioms, and the politics of the mid-Victorian empire.

A petty squabble amongst the officers of a British cavalry regiment posted in India, triggered when two officers refused to associate with another officer because he had married a divorcee, rapidly escalated into a major crisis within the British Army at home as well as in India. Lieutenant Colonel Thomas Crawley, the commanding officer of this regiment, the Sixth Inniskilling Dragoons, brought one of the officers before a court martial during the course of which one of the witnesses, Regimental Sergeant Major John Lilley, a popular and respected sergeant major, died having been placed under close arrest on Crawley's orders.[2] Lilley's wife Clarissa passed away not long after. While the initial court martial ostensibly had been called to deal with various accusations against Captain Smales, the regiment's paymaster, in particular a charge that he was trying to stoke up feelings amongst other officers against Colonel Crawley, who had only recently arrived to take command of the regiment, it quickly became a major scandal both in India and Britain, largely because of the circumstances surrounding the deaths of John and Clarissa Lilley. In fact, the original court martial case, involving accusations and counter-accusations between Crawley and Smales, was largely eclipsed by the attention paid to the Lilleys. It was no longer simply a matter of the internal administration of one regiment, albeit a prestigious one. Instead, it brought to the surface a number of questions about the management and discipline of the Indian Army, an institution whose strategic and symbolic importance had grown considerably in the aftermath of the 1857 Rebellion.

The trial, and with it the actions of some of the most senior officers in the British Army, notably General Hugh Rose (Commander-in-Chief in India, 1860–5), General William Mansfield (Commander-in-Chief of the Bombay Army, 1860–5, and Rose's successor as Commander-in-Chief in India, 1865–70), and even the Duke of Cambridge (Commander-in-Chief of the British Army, 1856–95, and cousin of Queen Victoria), came under intense public scrutiny, and these attentions in turn exposed a number of fault lines within the British military which, many feared, had the potential to further undermine imperial authority. Rumours circulated that Sir Hugh Rose, the Commander-in-Chief in India, and Sir William Mansfield, Commander of the Bombay Army, who had upheld the decision of the initial court martial, would soon be recalled.[3] As the then Secretary of State for India, Charles Wood, complained to the Viceroy, 'This Mhow Court Martial is a disagreeable business, and the further we get into it the worse everyone comes out of it.'[4] The grip that the Mhow Court Martial came to exert on the public imagination can be partially explained by its particularly melodramatic casting as well as its timing. The calamities and blunders of the Crimean War and the near-loss of India during the mutinies and revolts of 1857–8, the latter of which was popularly presented as struggles between lightness and darkness, Christian and heathen, civilization and barbarism, created a context which accentuated the dramatic aspects of the events at Mhow. The fact that the casualties included the wife of a soldier whose death was accelerated by the callousness of an officer only fuelled public outrage. One reason why this scandal was able to reverberate back and forth between India and Britain was because it touched upon a number of flash points—particularly gender and class—which had been rendered doubly sensitive in the aftermath of the 1857 Rebellion and the Crimean War.[5] That a court martial in an isolated cantonment in India, involving a British soldier and his wife, who were arguably amongst the most marginalized members of British society, could provoke such an outcry illustrates that empire could and did matter to Victorian society, even over such an apparently insignificant event. In the words of the *Penny Illustrated Paper*, it was 'one of those events which combine in no ordinary degree the elements of great personal interest and of high national importance.'[6] The intensity of the debates surrounding these trials, which began in India before being transferred to Britain, indicate that Victorian society was more sensitive to and influenced by developments in India than Bernard Porter's recent work might otherwise suggest.[7] Parallels can be drawn between the issues and anxieties which swirled around this case and contemporary debates over the introduction of the Contagious Diseases Acts in India, Britain, and elsewhere in the empire (1864, 1866, 1869).[8] While the Contagious Diseases Acts would produce a much more sustained public discussion which would spread throughout the British empire, they ultimately drew upon broadly similar questions about race, gender, class, and respectability that had featured in the Mhow Court Martial.

What is particularly intriguing about this case, beyond the tremendous interest it sparked in the British and Anglo-Indian press, is the pronounced swing that occurred in public opinion. When news of the Lilleys' deaths in custody reached Britain, British newspapers were not only nearly unanimous in demanding that Colonel Crawley be held accountable, but most had already convicted him of the crime of hastening the death of the Lilleys. The *Manchester Guardian* declared it to be an example of 'abominable injustice and unfeeling oppression.'[9] The rhetoric which surrounded this case grew particularly heated both in Parliament and on the printed page and there were a number of striking attempts to draw analogies between what happened to the Lilleys and previous atrocities. The Lilleys were described as having been forced to live in conditions similar to 'the hold of a slave ship or the Black Hole of Calcutta.'[10] Another paper, one that was particularly orientated towards Anglo-Indian (meaning British residents in India) readers, opined that 'this will assuredly be the most memorable court-martial of our time. It has assumed all the importance of a great state trial.'[11] It even made it into the *New York Times* which pointedly noted that, 'It is not for the purpose of a mere diversion from the absorbing topics of the time [the Civil War was then raging], that we call attention to the recent revelation of the common soldier's life in British India.'[12] So intense was media interest in this case that the *Illustrated London News* commissioned an artist to produce sketches of the trial that was being held at Aldershot as well as of the barracks in Mhow where it all began.[13]

The government reluctantly was forced to concede to the growing demand that Crawley be tried, and a second court martial was ordered, though this time it would be held in Aldershot in England. At over £20,000, it was also one of the costliest trials in nineteenth century Britain, as over a hundred witnesses, including several Indian civilians, had to be brought to Britain.[14] The sheer scale and expense of the trial guaranteed that it would remain in the public eye.

The Crawley trial is fine fun for the witnesses. There is a Parsee canteen keeper getting £70 a month and dashing about town in fine style at the expence of the income tax; and about 150 soldiers, two thirds of whom know nothing about the affairs but merely tendered themselves as witnesses in order that they might get the trip home.[15]

Colonel Crawley was initially cast as the villain in what became a melodrama observed by thousands through the pages of the major newspapers of the day in addition to the many who crowded the court room at Aldershot. Crawley came to symbolize all that was wrong with the mid-Victorian army: a stern martinet, vindictive, and heartless, his callous treatment of the men under his command led directly to the deaths of the Lilleys. Sergeant Major Lilley at the outset exemplified the professional soldier, whose sacrifices the public had come not only to appreciate but even idealize in the aftermath of the Crimean War and the 1857 Rebellion. Clarissa Lilley, by choosing to accompany her husband into close arrest and to die by his side, was assigned the womanly self-sacrificing role which Victorians were keen to promote. In the aftermath of the Crimean War, an aristocratic officer was the perfect target for, in the words of the *New York Times*, Crawley was 'intemperate, lazy, overbearing and neglectful of his duty.'[16] At the same time, memories of the 1857 Rebellion, which had only been suppressed five years previously, and which had been saturated with gendered readings of the civilizational differences between the British rulers and their Indian subjects, ensured that Clarissa Lilley could be easily cast as the tragic heroine. Yet Crawley was eventually acquitted of the charges and the Lilleys passed into obscurity. In the end, the Mhow Court Martial is an excellent example of the way in which a melodrama, even one which took place on the margins of the empire, lent itself readily to social commentary; yet as far as tropes were concerned, it had its limits. Stark distinctions between villains and victims in this case were incommensurable with the deeper structures and ideologies at work within the mid-Victorian empire, in particular the need to ensure that class and gendered hierarchies so vital to the empire in general and the army in particular were maintained. But we shall begin with the tragedy.

Act I: A Cantonment Scandalized

The first act in this tragedy begins in the dusty cantonment of Mhow in central India. The Sixth Inniskilling Dragoons, a regiment which had distinguished itself at the Battle of Waterloo and most recently won acclaim for its conduct in the Charge of the Heavy Brigade at Balaclava, had been posted to the Bombay Presidency in 1858.[17] As cavalry regiments go, it enjoyed considerable acclaim, ranking 16th in the army's list of precedence (as of 1881). As was common at the time, several of its officers, preferring the pleasures of life in Britain to the uncertainties of life in India, had transferred out of the regiment. The position of senior captain consequently passed to an officer, Captain Archibald Weir, who had been promoted from the ranks following distinguished service in the Crimean War. Several of the officers, including its commanding officer at the time, were not happy, and their discomfort grew when the latter resigned and Weir assumed temporary command.[18] While promotion from the ranks was not unheard of in the Victorian army, especially in wartime, it was unusual for such officers to attain regimental command. Most in fact were placed in more technical or clerical positions such as those of riding master or quartermaster. The deteriorating state of morale within the regiment can also be seen in the increased frequency of courts martial. Prior to their arrival in India, a total of 150 courts martial had taken place in the regiment and there were only 600 troops on its establishment.[19] The turbulence appeared to subside, at least temporarily, with the arrival of a new commanding officer in April 1861. Lieutenant Colonel Thomas Crawley had exchanged command of the Fifteenth Hussars, which he had purchased in 1858, for that of the Inniskilling Dragoons. Crawley was the son of an officer and a product of Sandhurst; he had impressed those under whom he had previously served by his zeal and commitment to maintain discipline. He had, however, not seen much service, only briefly experiencing combat during the Second Sikh War (1846–8). Nor was he a man of means, and like many before him, he found India appealing because he could maintain the lifestyle of an officer and gentleman and not bankrupt himself. Most importantly, he was not known for his tact and had an explosive temper. As one of his defenders would later remark, 'he is a man of strong feelings which sometimes overpower his judgment.'[20] One of his strongest feelings, as Crawley himself admitted, was that the officers of the regiment were 'neither officers nor gentlemen.'[21]

Expectations that relations within the officers' mess would improve were soon dashed with the arrival of another new officer. Captain Richard Renshaw joined the regiment in 1860 together with his wife. She, however, was a divorcee, having recently left her first husband, a solicitor, who had applied for a divorce under the recently approved Matrimonial Causes Act of 1857 on the grounds that she had been unfaithful to him—she had been having an affair with Renshaw.[22] For the first time, divorces could be secured from the courts without having to petition Parliament for special dispensation. Adultery was the only grounds under which a husband could sue for divorce, which, when coupled with the social stigma as well as the financial costs (it was estimated that a divorce through the courts cost upwards of £100), ensured that divorces were relatively few in number, only 200 or so a year by the 1870s. A divorcee was therefore a rarity, and in the hothouse environment of an Indian cantonment, where rumours and scandals were often the only distractions from the tedium of daily life, the arrival of Mrs Renshaw was bound to stir things up. One letter to the press from an officer in India referred disapprovingly to 'the social position of a lady married to an officer of the regiment, who had been previously divorced under the usual circumstances which entitle a husband to free himself from an erring partner.'[23] Anglo-Indian culture was both acutely status conscious and remarkably insular and nowhere was this more evident than in the confines of the officers' mess. As Mrinalini Sinha has persuasively shown, clubbability was one of the most cherished virtues in the Anglo-Indian world. Clubs, of which the officers' mess was arguably the ultimate distillation in its emphasis on the preservation of social hierarchies and the perpetuation of a particularly masculine definition of character, 'articulated the legitimate boundaries of an acceptable image of "whiteness."'[24] That the officers of this regiment would be outraged by Renshaw is not surprising.[25] It was, for example, widely known in India that the presiding judge in the divorce had described Mrs Renshaw as a 'singularly profligate woman'.[26] What is surprising, however, is that the situation grew steadily worse. Even newspapers that regularly dealt with the Anglo-Indian community were surprised at what they saw as the persistent prudishness of those officers who refused to associate with Renshaw and his wife.[27]

The regiment was scandalized, and the Renshaws were ostracized by most of the officers. According to one contemporary,

all the married officers of the Inniskillings, with the exception of Colonel Crawley, declined to concede any longer to the lady the local rank which she had hitherto usurped amongst their wives and daughters as an honest woman.[28]

The two most senior married officers went even further: regimental surgeon Gavin Turnbull and the regimental paymaster, Captain Thomas Smales, informed the Colonel that they were not willing to meet socially with either of the Renshaws. Crawley, despite his reputation as a martinet and his seeming obsession with maintaining proper hierarchies, had together with his wife regularly socialized with the Renshaws. He issued an order to the officers of the regiment that regimental harmony should not be jeopardized by treating the Renshaws as pariahs, but to little effect. Matters exploded when Crawley ordered that Smales open the pay office outside of normal hours to allow Renshaw to collect his pay. Smales refused; Crawley then tried to have him court martialled for insubordination, but the charges were thrown out.

Matters might have ended there had Smales not tried to gain the upper hand over Crawley by accusing him of a number of infractions, the most damaging of which was his claim that Crawley had signed muster rolls for inspection parades at which he had not been present. Even Smales' defenders concede that he lacked tact and was inclined to use intemperate and insubordinate language.[29] Smales hoped that by complaining to the War Office, he could persuade them to recall Crawley. However, there was no response to his first letter, so Smales decided to try again, this time though he followed official procedures and directed his complaints upwards through his commanding officer, who was none other than Colonel Crawley. The result: a court martial, though the defendant was not Crawley. Smales was instead tried for insubordination.

Normally, accusations such as those raised by Smales would have prompted the army to initiate a Court of Inquiry that would have examined the evidence and from it prepared a recommendation as to whether there were sufficient grounds for a court martial.[30] But proper procedures were not followed. Crawley instead convinced General

Farrell, the commander of the British garrison at Mhow, that Smales was not simply a trouble-maker but was more alarmingly the ringleader of a clique of discontented officers. Anglo-Indian society at this time was particularly susceptible to conspiracy theories: memories were fresh of the recent revolts in India (1857–8), and the army was still coping with the aftershocks of the White Mutiny, a less dramatic and violent but no less ominous display of unrest amongst the Company's European soldiers and officers in India who, following the winding up of the Company, were alarmed at the prospect of being transferred into the Royal Army.[31] Farrell, one of the oldest officers serving in India and rather uncharitably if not unfairly described by Smales as 'almost an imbecile'[32] in turn recommended to Major General William Mansfield, the Commander-in-Chief of the Bombay Army, that Smales be brought up on charges. Mansfield agreed for he too was eager to quell any signs of insubordination before they could spread beyond the regiment. Mansfield, aware of the poor state of morale in the regiment even before Crawley's arrival, was convinced that disgruntled officers in the Inniskilling Dragoons were pursuing a vendetta against Crawley. Mansfield tried to convince the Duke of Cambridge that not only was there a conspiracy at work within the Dragoons, but that such feelings could easily be goaded still further by a licentious press that was often too willing to accept officers' grievances, which would in turn spread disaffection to other regiments.[33] The military high command in India held very ambivalent views on the Anglo-Indian press: on the one hand, they, like the rest of the Anglo-Indian community, relied upon it not only as a source of information but also as a forum through which a sense of community could be nurtured. Yet given the preponderant position enjoyed by the army within Anglo-Indian society, newspaper proprietors and editors were all too often inclined to identify with and take up officers' grievances.[34] The role that the Anglo-Indian press played in the ensuing scandal provoked Mansfield to complain that, 'I have never known the press of this country to proceed with such effect and cruelty as in this case.'[35]

In adopting this course of action, Mansfield enjoyed the support of his immediate superior, General Hugh Rose, the Commander-in-Chief in India (1860–5), whom he informed that 'the provocation [Crawley] had received from all the parties who were working against him was sufficient to drive any man besides himself.'[36] Rose had distinguished himself in 1857–8 when he commanded a column to suppress the revolts that had broken out in central India, and in many respects was considered quite far-sighted and innovative. But he had his blind spots. He was described by Lord Elgin, the Governor General, as having been afflicted with a 'certain obliquity of vision which leads him, not infrequently, to take a perverse view of a case when it comes before him, and disables him from seeing his error when it is pointed out.'[37] Rose was also the subject of a number of scandalous rumours, some of which made it back to Britain. One of the women with whom Rose was reportedly besotted, and who rebuffed his attention, was the wife of Lieutenant Colonel Charles Shute, Crawley's predecessor as commanding officer of the Sixth Dragoons, and the officer upon whom Rose and Crawley would attempt to shift the blame for the regiment's poor state of discipline.[38] There was another scandal after an officer publicly complained about Rose's 'senile philanderings' at a banquet at the United Service Club.[39] Rose's reputation as being somewhat less than gallant would colour later discussions of the role he had played in the events which led to the deaths of John and Clarissa Lilley, for as one editor noted, 'Sir Hugh has the misfortune of most elderly ladies men of believing himself irresistible, and a petticoat is sure to be mixed up in any delicate or difficult affair in which Sir Hugh comes before the public'. The same article concluded that Rose's conduct during the course of the Mhow Court Martial would further undermine his reputation.[40] Reports circulated in Britain that Rose would be forced to resign, if for no other reason than to avoid being recalled in disgrace. The Secretary of State for India, Charles Wood, later confided to Lord Elgin, the Viceroy of India during this period, that Rose was lucky not to have been recalled, and that he personally had hoped that Rose would have resigned.[41] While officials in the India Office and the Horse Guards would express many misgivings about the course of action that Crawley and Farrell had decided upon once the news had reached them, the higher authorities in India closed ranks around Crawley, for they were still haunted by memories of previous acts of insubordination in India.[41] A court martial was ordered: Smales was the defendant, and the prosecutor was none other than Colonel Crawley.

ACT II: A CONTROVERSIAL COURT MARTIAL

The second act began on the first day of April 1862 when the court martial which would try Captain Smales was assembled at Mhow. It would prove to be one of the most costly and prolonged courts martial to take place in India. The court sat for 60 days and at the end of it all some 600 pages of evidence and testimony had been recorded. The president of the court was the commander of the Seventy-second Infantry; he was accompanied by four more lieutenant colonels, a major, and nine captains. By contemporary standards, it was a large tribunal. Moreover, the fact that there were five lieutenant colonels attests to the importance that Mansfield and others had attached to its proceedings. The charge levelled against Smales was the familiar and omnibus one of 'conduct highly insubordinate, most disgraceful, unbecoming the character of an officer and a gentleman, and to the prejudices of good order and military discipline.'[43] Military law, because it was less concerned with punishing individual malefactors and driven more by the need to impose collective discipline, frequently made use of sweeping articles such as 'conduct unbecoming', for it gave the court considerable latitude in deciding what constituted 'conduct unbecoming'. The basis for this charge were the letters which Smales had written in which he accused Crawley of failing to attend monthly musters, and which Crawley and Farrell (and later Mansfield and Rose) took as proof that Smales was trying to orchestrate a smear campaign against his commanding officer. Yet there was insufficient evidence to sustain a more serious charge of mutiny.

Smale's defence depended on his proving that Crawley had not attended the parades at which he had signed the inspection reports, and to do so he required corroborating evidence. This he hoped to secure from the non-commissioned officers who were always present at the parades, and he called upon Regimental Sergeant Major John Lilley and two other sergeants major to confirm Crawley's absence. Crawley reacted once again by invoking the spectre of a cabal being hatched against him and on 26 April placed the three witnesses under close arrest, thereby denying Smales access to them. General Farrell, his immediate superior officer, approved of the measure. And while Mansfield was convinced that there was a conspiracy brewing, he concluded that there was not enough proof and he eventually ordered that the two sergeant majors be released.[44] Lilley's release was also ordered shortly thereafter, but he died before these orders reached the regiment. Crawley defended the use of close arrest as not only necessary to prevent communication between these sergeants and any possible co-conspirators but also as a form of punishment for their insubordination.[45] Crawley, Farrell, and even Mansfield were convinced that these sergeants were part of a growing opposition to Crawley within the regiment.

At this point, the story shifts from what could still have been played out as a Thackeray-style farce to one more reminiscent of a Dickensian tragedy. Following his arrest, John Lilley, by all accounts a reliable and popular non-commissioned officer, was moved along with his wife Clarissa into even smaller quarters where they were placed under the constant surveillance of a 24-hour guard. Clarissa was suffering from the last stages of tuberculosis and required constant care. Much was made in subsequent accounts of the horrid conditions in which they lived, and the humiliation that they experienced by being under the sentry's constant gaze. As previously noted, newspapers drew analogies between the Lilleys' cramped and sweltering accommodations and the infamous Black Hole of Calcutta, as well as the conditions aboard slave trading vessels, and in so doing not only enhanced the pathos of their suffering but also emphasized their sacrifice in contrast to Colonel Crawley who was depicted as hot-tempered and callous in his treatment of those under his command. And if that was not enough, their two young children had passed away just before the trial commenced. Lilley and his wife were confined to their quarters during the hottest season of the year for the duration of the trial. Lilley died on 26 May 1862. Six weeks later his wife passed away.

Meanwhile, the trial against Smales proceeded, and the fact of whether or not Crawley had attended the parades became irrelevant for it was Smales and not Crawley who was on trial. Crawley attempted to discredit one of the witnesses, Lieutenant Fitzsimon, who had insisted that Crawley had not attended several of the parades in question, by declaring that the latter was so short-sighted that he could not be trusted. Yet it later emerged that Fitzsimon held a certificate as a first class rifle shot at a range of 600 yards.[46] Nevertheless, on 7 June Smales was found guilty by the court and dismissed from the service. Smales' problems did not end there: he and his family were stopped and searched while en route to Bombay from whence they were to set sail for Britain. He was charged with theft; the charge was thrown out, he was rearrested, and languished for several months in prison. He was eventually released, but military authorities in Bombay continued to pursue him. The basis for these charges was reports of deficiencies in the regimental accounts.[47] Smales would continue to bombard officials in the Horse Guards and in the War Office with petitions, and was finally released, the charges against him being dropped for want of evidence. Yet Rose and Mansfield continued to believe in his guilt, and when Smales later attempted to have his rank restored, Mansfield wrote to the Adjutant General to convince him that Smales' was not suited to be an officer.[48] Crawley meanwhile had incurred the wrath of many Anglo-Indian newspapers which, when combined with Smales' determination to secure a pardon and reinstatement, ensured that the controversy would spill over into the United Kingdom. Mansfield would later lament that the Anglo-Indian press had taken up the issue 'with such effect and cruelty'.[49]

Criticisms of the Mhow Court Martial were initially sparked by Smales' efforts to secure reinstatement into the army as well as compensation for his losses. By all accounts, Smales was not a sympathetic character. Even those who joined in the condemnation of Crawley were reluctant to give any support to Smales' claims. No matter how hostile the press had been to Crawley, they were quite unreceptive to Smales' situation and in fact repeated allegations that Smales had defrauded regimental accounts.[50] The Lilleys, however, could be easily cast as innocent victims; given the growing sanctity and sentimentality with which domestic spaces were viewed; their prolonged sufferings, incarceration, and tragic deaths were easily captured in melodramatic terms. Smales was astute enough to appreciate this, and in the pamphlet war which he instigated against Crawley as well as the several petitions he lodged with Horse Guards, he played up the sufferings inflicted upon the sergeant and his wife as a means of building his case against Crawley.

Crawley's situation was made even more precarious following the leaking of a memo from the Duke of Cambridge on the conduct of the Mhow Court Martial. In it, Cambridge found fault with the entire handling of the trial, and the fact that officers senior to Crawley had consented to several acts which were in violation of the Articles of War. In particular, the Articles required that no soldier or officer could be imprisoned for more than eight days without being formally charged. Neither Lilley nor the other two sergeants placed under close arrest were ever charged. Even more damning was Cambridge's conclusion that the deteriorating state of discipline within the Inniskilling Dragoons was due to Crawley's inability to earn the respect of those under his command.[51] Cambridge declared that Crawley was 'an officer not gifted with the special talent which unites with the firmness of command the tract which inspires confidence and creates goodwill'.[52] Crawley had incurred the Duke of Cambridge's anger with a speech that he had made in India regarding the trial in which he publicly denounced the officers he thought were in league against him, and which had been reported in the *Deccan Herald*. Mansfield had looked into the speech and its reporting by the Anglo-Indian press, and concluded that it was a 'speech which would have been better unsaid.'[53]

Rose and Mansfield were also singled out for criticism in the memorandum, especially for the readiness with which they and Crawley had tried to attribute Lilley's death to excessive drinking. Moreover, the Duke of Cambridge had given Rose and Mansfield permission to send Crawley back home to England, and while he would not order that course of action himself, he indicated clearly that he differed from them in his opinion of Crawley.[54] While Crawley would remain the focus of most of the criticisms, the reputations of Rose and Mansfield were also placed in the balance. Nowhere was this captured more poignantly than in a cartoon in *Indian Punch* from August 1863 with the caption 'The Living Rose Contemplating the Dead Lily: this could be my fate tomorrow.'[55] Cambridge's memorandum had a curious effect; it seemingly acknowledged that there were serious faults within the Indian Army but it offered little by way of constructive action. As one newspaper informed its readers, Cambridge's memorandum 'went too far to be agreeable to the Indian authorities and did not go far enough to satisfy public opinion in England.'[56] Cambridge was himself thrown on the defensive. As noted by the *Spectator*, 'So strong is public feeling in this matter, that the Duke of Cambridge rose in his place on Monday night to defend himself, stating...that he had only been aware of all the facts connected with this affairs for the past ten days, and alleging that the Commander-in-Chief in India was, in matters of discipline, by usage independent.'[57]

ACT III: THE VINDICATION OF COLONEL CRAWLEY

For act three, the setting shifts to London where public opinion had been outraged by reports of Crawley's treatment of Sergeant Lilley and his family. Rumours circulated that Lilley's surviving family members in the United Kingdom were considering criminal proceedings against Crawley.[58] As Mansfield ruefully noted, 'a concatenation of circumstances has with their assistance [the press and Parliamentary radicals] led in the most extraordinary manner to the curious persuasion of public opinion.'[59] A correspondent of the *Manchester Guardian* credited *The Times* with forcing the British public to take notice of what had happened at Mhow.[60] *The Times'* opening salvo included the following words:

A brave and honest soldier, with the best of character, 20 years of irreproachable service, was ordered into close arrest in a climate where such confinement implies the worst of torture, and then detained for 27 dreadful days. At the expiration of that time he perished miserably, and his wife, who had shared his incarceration, followed him to the grave a few days afterwards.[61]

The success of these efforts at dramatizing the sufferings of the Lilleys in the pages of the Anglo-Indian and later the domestic British press was due at least in part to the heightened concern for the physical and moral welfare of soldiers and their families, for the decade after 1857 was one in which the British rank and file enjoyed a brief period of popular respect. Whereas much of the public would have hitherto agreed with Wellington's description of them as the 'scum of the earth', the sufferings and sacrifices that British soldiers made during the Crimean War and 1857 Rebellion led to their being recast as Christian heroes. British war artists like Lady Butler, for example, began to feature soldiers as the subject of their paintings, rather than simply as a backdrop.[62] Journalists like William Howard Russell extolled their dedication and bravery, in India as well as in the Crimean peninsula, and frequently juxtaposed them against their less deserving officers.[63] And then there were the reports of Florence Nightingale which encouraged a much more sympathetic, if not always empathetic, public engagement with the lives of the rank and file. A large swath of the British public was convinced that the rot within the army was due to the arrogance and incompetence of the officers of the British Army.

Concerns for the well-being of Britain's soldiers were soon after extended to India where accounts of the fighting during the 1857 Rebellion fixed attention on the heroic sacrifices made by British soldiers. Such concerns became entangled with growing professional interest in sanitation and in the use of statistics in order to reduce the high mortality rates experienced by British soldiers scattered across the empire. It is no coincidence that 1863 was also the year in which Florence Nightingale's study of the sanitary state of the British Army in India was published.[64] The growing interest in the medical and moral well-being of Britain's soldiers often focused on living conditions within the barracks.[65] Much was made in the contemporary press of the living conditions experienced by the wives and families of married soldiers. Readers of the *Calcutta Review*, one of the leading periodicals in India, were told as early as 1845 that, 'We have seen young girls and married women, in the midst of drunken, half-naked men, hearing little but blasphemy and ribaldry, exposed to the extremes of heat and cold, surrounded by influences that render decency nearly impossible, and make devotion seem almost a mockery.'[66] *Colburn's United Service Magazine*, one of the principal platforms for military reformers, published a story in 1850 which featured a character named Lizzie Gould, and melodramatically charted her descent into debauchery on account of being forced to live in the barracks. Lizzie Gould was a country girl, pure, simple, and virtuous, who married a soldier and from there tumbled into the hell of barrack life. As its author warned her readers, 'however virtuously a girl may be brought up, however well disposed she may be in her womanhood, she cannot fail, if she marries a soldier, under the present system...to become acquainted with vice in every shape.'[67] Similar emotionally-charged tales that recounted the humiliating experiences of women in army barracks were picked up in middle-class journals like Dickens' *Household Words*.[68]

Given this intensified interest in the lives of British soldiers and their families overseas, the surge of attention given to the events in Mhow in 1862 becomes more comprehensible. One pamphleteer picked up on this theme,

Wives and mothers will, therefore, readily understand how it came to pass that Clarissa Lilley clung to the father of her dead little ones, and patiently elected to endure even the terrible indignities I have described, in order to secure to herself the melancholy consolation of dying in his arms.[69]

Much was made of the extent to which Mrs Lilley (and by extension her husband) were humiliated by being under constant scrutiny, especially given that Mrs Lilley, as a number of newspapers informed their readers, was suffering from extreme diarrhoea as well as tuberculosis. The *Manchester Guardian* took up the case against Crawley, and at least initially so did *The Times*, the *Spectator*, the *Examiner*, the *Saturday Review*, and the *Penny Illustrated Paper*. The *Illustrated London News*, described by one scholar as taking an interest in colonial affairs only 'whenever there was a suitably picturesque colonial war' dedicated much of one of its issues to detailing the trial in text as well as in illustrations, and with a circulation estimated at 100,000, it reached a large audience.[70] *Punch*, with a circulation of about 40,000, also joined in on the attack on Crawley. In one issue, it published a very maudlin poem about the sufferings of Lilley at the hands of Colonel Crawley which included the following stanza:

Dying man—dying wife—let them lie,
Close-pent in their casement of doom,
Night and day 'neath the sentinel's eye,
Though the sun to white-heat fire the room.[71]

Expressions of outrage were made on the floor of the House of Commons where several radical and reformist Members of Parliament (MPs), especially D.B. Fortescue and the Earl of Shaftesbury, were joined by MPs with a particular interest in reforming the military, notably General De Lacy Evans. The rhetoric of one of the MPs who took up the cause against Crawley became so overheated that the Speaker of the House of Commons had to caution him several times for his intemperate language.[72] So great was the outcry that the Duke of Cambridge, with the support of the War Office, reluctantly directed that Crawley be brought before a court martial in Britain.

The option of trying Crawley in India had been quickly rejected for it was widely believed in India as well as in Britain that he was being protected by Rose and Mansfield. Was Crawley to be tried in India and found innocent, it would not only confirm suspicions of the complicity of the Indian and Bombay Commanders-in-Chief, but also give credence to the belief that military law in practice favoured officers. As one journalist put it, it is impossible to treat courts martial with 'the respect that Englishman usually (and with much reason) accord to the administration of law.'[73] This conviction would linger throughout much of the period, prompting Lord Salisbury in 1875 to request that a report be prepared on the fates of officers tried by courts martial in India.[74] In fact, this report found that of 128 officers brought before a court martial, 99 were found guilty on all charges and 14 on at least one of the charges: only 15 officers were acquitted.

Nevertheless, in the case of Crawley, allegations of official favouritism had some substance. Mansfield had written to Cambridge, telling him that 'never was an army officer tried in this manner as Colonel Crawley has been, and that though he may at times have been intemperate and indiscreet, he had not been more so than many army officers habitually are.'[75] Mansfield confided to Rose that while the two of them were aware of the dangerous spirit of insubordination that prevailed in the Dragoons, the Duke of Cambridge appeared to be willfully blind to the threat.[76] In a letter marked 'very confidential', Mansfield complained that the Duke of Cambridge had weighed in and sent a blistering note to Rose in which Colonel Crawley was criticized for his intemperate language and conduct.[77] Revealingly, if somewhat hypocritically, Mansfield would during his term as Commander-in-Chief of the Indian Army criticize the practice of courts martial on the grounds that when it came to assigning a punishment, the courts tended to be more lenient on officers and much harsher on the rank and file.[78] He correctly attributed this to the fact that the courts martial was comprised of officers who could empathize much more easily with their fellow officers than they could with private soldiers and non-commissioned officers.

The trial proved to be a logistical challenge. Officials in the Bombay Army were directed to make the necessary arrangements to send to

Britain any Indian witnesses, British civilians as well as officers and soldiers from the Sixth Inniskilling Dragoons.[79] It was an expensive undertaking: the P&O Line charged Rs 50,000 alone to transport 13 officers and 129 soldiers to Britain for the trial.[80] There were, however, some difficulties in securing the agreement of the Indian witnesses to travel to Britain. The government solicitor was asked for his opinion as to whether Indian witnesses could be compelled to travel to Britain: he responded in the negative as he did to the follow-up query as to whether their depositions could be taken in India and read before the court.[81] In the end, three Indian witnesses appeared before the court martial at Aldershot: Ardaseer Framjee, a Parsi merchant or sutler, his clerk Cowasjee Mucherjee, also listed as a Parsi, and Salvador Lobo, a Goanese cook attached to the Sixth Dragoons. At one point, the possibility was raised that either the defence or the prosecution could demand that Rose and Mansfield appear as witnesses.[82]

The charges under which Crawley was arraigned before the court martial related to the incarceration and treatment of the Lilley family. The first charge was the familiar 'conduct unbecoming an officer, and to the prejudice of good order and military discipline' and related to his having placed Lilley under close arrest with 'unnecessary and undue severity, whereby the said Regimental Sergeant Major Lilley and his wife were subjected to great and grievous hardships and sufferings', and second and again 'For conduct unbecoming an officer and gentleman, and to the prejudice of good order and military discipline', though in this case for having tried to assign blame for the harsh treatment to the regimental adjutant rather than taking responsibility himself.[83]

The trial opened on 17 November 1863. It lasted just over a month, and on 24 December 1863 Crawley was acquitted of all charges. The case for the prosecution rested upon establishing Lilley's good character as well as Crawley's abuse of authority in ordering Lilley to be incarcerated in such terrible conditions. It was necessary for the prosecution to prove that Lilley was a dependable and sober soldier so as to counter the impression made in the earlier court martial that Lilley's excessive drinking was the cause of his death, and not the conditions in which he had been held. The *Examiner Weekly* reported that Lilley 'remained Sergeant Major of the Inniskellens for seven years, during the whole of which time he never was placed under arrest, or received a reprimand from any officer under whom he served.'[84] Colonel Shute took the stand and testified to Lilley's good conduct as did a number of his fellow sergeants and soldiers, all of whom referred to him with such flattering terms as 'industrious', 'sober', 'conscientious', and 'dependable'. One soldier who took the stand, Private Blake, had been a corporal at the time of Lilley's death, and asserted that when he had been ordered to post sentries at Lilley's quarters, he directed them to take up their position outside the door. He was reduced to the rank of private for failing to order the sentries to watch the prisoner from within his quarters.[85] On the seventh day of the trial, a number of witnesses claimed that when Sergeant Major Cotton queried Crawley as to the propriety of placing Lilley under close arrest when his wife was in such poor health, Crawley lost his temper and retorted that he 'did not care a damn, officer or NCO, an order was an order, and should be obeyed.'[86] The prosecutor at Crawley's trial drew attention to this outrage, reminding the court of Mrs Lilley's predicament, 'the fixed ever present knowledge in her mind that there was about her bed, and about her path, and spying out all her ways, a constantly shifting watchful male stranger, who seemed to be by law not only entitled always to be there, but whose duty it was to be so'.[87]

Crawley's defence did attempt to discredit these testimonials to Lilley's character, including by bringing in one witness who claimed that Lilley was a hardened drinker. No longer the sturdy and dependable cavalry sergeant, he was presented as an ill-educated, uncouth drunkard. The claim that Lilley hastened his own death through excessive drinking, which had first been raised in Mhow only to be discounted by the Duke of Cambridge, resurfaced at Aldershot. Two of the three Indians brought to England as witnesses were liquor sellers in the cantonment bazaar, and the defence relied upon them to provide irrefutable evidence of Lilley's intemperance.[88] Yet when called to the stand, Ardresser Franjee admitted that they had kept no receipts of what they had sold to Lilley, nor did he sell directly to Lilley.[89] Instead, the liquor was purchased by one of Lilley's servants. The prosecution continued to insist that the liquor was intended for Mrs Lilley and had been prescribed by the regimental doctor who provided corroboration in his testimony. However, Surgeon Turnbull had been singled out early on as one of the ringleaders in the alleged conspiracy against Crawley and so his word had been discredited in the initial trial.

More importantly, however, and the issues around which the finding of not guilty eventually hinged, was that Crawley acted appropriately in placing Lilley under close arrest, for these orders had not only been sanctioned by his superiors, but they were necessary to check a dangerous spirit of insubordination within the regiment that if allowed to pass untreated could spread to the rest of the army. It was Crawley's claim that he acted to prevent a mutiny which helps to account for the rapid swing by the press in his favour. As noted by *The Times*, 'a thoroughly insubordinate spirit existed among the officers; that this spirit was spreading downwards; and might have produced mutiny had it reached the men.'[90] In 1863, merely mentioning mutiny was enough to raise alarm, particularly but not exclusively at the margins of the British empire. Even in the metropole, memories of 1857–8 were sufficiently strong that the threat of mutiny had to be taken seriously.

The Times also took the position that Crawley should only be judged on the basis of the charges against him, namely whether he was justified in imposing close arrest on Lilley and whether that in turn contributed to his death. As far as the decision to place Lilley under arrest, Crawley defended himself by saying that the orders came from General Farrell, the garrison commander, and that they had been approved by General Mansfield. He also blamed the surgeons for not informing him of Lilley's deteriorating health, reminding the court that the surgeon had been one of the first to oppose him.[91] Crawley's statement of defence, which he read from notes, and was rumoured to have been written for him by Vernon Harcourt, a lawyer and eventually Chancellor of the Exchequer and who was acknowledged to be one of the best debaters in the House of Commons, took three hours, and was compared by one of Crawley's supporters as equal to Burke's speeches during the trial of Warren Hastings.[92] One of his more memorable statements was that 'Close arrest was necessarily a severe measure, but it was much milder than blowing soldiers from the guns.'[93]

The widespread public antagonism towards Crawley that was so apparent just weeks before dissipated quite quickly. Not surprisingly, a number of his fellow officers rallied to his defence. His legal expenses were picked up by contributions; the Earl of Cardigan, of Crimean War fame, alone was rumoured to have donated £100. As one of Crawley's most outspoken critics, Matthew Higgins, who wrote extensively on military and other topics for *The Times* as well as other papers under the pen name Jacob Omnium, would later lament, 'the popular breeze turned around...'.[94] Perhaps nowhere was this more noticeable than in the pages of *The Times*. It had, in common with much of the British public, taken a very hard line on Crawley's conduct. By the end of the trial, however, it had shifted to a position that was much more favourable to Crawley. In shifting course so dramatically, *The Times* angered Matthew Higgins who retaliated with a blistering attack on J. Walter, the publisher and proprietor of *The Times*. In return, Walter would single out Higgins as one of the people responsible for disseminating false and exaggerated stories that resulted in such an expensive trial.[95]

In seeking to exonerate Crawley of the charges that had been initially levelled against him, the circumstances surrounding the death of Clarissa Lilley were also rewritten to make her appear less the innocent victim of a heartless system. Rather, she was portrayed as a typical working class woman. In the more melodramatic treatments of her incarceration, much was made of the humiliation that she had to undergo, having liniment applied to her chest by her husband within eyesight of the guard. The reworked version, however, argued that given her class background, the standards of modesty that would have been assigned to a woman of better breeding were not applicable to her. *The Times* declared that

We may still pity Mrs Lilley, but it would be affectation to doubt that in many a lodging house of this great city, not to speak of barracks, of workhouses, and of overcrowded cottages, there are many female sufferers subjected to equal indignities and far greater privation without making any demands on our sympathy.[96]

The *Spectator*, which like *The Times*, had initially joined in the condemnations of Colonel Crawley, made a similar point when reflecting upon the verdict of the court martial; it declared that 'Lilley, after all, had risen from the ranks, [and] that the life of a married private soldier is unfortunately not consistent with very fastidious notions of domestic privacy.'[97] Crawley went even further, insisting that having allowed Clarissa to join her husband in close arrest was actually an indulgence—he need not have allowed that. As put forward by his defence counsel, 'What is the proposition of the prosecution? Is it that a man of plethoric habits, who happens to be married, and whose wife may chance to be sick, cannot be subjected to the same military discipline as others? Because, if so, the sooner such men leave the army, the better.'[98] In taking this tack, the defence counsel touched upon an unresolved debate within the army over the costs and benefits of marriage. For every officer who argued that allowing marriage would improve the moral tone and discipline of the army were a number who insisted that marriage weakened the fighting spirit of soldiers and distracted them from their duties.[99]

Anglo-Indians rallied to Crawley in part because of what they argued was the unwarranted interference by the Duke of Cambridge who to them symbolized the gulf which separated them from the British government, and which was characterized by the government's failure to acknowledge what they felt to be their unique circumstances as a beleaguered yet conquering race. One paper expressed this frustration as follows: 'So Lieutenant Colonel Crawley is to be tried in England in order to satisfy public opinion. Another sad proof that India is being governed in the city of Westminster...'[100] The Times of India, which had initially come out strongly against Crawley, had by the time the trial started swung round in his favour, largely because it had realized that it was out of step with Anglo-Indian opinion in India.[101] British readers were told that 'the private letters of many military men from India indicate a state of opinion there more favourable to the accused than could have been considered possible here if a tithe of what has been alleged against him be true.'[102] The Mofussilite, a newspaper from northern India that was particularly popular with army officers, argued in defence of Crawley that 'he is one of the most gentlemanlike, generous, openhanded, humane men that ever was encountered.'[103] Another Anglo-Indian newspaper insisted that Lilley was 'a drunken sot, whose death was hastened, if not altogether caused, by his intemperance.'[104]

Contemporaries were surprised at just how quickly the trial was concluded, particularly given the heated rhetoric of the public discussions that preceded it. Yet if we look closely at public opinion, we find that the boundary between those who defended Crawley and those who opposed him was itself unstable and ultimately could not be maintained. This situation was reminiscent of the trials of other British colonial officials who stood accused of flagrant abuse of power. The Times drew an explicit parallel between this trial and the impeachment of Warren Hastings nearly 100 years before, arguing that 'The moral significance, however, of the two proceedings is essentially the same, and the popular indignation which demanded a most costly investigation into the death of an English soldier was a lesser outburst of the same spirit which dragged the great proconsul to the tribunal of public justice.'[105] But not everyone was as persuaded of Crawley's innocence in the broadest sense. The Manchester Guardian, for example, concluded that while he was technically innocent of the charges brought against him, they were not convinced that he was not guilty of malice and poor leadership.[106] And in Punch, the verdict was reported under the heading of 'The Inniskillings and the Lilleykillings'.[107] Echoes of such sentiments can also be detected in the public reaction two years after Crawley's court martial to the brutal suppression of the Jamaican protest by Governor Eyre in 1865.[108] While the cleavages occasioned by the latter episode penetrated much more deeply into British society, the characteristics of the fault lines were very similar in the ways in which moral and ethical concerns of Eyre's critics were juxtaposed against the security imperatives claimed by his defenders. And both cases triggered debates over the appropriateness of the legal processes in use.

Within a remarkably short period of time, Crawley had been partially rehabilitated—on the day of his acquittal, *The Times* opined 'that he was more sinned against than sinning, and succeeded to a command which would have tried the sagacity of a statesman and the patience of a saint.'[109] The pendulum had swung back. In the words of one newspaper editor, 'It is probably as far from the truth that Colonel Crawley has been scandalously maligned and persecuted, as that he is the monster of cruelty and iniquity that he was at one time represented to be.'[110] The irony was not lost on the editors of *Colburn's United Service Magazine*, a journal popular amongst reform-minded military officers in Britain and India. In their retrospective account of the trial, they sarcastically noted that:

> for fifteen months, no epithets have been too harsh to be applied to Colonel Crawley, no punishment too great for his crimes; now the re-action will run its usual course, and the incarnation of military tyranny be pronounced to have been but the firm, conscientious upholder of necessary military discipline, a modern St Sebastian, who from a sense of duty has submitted in silence to be pierced by the arrows of calumny.[111]

Colonel Crawley's subsequent career, while short, was not adversely affected, even though the Duke of Cambridge pointedly refused to exonerate him completely. He rejoined his regiment on its return from India and accompanied them to their next posting at York. He retired with the rank of Major General in 1868, dying 12 years later. Elaborate memorial tablets to him and his wife were placed in the church of St Stephen's, Hackington, near Canterbury, Kent. The same cannot be said for General Mansfield: the fact that his name did not appear on the list for the Order of the Bath in 1867 was attributed to his involvement in the Crawley case.[112] Crawley's antagonists, who initially had been cast as the victims of this tragedy, did not fare so well. Smales, through the intervention of Queen Victoria, had secured some of his back pay and emigrated to Australia. He was given a pardon, despite Mansfield's protestations, but was never given another posting.[113] The reason for the pardon was that the Judge Advocate General declared that the 'trial at Mhow had not been a fair one', and in particular that Smales never had the opportunity to call for his own witnesses for they had been placed under house arrest.[114] The Lilleys, without whom there would not have been such a high level of public engagement, were quickly forgotten.

The family was buried in Mhow, and discussions of the tragedies that had befallen them quickly faded. A subscription was started at Mhow to erect a monument over the family's grave, but a shortage of funds meant that it was only partially completed.[115] His impoverished parents did receive a small pension of 2s 6d a day.[116] Many of the other officers with whom Crawley had tangled were transferred out of the regiment.

Epilogue

The Lilley family was initially cast as the innocent victims of a cruel and capricious regime, an impression which was well-suited to an era in which institutions such as the British army were coming under harsh criticism from social and political reformers. It had all the characteristics of a political scandal according to the explanation offered by Anna Clark, namely that they 'could have a long-lasting political impact only when they transcended their instigators and protagonists to focus on wider issues, and when they generated political associations with the power to pressure Parliament.'[117] Yet this was a scandal that ultimately lost momentum. Its more melodramatic aspects did not play well with all its audiences, and even those who initially had a hand in its writing, such as The Times, felt that it was necessary to pull back. The public might have more sympathy with the Lilleys than with Crawley, but what Crawley stood for (discipline, order, hierarchy) ultimately mattered more within an imperial context and so in the final editing, the Lilley family was recast as an imperial lumpen proletariat, their deaths tragic, but unavoidably so. Sympathy could be elicited for them but not empathy. In the words of The Times, 'Privacy is a relative term; a sergeant's wife is not accustomed to the same sort of privacy as a fine lady.'[118]

Anglo-Indian society was largely military and hence any tendencies that were thought to undermine military discipline ultimately threatened the safety of the empire. Recent events in India were a constant reminder of just how dependent the British Raj was upon its European soldiers. Consequently, 'The notion in Colonel Crawley's mind was that he had to deal with a mutiny. There had been a mutiny in India, so mutiny was always to be apprehended in India. There had been mutiny in native forces, so mutiny was likely to break out in an English regiment.'[119] When placed in such stark terms, the reasons for this scandal losing momentum become more understandable. In the end, Colonel Crawley was exonerated, for no matter how unsympathetic a character he was, it was what he stood for that ultimately mattered most.

230 Fringes of Empire

I would like to thank Patricia Gordon and Graeme Miller for their assistance in combing through volumes and reels of contemporary newspapers and periodicals. Financial support for the research underpinning this study came from the Social Sciences and Humanities Research Council of Canada.

NOTES AND REFERENCES

1. *Allen's Indian Mail*, 16 July 1863, p. 622.
2. The most recent efforts to recount these events can be found in Byron Farwell, 1989, *Armies of the Raj: From the Mutiny to Independence, 1858–1947*. New York: Norton; and Arthur Hawkey, 1969, *Last Post at Mhow*, London: Jarrolds. The latter is the most extensive study to date, but it is difficult to trace the source of his information as he does not provide any citations. A very brief bibliography indicates that he has used contemporary newspapers and War Office files, but he does not appear to have consulted any private papers, nor a number of the critical pamphlets put out by the protagonists. Of particular interest here are M. Higgins, 1864a, *Correspondence Between J. Walter esq M.P. and J.O. (M. Higgins, esq.)*. London: Thomas Brettell; 1864b, *The Story of the Mhow Court-Martial, with notes and an appendix. By J.O. [Jacob Omnium, pseud., i.e. M.J. Higgins.]*, London: np; and Thomas Smales, 1863, *The Mhow Court Martial on Paymaster Smales. Correspondence Between the Military Authorities and Paymaster Smales, etc.* London: np. Matthew Higgins, who wrote under the pseudonym Jacob Omnium, was an outspoken advocate of military reform, and championed the abolition of the purchase system through pamphlets as well as articles in *The Times*. See, for example, 1857, *Observations on the Purchase System in the Army and on Jacob Omnium's Letters to 'The Times'*. London: George Earle.
3. *Mofussilite*, 17 July 1863.
4. Wood to Elgin, 3 July 1863, MS Eur F78/L.B.13, Oriental and India Office Collections (hereafter OIOC).
5. The heavily gendered readings of the Indian Rebellion of 1857–8, and particularly the prevalence of reports of European women being raped by Indian rebels despite the absence of any evidence, has been studied in Nancy L. Paxton, 1998, *Writing under the Raj: Gender, Race, and Rape in the British Colonial Imagination, 1830–1947*, New Brunswick, NJ: Rutgers University Press; Jenny Sharpe, 1993, *Allegories of Empire: The Figure of Woman in the Colonial Text*, Minneapolis: University of Minnesota Press; and Alison Blunt, 2000, 'Embodying War: British Women and Domestic Defilement in the Indian "Mutiny" 1857–8', *Journal of Historical Geography*, vol. 26, pp. 403–28.
6. *Penny Illustrated Paper*, 21 November 1863, p. 1.
7. Bernard Porter, 2004, *The Absent-Minded Imperialists: Empire, Society and Culture in Britain*, Oxford: Oxford University Press.

8. Philippa Levine, 2003, *Prostitution, Race and Politics: Policing Venereal Disease in the British Empire*, London: Routledge.
9. *Manchester Guardian*, 9 June 1863, p. 2.
10. *Examiner Weekly*, 21 November 1863, p. 746.
11. *Allen's Indian Mail*, 21 November 1863, p. 1007.
12. 'The British Common Soldier', *New York Times*, 28 June 1863. While the *New York Times* obviously found the story of the Mhow Court Martial to be of interest to its readers, it did manage to mangle some aspects of the story. For example, they set the original scandal and trial in Calcutta rather than Mhow.
13. *Illustrated London News*, 29 November 1863, p. 541 and 544; 12 December 1863, p. 584.
14. *The Times*, 2 June 1866.
15. *Manchester Guardian*, 1 December 1863, p. 3. The same article reported that American crimps or recruiters were hanging about Aldershot trying to recruit experienced cavalrymen for service in the Union Army.
16. 'The British Common Soldier', *New York Times*, 28 June 1863.
17. It was nicknamed the Black Dragoons on account of their black facings on their uniforms. The regiment was first raised in the late seventeenth century. For its history, see E.S. Jackson, 1909, *The Inniskilling Dragoons: The Records of an Old Heavy Cavalry Regiment*, London: Arthur L. Humphreys.
18. Mansfield to Rose, 7 July 1862, Add. MS 42806 British Library (hereafter BL).
19. Mansfield to Rose, 4 June 1863, Add. MS 42806 BL.
20. Mansfield to Rose, 7 July 1862, Add. MS 42806 BL.
21. Matthew James Higgins, 1864, *The Story of the Mhow Court-Martial, with notes and an appendix. By J.O. [Jacob Omnium, pseud., i.e. M.J. Higgins.]*, London: np, p. 3.
22. *The Times*, 14 May 1858.
23. *Homeward Mail*, 22 August 1862, p. 701.
24. Mrinalini Sinha, 2005, 'Britishness, Clubbability, and the Colonial Public Sphere', in Tony Ballantyne and Antoinette Burton (eds), *Bodies in Contact: Rethinking Colonial Encounters in World History*, Durham, NC: Duke University Press, p. 187.
25. One of the best, if often sanctimonious, treatments of cantonment life in this period is offered by W.D. Arnold, 1854, *Oakfield; or Fellowship in the East*, 2nd edn, London: Longman, Brown, Green, and Longmans. Elizabeth Buettner's work provides an important examination of the place of rank and status in the late nineteenth and early twentieth century Anglo-Indian world; 2004, *Empire Families: Britons and Late Imperial India*, Oxford: Oxford University Press. With the exception of works by Myrna Trustram and Noel Williams, the lives of soldiers' wives have largely been neglected. Myrna Trustram, 1984, *Women of the Regiment: Marriage and the Victorian Army*, Cambridge: Cambridge University Press; Colonel Noel T. St John Williams, 1988, *Judy O'Grady and the Colonel's Lady: The Army Wife and Camp Follower since 1660*, London: Brassey's Defence Publishers.
26. *Homeward Mail*, 16 November 1863, p. 974.

27. *Homeward Mail*, 5 November 1863, p. 945.

28. Higgins, *The Story of the Mhow Court-Martial*.

29. Ibid., p. 8.

30. One of the standard authorities in nineteenth century British military law was William Hough; 1825, *The Practice of Courts Martial*, 2nd edn, London: Kingsbury, Parbury and Allen; 1836, *Simplification of His Majesty's and Hon'ble E.I. Company's Mutiny Acts and Articles of War*, Calcutta: Huttmann; 1839, *Military Law Authorities*. Calcutta: W. Thacker; 1855, *Precedents in Military Law: Including the Practice of Courts Martial*, London: W.H. Allen.

31. For the White Mutiny, see Peter Stanley, 1998, *White Mutiny: British Military Culture in India*, London: Hurst. The operation of military law in post-rebellion India is the subject of Kaushik Roy, 2006, 'Spare the Rod, Spoil the Soldier? Crime and Punishment in the Army of India, 1860–1913', *Journal of the Society for Army Historical Research*, vol. 84, pp. 9–33. Roy provides some fascinating evidence of the willingness of some British soldiers to commit crimes as a means of getting out of India and out of military service.

32. Thomas Smales, 1863, *The Mhow Court Martial on Paymaster Smales. Correspondence between the Military Authorities and Paymaster Smales, etc.* London: np, p. 10. According to the Manchester Guardian, Farrell, was an 'aged and broken-down man', *The Manchester Guardian*, 15 June 1863, p. 4.

33. Mansfield to Rose, 11 January 1863, Add. MS 42806 BL.

34. These relationships are more closely in Douglas M. Peers, 1997, '"Those Noble Exemplars of the True Military Tradition"; Constructions of the Indian Army in the Mid-Victorian Press', *Modern Asian Studies*, vol. 31, pp. 109–42.

35. Mansfield to Rose, 30 November 1862, ff.146 Add. MS 42806 BL.

36. Ibid.

37. Elgin to Wood, 23 September 1862, MS Eur F83/4 OIOC.

38. *Manchester Guardian*, 15 June 1863, p. 4.

39. *Allen's Indian Mail*, 27 October 1862, p. 851; see also *Homeward Mail*, 5 November 1863, p. 951.

40. *Manchester Guardian*, 9 June 1863, p. 2.

41. Wood to Elgin, 2 May 1863, MS Eur F78/L.B.13 OIOC.

42. The politicization of the officers of the Indian Army is an issue taken up in a number of works, including Raymond Callahan, 1972, *The East India Company and Army Reform, 1783–1798*. Cambridge, Mass.: Harvard University Press; and Douglas M. Peers, 1995, *Between Mars and Mammon: Colonial Armies and the Garrison State in Early-Nineteenth Century India*, London: Tauris.

43. Thomas Smales, *The Mhow Court Martial on Paymaster Smales*, p. 9.

44. Mansfield to Rose, 5 August 1863, Add. MS 42806 BL.

45. *The Times*, 21 December 1863, p. 8.

46. *Manchester Guardian*, 15 June 1863.

47. Letter from the Military Accountant, Bombay Military Proceedings, no. 1902, 26 June 1863, P/366/6 OIOC.

48. Mansfield to Rose, 24 June 1863, Add. MS 42806 BL.

49. Mansfield to Rose, 30 November 1862, Add. MS 42806 BL.

50. *Bengal Hurkaru*, 15 October 1863.

51. *Examiner Weekly*, 6 June 1863, p. 354.
52. Higgins, *Story of the Mhow Court-Martial*, p. 67.
53. Mansfield to Rose, 11 January 1863, Add. MS 42806 BL.
54. Mansfield to Rose, 20 January 1863, Add. MS 42806 BL.
55. *Indian Punch*, 1 August 1863, p. 84.
56. *Mofussilite*, 17 July 1863.
57. *Spectator*, 20 June 1863, p. 2138.
58. *Spectator*, 27 June 1863, p. 2162.
59. Mansfield to Rose, 24 June 1863, Add. MS 42806 BL.
60. *Manchester Guardian*, 24 June 1863, p. 2.
61. *The Times*, 15 June 1863, p. 9.
62. J.M. Hichberger, 1988, *Images of the Army: The Military in British Art, 1815–1914*, Manchester: Manchester University Press.
63. Many of his writings have been collected into William Howard Russell, 1957, *My Indian Mutiny Diary*: London: Cassell and 1855, *The War from the Landing at Gallipoli to the Death of Lord Raglan*, London: George Routledge.
64. Jharna Gourlay, 2004, *Florence Nightingale and the Health of the Raj*, London: Ashgate. But see Mark Harrison, 1994, *Public Health in British India; Anglo-Indian Preventive Medicine, 1859-1914*, Cambridge: Cambridge University Press, for a more critical assessment of Nightingale's impact. On the subject of the health of British troops, see also Philip D. Curtin, 1989, *Death by Migration; Europe's Encounter with the Tropical World in the Nineteenth Century*, Cambridge: Cambridge University Press; and Douglas M. Peers, 1999, 'Imperial Vice: Sex, Drink and the Health of British Troops in North Indian Cantonments, 1800-1858', in David Killingray and David Omissi (eds), *Guardians of Empire: the Armed Forces of the Colonial Powers, c.1700-1964*, Manchester: Manchester University Press, pp. 25–52.
65. For example, *Homeward Mail*, 5 October 1863. See also Florence Nightingale, 1863, chapter on soldiers' wives which appeared in her *Observations on the Evidence contained in the Stational Reports submitted to her by the Royal Commission on the Sanitary State of the Army in India*, London: Edward Stanford, pp. 82–90.
66. Anon., 1845, 'English Women in Hindustan', *Calcutta Review*, vol. 4. p. 126–7.
67. Mrs Ward, 1850, 'Married Soldiers in the Army', *Colburn's United Service Magazine*, vol. 3, p. 49.
68. See for example Henry Morley and W.H. Wills, 1855, 'The Soldier's Wife', *Household Words*, vol. 265, pp. 278–80.
69. Higgins, *Story of the Mhow Court-Martial*, p. 29.
70. Porter, *Absent-Minded Imperialists*, p. 84.
71. 'Crawley and Lilley', *Punch*, 20 June 1863, pp. 256–7.
72. *Homeward Mail*, 19 June 1863, p. 522.
73. *Penny Illustrated Paper*, 21 November 1863, p. 2.
74. Memorandum of Officers tried by Courts Martial in India, 1861–75, 1875, L/MIL/5/674 OIOC.
75. Mansfield to Rose, 11 January 1863, Add. MS 42806 BL.
76. Ibid.

77. Mansfield to Bruce, 1 March 1863, Add. MS 43992 BL.
78. Roy, 'Spare the Rod', pp. 18–19.
79. Judicial Letter to India, 3 July 1863, no. 35, Bombay Military Proceedings, 30 July 1863, no. 2272, P/366/6 OIOC.
80. Letter from the Quartermaster General, no. 1893, 27 August 1863, Bombay Military Proceedings, no. 2644, 4 September 1863, P/366/6 OIOC.
81. Letter from the Adjutant General, no. 1342, 21 August 1863, Bombay Military Proceedings, no. 2662, 7 September 1863, P/366/6 OIOC.
82. Wood to Elgin, 3 July 1863, MS Eur F78/L.B.13 OIOC.
83. 'Editor's Portfolio', 1863, Colburn's United Service Magazine, no. 121, p. 575.
84. Examiner Weekly, 16 May 1863, p. 308.
85. Examiner Weekly, 21 November 1863, p. 746.
86. Examiner Weekly, 28 November 1863, p. 761.
87. The Times, 21 December 1863, p. 8.
88. Allen's Indian Mail, 14 December 1863, p. 1063.
89. Homeward Mail, 14 December 1863, p. 1073.
90. The Times, 15 January 1864, p. 8.
91. The relationship between Crawley and the medical establishment needs to be examined more closely—there were insinuations that he regularly ignored their advice when it came to the health and comfort of troops under his command.
92. Anon., 1864, 'The Court Martial of Colonel Crawley', Colburn's United Service Magazine, vol. 1, p. 119.
93. Homeward Mail, 23 December 1863, p. 1096.
94. M. Higgins to J. Walter, 18 January 1864, in M. Higgins and J. Walter, Correspondence between J. Walter Esq M.P. and J.O. (M. Higgins, Esq.), London: Thomas Brettell, pp. 4–5.
95. J. Walter to M. Higgins, 31 January 1864, Correspondence between J. Walter Esq M.P. and J.O. (M. Higgins, Esq.), London: Thomas Brettell, p. 11.
96. The Times, 8 December 1863, p. 9.
97. Spectator, 26 December 1863, p. 2910.
98. The Times, 8 December 1863, p. 8.
99. Douglas M. Peers, 2006, 'The Raj's Other Great Game: Policing the Sexual Frontiers of the Indian Army in the First Half of the Nineteenth Century', in Anupama Rao and Stephen Pierce (eds), Discipline and the Other Body: Correction, Corporeality, Colonialism, Durham, NC: Duke University Press, pp. 115–50. See also Trustram, Women of the Regiment, pp. 29–50.
100. Mofussilite, 28 July 1863.
101. Excerpts from Indian newspapers in Homeward Mail, 21 October 1863, p. 902.
102. Homeward Mail, 29 October 1863, p. 927.
103. Mofussilite, 17 July 1863.
104. Allen's Indian Mail, 27 October 1862, p. 851.
105. The Times, 8 December 1863, p. 6. For a recent discussion of the metropolitan ramifications of imperial scandal, see Nicholas Dirks, 2006, The Scandal

of *Empire: India and the Creation of Imperial Britain*, Cambridge, Mass.: Harvard University Press.
106. *Manchester Guardian*, 26 December 1863, p. 4.
107. *Punch*, 23 January 1864, p. 34.
108. Qualms over the legal processes unleashed with the prosecution of Governor Eyre are the subject of R.W. Kostal, 2005, *A Jurisprudence of Power: Victorian Empire and the Rule of Law*, Oxford: Oxford University Press.
109. *The Times*, 24 December. 1863, p. 8.
110. *Homeward Mail*, 23 December 1863, p. 1090.
111. Anon., 'The Court Martial of Colonel Crawley', pp. 104–5.
112. Ripon to Mansfield, 16 March 1867, Add. MS 43619 BL.
113. Memorandum by Lieut General Sir W.R. Mansfield, 1864, Add. MS 42806 BL.
114. Higgins, *Story of the Mhow Court-Martial*, p. i.
115. A drawing of the monument can be seen in *Illustrated London News*, 29 November 1863, p. 544.
116. *The Times*, 3 July 1863, p. 12.
117. Anna Clark, 2003, *Scandal: The Sexual Politics of the British Constitution*. Princeton: Princeton University Press, p. 210.
118. *The Times*, 24 December 1863, p. 8.
119. *Examiner Weekly*, 26 December 1863, p. 825.

Literary Production at the Edge of Empire
The Crisis of Patronage in Southern India
under Colonial Rule

Lisa Mitchell

> In many villages where formerly there were schools, there are now none;
> and in many others where there were large schools, now only a few children
> of the most opulent are taught, others being unable, from poverty, to attend,
> or to pay what is demanded.
>
> A.D. Campbell, Collector of Bellary District, 1823[1]

> They now read proofs at printing shops just to stay alive,
> Or teach Telugu to the white Huns,
> Expound religion in the houses of those grocers who give them credit.
> Phenomenal scholars have been humbled. Times have changed.
>
> Cellapilla Venkata Sastri (1870–1950)[2]

The nineteenth century has been celebrated as a period of unusually
dynamic literary activity within the British-ruled Indian subcontinent.
The rise of printing in vernacular languages, the formation of new
native literary societies and library movements, the appearance of the
essay and the novel as new literary forms in Indian languages, and the
circulation of vernacular newspapers and journals have all been cited
as evidence of a new 'Golden Age' of vernacular literary production
during the period of British imperial rule.[3] Implicit in the accounts—
both Indian and foreign—that celebrate the dynamism of nineteenth
century transitions in Indian textual production is the recognition of the

colonial presence as the motivating force for dispelling the preceding 'Dark Ages' and creating the conditions necessary for the cultivation of the many new changes in literary production. Works in both English and Indian languages have documented in great detail the European influences on particular genres of vernacular literary production.[4] Yet even the more critical and less celebratory strains of scholarship that have focused on the reconfiguration of local forms of knowledge under colonial rule have devoted their attention primarily to those practices, genres, and domains that were of interest to the colonial state and its British representatives. They pay little attention to the lives and concerns of nineteenth century Indian poets, writers, and scholars beyond their service to the colonial administration and project of modernization, and offer no attention at all to those activities and domains in which the British took little interest.

Bernard Cohn, for example, concludes his path-breaking and highly influential essay, 'The Command of Language and the Language of Command'—which laid the basis for further explorations of the influences of colonialism on the emergence of new forms of Indian knowledge—with an acknowledgment of this neglected focus.[5] His final paragraph is the only place in his entire article where he pays any attention at all to what Indian poets, manipulators of other textual forms, and influencers of local opinion may have been up to during the many decades spent under colonial rule. In his final sentences, Cohn concludes his discussion of European domestication of Indian languages by commenting that:

The delineation of the cumulative effect of the results of the first half-century of the objectification and reordering through the application of European scholarly methods on Indian thought and culture is beyond the scope of this essay. The Indians who increasingly became drawn into the process of transformation of their own traditions and modes of thought were, however, far from passive. In the long run the authoritative control which the British tried to exercise over new social and material technologies was taken over by Indians and put to purposes which led to the ultimate erosion of British authority. The consciousness of Indians at all levels in society was transformed as they refused to become specimens in a European-controlled museum of an archaic stage in world history.[6]

In short, although he acknowledges the existence of dynamics beyond the scope of his article, Cohn's work, and the English writings of those who have followed him, have left us with a clear picture only of the British themselves, their concerns and agendas, and the domains of Indian culture and practice that they explicitly patronized and took interest in, even as they have examined the new forms of knowledge produced by colonialism. Such writings have given us virtually no insight at all into those domains in which the British took no interest— those domains at the very fringes of imperial concern. With a few very narrow exceptions discussed later, these marginalized domains included, but were not limited to, both vernacular education and vernacular literary production.

While scholars of medieval and early modern South Asia have made significant interventions in countering this representation of the nineteenth century as a uniquely dynamic era of textual production, they have done so primarily by making us aware of the literary dynamism of the period immediately prior to the East India Company's administrative ascendance. Velcheru Narayana Rao and David Shulman, for example, have drawn our attention to the richness of literary production in southern India during the immediate pre-colonial period.[7] Yet one can forward a similar argument using evidence from the nineteenth century itself. Focusing on nineteenth century Telugu literary and other textual production within the Madras Presidency as a case in point, I offer in the following pages evidence that (a) nineteenth century vernacular literary and textual domains were at the very fringes of the colonial empire's concerns; (b) when viewed from the perspective of Indian literary and textual cultures, the nineteenth century can best be characterized as a crisis of patronage, exacerbated by a decline in accessibility to education; and (c) literary and other forms of textual production appear to be so dynamic within the nineteenth century in large part due to the new reorganization of textual forms of knowledge, literary canons, and audiences along strictly linguistic lines by the end of the nineteenth century.

Of these three interrelated arguments, it is the second point which can be seen to have had the most significant and obvious ramifications. What I am calling the 'crisis of patronage' within vernacular literary production is not fully resolved until the formation—at first experimental, and later more substantial and enduring—of new audiences capable of acting for the first time as collective patrons, replacing the individual rulers and other patrons of literature of earlier eras. Indeed, I argue that it is the creative responses of members of the south Indian literati, displaced from their earlier sources of patronage, who are largely responsible for the creation of the new collective patrons who eventually come to see themselves as groups with common shared interests defined in relation to particular languages. In other words, it is due to these individuals that entities now regarded as natural collectives, such as the 'Telugu people', the 'Tamil people', the 'Kannada people', and so forth, were first imagined and brought into being. What appear in retrospect to be the emergence of vibrant new vernacular literatures, are, in fact, the regrouping of oral and textual forms—some new and some old—in relation to particular vernacular languages and the new audiences actively created in relation to these languages. As such, the crisis of patronage and its resolution form the beginning and end points for my discussion in this essay.

THE CRISIS

What I have identified as a crisis in patronage is linked to a larger transitional crisis in literary and textual production in southern India that occurred during the nineteenth century. One feature of the larger intellectual landscape that influenced textual production was the marked decline in education that had appeared by the early decades of the nineteenth century. Although rarely acknowledged by either colonial or post-colonial writers, the East India Company's economic policies had very real negative implications for the access to educational opportunities on the part of the colony's subjects. In an uncommon moment of colonial acknowledgment of British responsibility for the impoverishment of the subcontinent, A.D. Campbell—then Collector of Bellary District—wrote in 1823 of the ways in which the East India Company's policies and practices had diminished native education. 'Imperfect, however, as the present education of the natives is,' wrote Campbell, 'there are few who possess the means to command it for their children.'[8] It had not always been this way, he continued, writing that today, 'of nearly a million souls in this district, not 7,000 are now at schools',[9] a dramatic decrease from earlier days.

That the source of this deterioration lay in the hands of the Company government is something about which Campbell is quite clear, and his comments therefore deserve to be quoted at some length:

I am sorry to state, that this is ascribable to the gradual but general impoverishment of the country. The means of the manufacturing classes have been of late years greatly diminished by the introduction of our own European manufactures in lieu of the Indian cotton fabrics. The removal of many of our troops from our own territories to the distant frontiers of our newly subsidized allies has also, of late years, affected the demand for grain; the transfer of the capital of the country from the native governments and their officers, who liberally expended it in India, to Europeans, restricted by law from employing it even temporarily in India, and daily drawing it from the land, has likewise tended to this effect, which has not been alleviated by a less rigid enforcement of the revenue due to the state. The greater part of the middling and lower classes of the people are now unable to defray the expenses incident upon the education of their offspring, while their necessities require the assistance of their children as soon as their tender limbs are capable of the smallest labour.[10]

Such observations suggest that the crisis in literary production that I have identified extended from both the very bottom of the production chain—the availability of basic primary education, to the very top—the sources of patronage which acted as sponsors, discussed in the next section, affecting in the process the entire system involved in producing and sustaining a literary culture.

The early decades of the nineteenth century also saw the use of printing presses—which had been restricted within the Madras Presidency during the second half of the eighteenth century to the printing of single sheet forms, proclamations, and pamphlets—expand to the printing of periodicals and books. The first printing press in the Madras Presidency was acquired during the British siege of French-controlled Pondicherry in 1761, and carried to Madras.[11] Because the East India Company administration was not interested in maintaining the press themselves, they gave it to missionaries of the Society for the Promotion of Christian Knowledge (SPCK) in Vepery, on the outskirts of Madras town, where it could be used by the missionaries whenever it was not needed for official jobs.[12] Initially, the press seems to have been little used for the printing of books. As B.S. Kesavan has written, the press was used primarily for 'proclamations and such for the Company, alphabets and calendars for the missionaries.'[13] Some of the only printed items that have been preserved from this period are 'a single-sheet powers of attorney in English and a page of herbal remedies in Portuguese, both from 1764,' and a calendar for 1767.[14] Graham Shaw has found evidence that Francis W. Ellis, who was at the time employed by the Madras Mint, may have been the first to prepare a set of Telugu type in 1800. But parallel to the very limited use of English typesetting only for things like government forms, bills of credit, and flyers, Ellis apparently used his new Telugu type initially in November of 1800 to prepare 2,000 copies of a 'Government advertisement respecting inoculation.'[15] No copies have survived. Katharine Smith Diehl has also suggested that unlike the College of Fort William in Calcutta, which had a variety of independent printers it could rely upon, the Government at Fort St George in Madras was more limited in its options. She has found evidence that much of the government's early printing was done by the Orphan Asylum Press (also referred to as The Madras Male Asylum Press, or simply The Asylum

Press) in Egmore, Madras.[16] It is not clear exactly when the Government of Madras first acquired and began using a press of its own under its own name.[17] However, in 1812, the same year that the College of Fort St George was established by the Madras government, money was also made available for the establishment of a college press.[18] A.D. Campbell's *A Grammar of the Teloogoo Language*, apparently one of the very first books printed by the College Press, was published in 1816. Yet none of these earliest printing efforts were intended for the education of the native population of Madras Presidency; rather, even the grammars and textbooks produced were intended only for the East India Company's civil servants who had just arrived from England.

It was not until 1820, and the formation of the Madras School Book Society, that efforts first began to be directed toward the production of schoolbooks for use by local students. Supported primarily through donations and subscriptions from private citizens, many of whom were also civil servants, the government was not yet officially involved in the publication of textbooks for native education, their priority being textbooks for use by European civil servants acquiring vernacular languages. In 1826, Thomas Munro, then Governor of the Madras Presidency and a supporter of native education, allocated Rs 700 a month to the School Book Society specifically for the printing of textbooks to be used for native education, and for the salaries of teachers willing to prepare them, though this was slow to be implemented.[19] The little attention that was given to vernacular education was directed toward 'pruning Oriental literatures of their undesirable elements.'[20] Although, as Gauri Viswanathan has carefully pointed out, 'political philosophy and cultural policy converged to work toward clearly discernible common ends' during the first two-and-a-half decades of the nineteenth century, this period of British rule, 'appears as a period of relative inactivity in education.'[21] The very few actions taken in the first half of the 1820s to reform the teaching of language in native schools were a combination of local and private European initiative, and were not under official patronage of the East India Company administration. By the time the government administration did decide to take a hand in native education, debates over the most appropriate medium of instruction had resolved themselves in favour of English (with the English Education Act of 1935), and all pretence of support for vernacular education was abandoned by the colonial state.[22] Even the Telugu and other language pundits hired by the College of Fort St George were appointed only for the benefit of the language-learning goals of British officials. The limited state patronage given to the publication of Telugu (and other vernacular languages) books was similarly directed toward the benefit of European students of language rather than native students, suggesting that vernacular textual production was indeed on the very fringes of imperial concern.

NINETEENTH CENTURY PATRONAGE

Additional evidence that the colonial state failed to act as an effective patron of vernacular literary, scholarly, and other textual production can be seen both through the occasional writings of Telugu literary historians and through a close examination of the lives of nineteenth century writers affected by the crisis as they creatively struggled to find and bring into existence new sources of patronage. In his 13-volume history of Telugu literature, *Samagra Andhra Sahityam (Complete Telugu Literature)*, the twentieth century literary historian Arudra designates the period typically viewed as high colonialism—from the mid-nineteenth to the early twentieth century—as the *Zamindari Yugam*, or the era of landlord-estates.[23] His emphasis on the *zamindari* rather than the colonial state in his characterization of the era is surprising in light of the overwhelming emphasis on British colonial influences during this period made by most other writers. His periodization is even more striking given his labelling of the preceding era as the *Kumpini Yugam* (Company Era), with its explicit reference to the British East India Company. Indeed, his labels only make sense if we take into account what would have been the single most significant factor in a nineteenth century poet or writer's life—the availability of a patron to provide a livelihood and support an author's creative efforts. From Arudra's account, it is clear that what is most significant in defining this period are the increasingly diminishing sources of patronage available to scholars and poets.

Velcheru Narayana Rao echoes Arudra's recognition of the reorganization of literary patronage around the growing emasculation and impoverishment of princes, petty rulers, landlords, and tax farmers of the era when he writes:

During the late nineteenth and early twentieth centuries, literary and cultural patronage centred around small kings. These royal patrons were mainly tax farmers for the British rulers. In the absence of real power, these little kings tried to make up for it in the world of literature and culture. Following the style of the royal patrons of the past centuries, they supported scholars and poets within their limited resources. But their world was shrinking as more and more urban centres were opening to English education and the benefits of modern learning. Some of the zamindars themselves began to patronize new learning by supporting English educational institutions, while others entertained Sanskrit and Telugu alone. If the colonial cities and institutions received direct impact of the social reforms...the zamindari centres gave rise to a more nuanced response to science, history, and morality while trying to keep their respect for the indigenous practices.[24]

In his *The Hollow Crown*, Nicholas Dirks has similarly emphasized the displacement of energy into cultural arenas of representation as a response to the British colonial practice of maintaining Indian princes and petty rulers as symbolic heads of state while simultaneously emptying them of all political power, authority, and decision making.[25] In the context of Bengal, Satyajit Ray's famous film, *Jalsaghar (The Music Room)*, paints a portrait of the zamindari investment in the cultural domain in the face of lost political power.[26]

As these works make clear, there is no doubt that the interests, policies, and agendas of British rule made a profound impact on the relationship between literary production and power in southern India. Yet rather than regarding this statement as an endpoint in itself and viewing vernacular literary production as an impotent domain existing only in lieu of 'real' power, unworthy of serious investigation, this essay takes these observations as its starting point. By considering the nineteenth century literary activities of those excluded from the purview of the colonial state as worthy of sustained analysis despite their marginality in the eyes of the state, this essay seeks to better understand how vernacular writers and scholars on the fringes of the colonial state used their literary activities and efforts to adapt to their changing circumstances. In the process, these scholars effectively helped to reshape the very conditions of knowledge production in southern India.

In response to the unprecedented crisis of patronage that occurred during the nineteenth century, local scholars and poets put tremendous creative energy into trying to generate new sources of support and patronage. In the remainder of this section I discuss two individuals who represent two endpoints of the creative energies—not all of which were successful—that went into attempting to bring into being new formations of patronage. Although some of these efforts included the colonial state or its individual administrators among the targets of the appeals made for support, it is nevertheless clear that these efforts were occurring on the fringes of empire.

Although ultimately his efforts may not have been completely successful, one of the earliest and arguably most creative responses to the crisis of patronage can be seen in the life and activities of Kavali Venkata Ramaswami. Born in the last decades of the eighteenth century, Ramaswami belonged to a community of south Indian *karanams*—multilingual village-level document writers, accountants, and administrative advisors well-versed in matters of land use, local history, and dispute settlement, and accustomed to acting as advisors to rulers and landlords.[27] His father descended from a line of hereditary ministers to the Vijayanagaram sovereigns, suggesting a long history of dependency upon official patronage. Two of Ramaswami's elder brothers, Kavali Venkata Boraiah and Kavali Venkata Lakshmaiah, carried on this lineage of dependency on official patronage by becoming two of the most important assistants to Colonel Colin Mackenzie, the first Surveyor General of India. In addition to his official duties, Mackenzie spent much of his energy amassing an enormous archive of local history, manuscripts, inscriptions, and other forms of local knowledge with the help of an army of assistants like the Kavali brothers.

Although we know from Mackenzie's correspondence that Ramaswami never occupied the same position of importance that his two brothers did, it is clear that he was also employed by Mackenzie at some point during the first two decades of the nineteenth century, and when Mackenzie left the Madras Presidency in 1818 for Calcutta, it appears that Ramaswami also followed him there. When Mackenzie died in 1821, or possibly even earlier than this, Ramaswami found himself without a patron, and it was only then that his ingenuity appears to have really kicked in as he struggled to invent new sources of patronage to replace the single individuals who had provided patronage to his forebears and elder brothers. Ramaswami spent the next three decades collecting subscriptions for a wide range of publications which appear calculated to appeal to his new subscriber/patrons—a mixture of Europeans and prominent Indian merchants. Despite this clear ingenuity, it is not completely clear that Ramaswami was successful, and his published works leave a trail that finds Ramaswami in Calcutta in the 1820s, Madras in the 1830s, and Bombay in the 1840s, possibly attesting to the difficulty he had in finding patrons to sustain him. Most of his publications bear the names of long lists of subscribers at the back of each edition—sometimes well over 100 per publication. And just as earlier poets flattered and glorified a king or other single wealthy patron and his lineage, Ramaswami and those who followed him similarly can be seen to be attempting to flatter the sensibilities of their new collective audience/patrons by creating and glorifying a common shared history for them.

Ramaswami is arguably one of the first Indian writers to attempt to appeal to a collective audience rather than composing works on behalf of a single powerful patron. His earliest publications were a set of three items published in 1827–9, using the Deccan region as the foundation for their content. All three used materials collected as part of the Mackenzie manuscripts, suggesting that Ramaswami either kept copies for himself or, more likely, continued to have access to the manuscript collection following Mackenzie's death. It is significant that Mackenzie himself never published anything from his collection, so, in this, Ramaswami shows initiative in utilizing the collection for particular ends—ends quite different from those Mackenzie may have intended. In 1827—the same decade in which A.D. Campbell remarked on the deterioration of education in the Madras Presidency—Ramaswami produced what was likely the first, or at least one of the very first, privately commissioned lithographed maps in India, given that the lithographic technology had only recently been introduced in India. His effort was entitled *A New Map of the Ancient Division of the Deckan.*[28] The following year, in 1828, he published a companion to this work, entitled *Descriptive and Historical Sketches of Cities and Places in the Dekkan*, a region defined by Ramaswami as 'that part of India which lies south of the Vyndhia mountains.'[29] And in 1829, Ramaswami published his third work, entitled *Biographical Sketches of Dekkan Poets*, containing descriptions of poets from a wide range of time periods who composed in Sanskrit, Telugu, Tamil, or Marathi, whose only connection was that all had lived within the Deccan at some point in the past.[30]

What is unique about all three of these texts is their reliance on the geographical territory of the Deccan as the foundation for organization and inclusion of the content presented. Never before had there been an attempt to organize history writing or anthologize literary production solely with reference to a geographical territory that did not explicitly correspond with a political entity. The region Ramaswami identifies as the Deccan on his map and within his *Descriptive and Historical Sketches* includes portions of many different political territories of the nineteenth and earlier centuries, not any single one, and his *Biographical Sketches* includes discussions of literary figures who composed in at least four different languages. Both historical narratives and literary production up until the nineteenth century were typically organized around either a particular ruler, court, or dynasty, or in relation to a particular sect, religious leader, or lineage (genealogical or intellectual). Texts were associated with particular geographical territories only to the extent that those territories reflected the domain of a ruler or dynasty, with the territory being secondary to the dynasty as the foundational organizing principle. Indeed, a poet's decisions regarding content were usually shaped such that his patron's sensibilities were effectively flattered, emphasizing notable ancestral or political connections to present a dynasty's history in a way that created and enhanced its power, and 'forgetting' less successful or less flattering forebears. It is my argument that Ramaswami employed many of these same strategies in attempting to cultivate and appeal to a reading public as a new form of collective patron that would find the Deccan a recognizable basis for identity and be able to relate themselves and their own pasts to its poets, places, and cities.

While Ramaswami's attempts to use the Deccan region and its poets as a constructed lineage for his new collective of patrons may not have succeeded in the long run, later attempts to construct collective lineages on the basis of vernacular languages rather than multilingual regions clearly were successful. During the first half of the nineteenth century, the emergence of linguistic regions as the defining basis for collective audiences capable of acting as patrons was by no means already a foregone conclusion, regardless of how natural such entities may appear today. It is not until the very last decades of the nineteenth century that we first begin to see the initial very hesitant attempts to imagine such audiences-cum-collective patrons along explicitly linguistic lines.[31]

In 1893, the writer Guruzada Sri Ramamurti opened the preface to the second edition of his *Kavi Jivitamulu*, or *Lives of Poets*, with an appeal (*vijnapanamu*) addressed to all those having affection for the language of the Telugu country (*telugu desa bhasha abhimanulu*).[32] In doing so, he was arguably one of the very first (if not the first) to imagine, address, and explicitly solicit support from a group of patrons defined solely through their shared relationship to the Telugu language. Yet it is clear that his hope that his intended audience—those who shared affection for the Telugu language—might collectively recognize a glorious shared past in reading his literary history of exclusively Telugu poets, and that they might identify with this past and claim it as their own lineage, was something Sri Ramamurti was uncertain about. Indeed, his uncertainty attests to the fact that imagining such an entity was an absolute novelty. In other words, an already recognizable and self-conscious Telugu 'people' clearly did not already exist as such. We can see this uncertainty in his descriptions of the first 1878 edition of his *Kavi Jivitamulu* which he describes in his preface to the second edition. He writes in his 1893 second edition that his earlier edition had been an experiment to discover whether there was indeed interest in such a work among his fellow countrymen (*desastulu*).[33] In other words, he was not yet certain that language was enough of a shared commonality for his audience to recognize itself and constitute a shared heritage it could claim as its own collective past. This was something new—not yet tested. But ultimately it was also wildly successful. Sri Ramamurti succeeded in flattering the sensibilities of his audience and giving them a new collective lineage of which they could be proud; over the course of the next few decades there was a flurry of new histories that all served to create and glorify the lineage not of an individual patron, but of a community defined solely by their relationship to the Telugu language. In effect, with the discovery and cultivation of an audience willing to recognize itself as a collective entity with a common linguistic identity, the crisis of patronage had ended.

THE CRISIS OF PATRONAGE AND THE MAKING OF A TELUGU PEOPLE

Guruzada Sri Ramamurti was not the only one to conceive of the idea of publishing a collection of biographies of Telugu poets during the last decades of the nineteenth century. In 1887, midway between the first and second editions of Sri Ramamurti's *Lives of Poets*, Kandukuri Viresalingam published the first of his three volume *Andhra Kavula Charitramu (History of Andhra Poets)*, a text that eclipsed Sri Ramamurti's to such an extent that many later literary historians cite it not only as the very first history of Telugu poets, but also as the first history of Telugu literature.[34] Viresalingam's first (1887) volume was selected for inclusion in the syllabus for the First Examination in Arts at Madras University in 1890. The second and third volumes appeared in 1894 and 1897, respectively.

Prior to these last decades of the nineteenth century, such a catalogue of literary production organized around the Telugu language had never before existed, possibly never even been imagined. Yet these texts anticipated a flood of subsequent works—histories, biographies, anthologies, encyclopaedias, and compendia—that were explicitly organized and written in relation to the Telugu language. What caused each of these two men to independently begin works—at almost exactly the same time—that had likely never before been imagined? Just as Telugu defined the audience imagined by Sri Ramamurti—an audience he needed to test, as he did not yet have a sense of its actual existence in practice—the Telugu language was by the end of the nineteenth century becoming a fundamental category through which many different forms of knowledge were beginning to be reorganized and imagined. These included literary production, the writing of history, collective geographical imagination, and even identities. By the 1890s such a foundational organizational category may well have already appeared to be completely natural, though arguably it did not exist in practice even a quarter of a century earlier. Prior to the last decades of the nineteenth century there is little evidence that the Telugu language was considered an object empowered to act as the foundation or basis for anything. This is not to say that people did not have an appreciation of particular named languages and their usages, for clearly there existed a highly developed sense of aesthetics, exemplified most strongly in the playfulness of poetic composition and the demonstrations of virtuosity implicit in the accomplishment of complicated linguistic feats.[35] Yet many—if not most—of those who were equipped to participate in such verbal play and demonstrations of virtuosity typically possessed mastery of a large repertoire of different registers and languages, not just one, and often performed for an audience equally heteroglossic and accomplished.[36] As such, there was little basis for linking the literati with a single language. Indeed, to be literate meant having command of a wide range of these registers and languages, a meaning quite different from today's understanding of literacy as simply a basic ability to read and write the language that you speak. Nor is it to say that certain territories or dynasties were not associated or identified with the Telugu language. What is clear, however, is that even for kings who associated themselves with a particular language, the language never provided the foundation for the definition of their territory or domain, their subjects, their boundaries, or their history.[37] There were always others who used the language in question who lay outside of the dynastic domain in question. In short, the emergence of Telugu as a foundational category for the reorganization of a wide range of knowledge marks a significant shift in the way in which language was perceived and experienced in southern India.

We can see this transition quite vividly in the genre of narratives identifiable as *charitras*—biographical narratives. Until the late nineteenth century, charitras had almost exclusively been composed to glorify single high status beings represented as ideal models for human action and behaviour—for example, kings, saints, and sectarian leaders. So, in Sanskrit, one of the earliest charitras was the *Buddha Charitra*, and in Telugu, the *Prataparudra Charitramu*, composed by Ekamranatha in the sixteenth century to glorify the lineage of the king Prataparudra. Only toward the end of the nineteenth century do we begin to see a shift in the topics of charitras. In the 1870s the first Telugu novels use the term charitra (alt. charitramu) in their titles, suggesting that for the first time their fictional ordinary protagonists, who are nevertheless models for new forms of ideal behaviour and character, are worthy of biographical narratives. So we see in 1872, Narahari Gopalakrishna Chetty's *Sri Ranga Raja Charitramu*, and in 1878, Kandukuri Viresalingam's *Rajasekhara Charitramu*, both with protagonists with whom readers can easily identify themselves, but who offer a new ideal with which to compare one's own actions.[38] In writing about *Rajasekhara Caritramu*, D. Anjaneyulu marks this break with earlier literary protagonists, writing that 'From the traditional preoccupation with mythology, legend and romance among the writers of the day, we have come down here to social life in all its realism. The prince of noble birth, who used to be the traditional hero of the *Prabandhas* and the *Kavyas* [has] given place here to the average householder, so familiar in life to the contemporary reader.'[39] Indeed, Anjaneyulu's description identifies this type of protagonist as a completely new phenomenon within the literary production of southern India.

In 1887, when Kandukuri Viresalingam published his edition of the lives of Telugu poets, *Andhra Kavula Charitramu*, we see the idea of a biographical narrative of a collective group beginning to take hold. Viresalingam's narrative differs from Guruzada Sri Ramamurti's earlier *Lives of Poets (Kavi Jivitamulu)*—which significantly does not include the term charitra in its title—in its effort to organize its poets into a single chronological narrative organized in relation to the linear progression of time. In an essay published in 1896, the literary scholar and historian Jayanti Ramayya, made a striking comparison between the few representations of the lives of poets which had thus far been produced.[40] He hastily dismissed the aforementioned Kavali Venkata Ramaswami's 1829 *Biographical Sketches of the Deccan Poets* (which included poets who composed in Sanskrit, Telugu, Tamil, and Marathi, but did not yet explicitly organize poets on the basis of language), as well as Guruzada Sreeramamurti's 1878 *Kavi Jivitamulu*, as lacking in historicity. He writes, 'neither of these works is exhaustive and no attempt has been made in either to fix the chronology of the poets. They merely record some of the local traditions and anecdotes regarding the poets with brief notices of their principal works.'[41] In contrast to these two works, Kandukuri Viresalingam's 1887 *Andhra Kavila Caritramu* is the recipient of Ramayya's great praise. Ramayya writes,

The next attempt has been made by Rao Bahadur Kandukuri Veeresalingam Garu whose work I consider to be the best of its kind. His book is arranged chronologically and he has attempted, with [a] great deal of success, to fix the time at which each poet lived. He has also, where possible, given brief sketches of the lives of the poets.[42]

In emphasizing the importance of a linear chronology linking, or 'fixing' as Ramayya puts it, the lives of each poet within a larger narrative of the progression of Telugu language and literature—something he feels Viresalingam does, but Ramaswami and Sri Ramamurti do not— Ramayya betrays the entry of a new value into the discourse of Telugu intellectual circles, a value reflected in the use of the term charitra within Viresalingam's title.

In 1890, we see the first *Desa Charitra* or biographical narrative of the Telugu region.[43] And in 1896, P. Gopala Rao Naidu's *Andhra Bhasha Charitra Sangrahamu*, the first biographical narrative of the Telugu language, creates for the language a birth, reflects the shared fear of its possible death, and suggests that language, too, has a life. Such a biographical narrative paves the way for the explicit personification of the Telugu language, complete with an elaborate kinship network, which occurs in the following decade in the form of Telugu Talli ('Mother Telugu'). And finally, in 1910 we see the first charitra of the Telugu people in Chilukuri Veerabhadra Rao's three volume *Andhrula Charitramu*.[44] And by this time, the decade in which the movement for a separate Telugu linguistic state is launched, it is clear that the audience only hesitantly and experimentally imagined by Guruzada Sri Ramamurti in his 1878 and 1893 publications has recognized itself and come into being—both as patron and as very powerful historical actor. The crisis of literary production—or literary patronage more particularly—has passed, and a new hero of historical narratives has been born to replace the kings and saints of an earlier era—in this case, the Telugu 'people'—an entity both celebrated in its symbolic power, and, ultimately, by the mid-twentieth century, powerful in practice, as well.

Velcheru Narayana Rao and David Shulman have written about the tremendous and very literal creative capacity of language during the sixteenth to eighteenth centuries—not simply its ability to reflect power, but also to constitute it.[45] Poets during this period, they argue, were literally (not simply figuratively) capable of creating kings and other high status beings. In return, poets received patronage from the kings, landlords, and merchants whose status and power they flattered and helped to create. By the beginning of the nineteenth century, royal courts had largely been replaced by the colonial state. Although willing to patronize certain very limited kinds of writing, including grammars and textbooks for their own administrators which offered some practical benefit, the colonial state was in many ways a less reliable patron, with an attitude toward language and those who manipulate it very different from their pre-colonial predecessors. For the heirs to the literary traditions of southern India, new sources of patronage therefore needed to be brought into existence. This meant that if sources of patronage didn't already exist, they needed to be created. The introduction of print technology revolutionized literary production, and it is here that we see first geography, and then language, being invoked as a potential foundation for defining and cultivating new sources of patronage, located no longer in a single patron, but for the first time in *communities* of patrons. If these potential audiences/communities of patrons did not already exist, then especially innovative people like Ramaswami and Sri Ramamurti found ways to bring them into existence.

This shift to appealing to communities of patrons rather than individual patrons did not happen all at once, and arguably not all attempts—including Ramaswami's—were completely successful. Dedications to potential individual patrons continued to appear throughout the nineteenth century, and poetic compositions extolling the virtues of Britain's queen and colonial officials were not uncommon. Yet it is clear that new efforts were being made to appeal to audiences in previously untested ways. In fact, I would argue that Narayana Rao and Shulman's description of the capacity for language to create literally the power of its patrons in the sixteenth to eighteenth centuries is no less relevant in the nineteenth century, though it has seldom been recognized. It is through historical narrative and the appeal to patrons on the fringes of empire that newly imagined communities, including by the end of the century, the 'Telugu' people, have literally been brought into being.

NOTES AND REFERENCES

1. A.D. Campbell, 1832-3, 'Report of A.D. Campbell, 17 August 1823', in House of Commons, *Committee on the Affairs of the East India Company*, 1832-3, Public Proceedings 1.2, vol. 12. Reprinted as A.D. Campbell, 1833-4, 'On the State of Education of the Natives in Southern India', *Journal of the Madras Literary Society*, vol. I, p. 355.

2. Translated by Velcheru Narayana Rao and David Shulman, 1999, *A Poem at the Right Moment: Remembered Verses from Premodern South India*, New Delhi: Oxford University Press, p. 47. See also Velcheru Narayana Rao (ed. and trans.), 2002, *Twentieth Century Telugu Poetry: An Anthology*, New Delhi: Oxford University Press, pp. 293-5, for a discussion of Cellapilla Venkata Sastri.

3. In the case of Telugu, this is true not only of early literary historians like P. Chenchiah and M. Bhujango Rao who, writing in 1925, characterized the immediate pre-colonial period beginning in 1630 as 'The Period of Stagnation', relieved by 'The Modern Period' beginning in 1850 (1988, *History of Telugu Literature*, Delhi: Asian Educational Service), and G.V. Sitapati, writing in 1968,

252 Fringes of Empire

but also of more recent historians. Sitapati (1968, *History of Telugu Literature*, New Delhi: Sahitya Akademi) celebrates the influence of English ideas, literary forms, and styles of writing as central to the literary transitions that occurred during the nineteenth century, stating that 'But for the English education, the country would have been in blissful ignorance of modern culture' (p. 107). More recently, G.K. Subbarayudu and C. Vijayasree have written that 'Telugu literature describes a sharp decline in the seventeenth and the eighteenth centuries with mediocre imitations of *prabandha*s ruling the day. The revival came in the nineteenth century through the efforts of Charles Philip Brown, the Orientalist lexicographer (who was also an East India Company administrator), who brought many Telugu classics into edition and print and gave Telugu its first authoritative dictionary as well' (1996, 'Twentieth-Century Telugu Literature', in Nalini Natarajan (ed.), *Handbook of Twentieth-Century Literatures of India*, Westport, CT: Greenwood Press, p. 306). The many biographies and hagiographies of C.P. Brown perform similar claims of the revival of Telugu literature in the mid-nineteenth century under C.P. Brown's influence.

4. In the context of Telugu see, for example, Kottapalli Veerabhadra Rao, 1960, *Telugu Sahityamupai Inglisu Prabhavamu: The Influence of English on Telugu Literature*, Secunderabad: Ajanta Printers; and J. Mangamma, 1975, *Book Printing in India: With Special Reference to the Contribution of European Scholars to Telugu, 1746–1857*, Nellore: Bangorey Books.

5. Bernard Cohn, 1985, 'The Command of Language and the Language of Command', in Ranajit Guha (ed.), *Subaltern Studies IV*, New Delhi: Oxford University Press, pp. 276–329.

6. Ibid., p. 329.

7. Velcheru Narayana Rao, David Shulman, and Sanjay Subrahmanyam, 1992, *Symbols of Substance: Court and State in Nayaka-Period Tamil Nadu*, New Delhi: Oxford University Press; and Velcheru Narayana Rao, 2003, 'Multiple Literary Cultures in Telugu: Court, Temple, and Public', in Sheldon Pollock (ed.), *Literary Cultures in History: Reconstructions from South Asia*, New Delhi: Oxford University Press, pp. 383–436.

8. Campbell, 'Report', p. 354.

9. Ibid., p. 355.

10. Ibid.

11. Government of India, 1873, *Census of the Town of Madras, 1871*, Madras: The Government Press, p. 48. See also Mangamma, *Book Printing*, pp. 38–42. Mangamma speculates that the East India Company must have had earlier access to a printing press in Madras, despite official accounts which cite the press captured from the French in 1761 as the first press to be established in Madras. She also provides a good discussion of earlier presses in southern India, including the press established at Tranquebar in 1711 by the Society for the Promotion of Christian Knowledge (SPCK), used almost entirely for missionary work.

12. Ibid.

13. B.S. Kesavan, 1985, *History of Printing and Publishing in India: A Story of Cultural Re-awakening*, vol. I, New Delhi, National Book Trust, p. 62. Kesavan notes that the French, who had brought the press to Pondicherry in 1758, had used it primarily for printing notes of credit.

14. Ibid.
15. Correspondence from Graham W. Shaw, India Office Library, cited in Kesavan, *History of Printing*, p. 414.
16. Katharine Smith Diehl, 'Early Madras-Printed Books', http://www.intamm. com/l-science/smith.htm, accessed 29 July 2003.
17. Mangamma suggests that this did not occur until 1831 and that the government obtained a press then solely for the purpose of publishing the Fort St George Gazette, a periodical first issued in 1832. The government press apparently printed 'general military orders, Queen's orders and job-work on a very limited scale' (p. 112). The government press did not begin to print books until Company rule had ended in 1858. Thereafter, government involvement in book-printing rapidly expanded, with a press in every district by 1859 (p. 108). See also Kesavan for a similar discussion.
18. Mangamma, *Book Printing*, p. 101. There is no evidence of anything being printed by this press until 1815–16, as books were initially obtained from the College of Fort William in Calcutta.
19. Thomas Munro, 1930, 'Minute on Native Education', 10 March1826, in G.R. Gleig (ed.), *The Life of Major-General Thomas Munro, Bart. and K.C.B., Late Governor of Madras, with extracts from his correspondence and private papers*, vol. II, London: Colburn and Bentley, p. 410.
20. Gauri Viswanathan, 1989, *Masks of Conquest: Literary Study and British Rule in India*, New York: Columbia University Press, p. 34.
21. Ibid.
22. Ibid., pp. 41–4.
23. Arudra, 1991, 'Zamindari Yugam', *Samagra Andhra Sahityam* (*Complete Telugu Literature*), *Volume 11*, Vijayawada: Praja Shakti Book House, pp. 1–71.
24. Narayana Rao, *Twentieth Century Telugu Poetry*, p. 293.
25. Nicholas B. Dirks, 1993, *The Hollow Crown: Ethnohistory of an Indian Kingdom*, Second Edition, Ann Arbor: University of Michigan.
26. For a good discussion of the film and its portrayal of the dying zamindari community, see the recent work of Dard Neuman, 2004, 'A House of Music: The Hindustani Musician and the Crafting of Traditions', unpublished PhD dissertation, New York: Columbia University.
27. See Velcheru Narayana Rao, 2004, 'Print and Prose: Pundits, *Karanams*, and the East India Company in the Making of Modern Telugu', in Stuart Blackburn and Vasudha Dalmia (eds), *India's Literary History: Essays on the Nineteenth Century*, New Delhi: Permanent Black, pp. 146–66.
28. C.V. Ramaswamy, (Kavali Venkata Ramaswami), 1827, *A New Map of the Ancient Division of the Deckan Illustrative of the History of the Hindu Dynasties with Discriptions* [sic] *of the Principle Places*, Calcutta: Asiatic Lithographic Press. On the introduction of lithography within India, see Andrew S. Cook, 1989, 'The Beginning of Lithographic Map Printing in Calcutta', in Pauline Rohatgi and Pheroza Godrej (eds), *India: A Pageant of Prints*, Bombay: Marg Publications. The first lithographic press was introduced to India in 1822, and experiments in reproducing maps began in March of 1823. Local climatic conditions meant that it took some time for adjustments to the

European process and initially only the government made use of the earliest presses. Ramaswami's map in 1827 was likely one of the earliest applications of lithographic technology issuing from a non-governmental source in India.

29. Cavelly Venkata Ramaswami (Kavali Venkata Ramaswami), 1828, *Descriptive and Historical Sketches of Cities and Places in the Dekkan*; to which is prefixed, *An Introduction, containing a brief description of The Southern Peninsula, and A Succinct History of its Ancient Rulers: The Whole Being to Serve as a Book of Reference to A Map of Ancient Dekkan*, Calcutta: n.p., p. vii.

30. Cavelly Venkata Ramaswamie (Kavali Venkata Ramaswami), 1829, *Biographical Sketches of Dekkan Poets*, Calcutta: n.p.

31. In addition to the following discussion, see also Sumathi Ramaswamy, 1997, *Passions of the Tongue: Language Devotion in Tamil India*, Berkeley: University of California Press, which, significantly, begins in 1891, and Lisa Mitchell, 2009, *Language, Emotion, and Politics in Southern India: The Making of a Mother Tongue*, Bloomington: Indiana University Press.

32. Guruzada Sri Ramamurti, 1893, *Kavi Jivitamulu*, Chennapattanamu: Empress of India Press, p. 1.

33. Ibid.

34. Sitapati, for example, in his *History of Telugu Literature*, writes 'Viresalingam Pantulu is again the first in the writing of History of Telugu Literature but what he actually wrote was *Andhra Kavulu Caritra* (Biographical Lives of Telugu Poets) arranged in chronological order.... About the same time Guruzada Sri Ramamurti wrote his Lives of Telugu Poets under the title of *Kavi Jivitamulu*. But he did not arrange them according to the chronological order. He classified them under headings such as *Purana Kavula, Prabandha Kavulu*, etc. and he selected only the leading poets' (p. 254). Arudra, however, gives a different picture. He writes, 'Sri Ramamurti's *Kavi Jivitamulu* prompted the writing of other works of that sort. In 1887, Kandukuri Viresalingam published the first part of his *Andhra Kavulu Caritramu*. Sri Ramamurti acknowledged that Viresalingam's work contained many poets' names which his own work did not. Therefore, in the literary world Viresalingam's book gradually became established as the authoritative work. Sri Ramamurti's composition gained a name as a bundle of myths and legends. But in reality, Sri Ramamurti also did not fail to discuss historical matters' (*Samagra Andhra Sahityam [Complete Telugu Literature], Volume XI*, p. 76, my translation).

35. See, for example, Velcheru Narayana Rao and David Shulman, 1998, *A Poem at the Right Moment: Remembered Verses from Premodern South India*, Berkeley: University of California Press. Elsewhere, Velcheru Narayana Rao writes that in classical forms of Telugu, 'literary riddles test the intellectual skills of adults, their wit and wisdom, and, above all, their ability to play with language'. He goes on to list the numerous types of linguistic play found in classical literature: 'Used in royal courts of medieval Andhra as demonstrations of cultural excellence, there is a variety of forms of literary riddles: they include *slesa padyamulu* (punning verses), *citra kavitvamu* (picturesque verses), *garbha kavitvamu* (verses including other verses within them), *camatkara catuvulu* (riddling verses), and *samasyalu* (tricky statements),' (Velcheru Narayana Rao,

1996, 'Texture and Authority: Telugu Riddles and Enigmas', in Galit Hasan-Rokem and David Shulman (eds), *Untying the Knot: On Riddles and Other Enigmatic Modes*, New York: Oxford University Press, p. 196).

36. Narayana Rao, Shulman and Subrahmanyam, *Symbols of Substance*, p. 334; Narayana Rao and Shulman, *A Poem*, pp. 186–7. Phillip Wagoner's translation and ethnohistorical analysis of the Telugu *Rayavacakamu*, a text composed in the late sixteenth or early seventeenth century also presents a picture of the multilingual nature of courts of this period. In particular, he includes a passage taken from an earlier mid-sixteenth century literary work in which a list of instructions is provided for the king. Many of these instructions relate to the literary ability expected of a king, including that he 'be skilled in the eight languages, which are Sanskrit, Prakrit, Shauraseni, Magadhi, Paishachi, Chulika, Apabhramsa, and Tenugu [*Telugu*]' 1993, *Tidings of the King: A Translation and Ethnohistorical Analysis of the Rayavacakamu*, Honolulu: University of Hawaii Press, p. 93. One must be careful not to imagine the labels of the speech of different characters as equivalent to 'languages' as we think of them today. In fact, it might be more accurate to refer to them as registers, or 'forms of speech'. These forms of speech were also widely used in dramas of the period, with a different one being used for each type of character. An audience would have been expected to understand all of these forms of speech, and as much information would have been conveyed to the audience through the form of speech each character used, as would have been communicated through the actual content of speeches.

37. For example, the Kakatiya dynasty which emerged in the late twelfth century has long been associated with the Telugu language; however, there was never a time when all of the regions where Telugu was spoken were imagined to be included within the Kakatiya dynasty. In other words, although the Kakatiya kingdom may have been thought of as a Telugu kingdom at the time of its existence (and was certainly thought of in that way later on), it was not the only territory thought of as Telugu, and the Telugu language was never the basis upon which the Kakatiya dynasty was organized, delineated, and defined. Likewise, many medieval Sanskrit texts refer to an Andhra region where Telugu was spoken, but they also refer to a Kalinga region, where Telugu was also spoken. Kalinga and Andhra clearly referred to two separate and distinct regions, and both were identified with Telugu. The point here is that although Telugu was used in both of these regions, at no point during the medieval period did it ever form the foundation upon which either region was defined or constituted. Even when the fourteenth century Vidyanatha called the last Kakatiya king Prataparudra 'the lord of the Andhra realm' (Somasekhara Sarma, 1945, p. 2, cited in Cynthia Talbot, 2001, *Precolonial India in Practice: Society, Region, and Identity in Medieval Andhra*, New Delhi: Oxford University Press *Precolonial India*, p. 36), he clearly did not intend to suggest that he was also the lord of the neighbouring Telugu-speaking Kalinga region, then ruled by the Eastern Ganga dynasty. Such evidence causes us to reconsider the approach taken by Cynthia Talbot, *Precolonial India*, which argues that 'Telugu' and 'Andhra' were synonymous for everyone from the late twelfth century onwards (p. 36), that 'the language, the physical territory, and the culture are all conflated into one' (p. 37), and that inscriptions show a

clear 'consciousness of unity based on the use of Telugu' (p. 36). Indeed, what makes it possible to sustain the arguments that 'languages [were constituted] as significant boundaries between communities' (p. 211) in medieval India, that 'language [was] the central component of group identity' (p. 8), and that 'Andhra and Telugu were interchangeable' (p. 211), is the exclusion of Telugu inscriptions in the Kalinga region (now part of contemporary Andhra Pradesh) from consideration (p. 110), and the inclusion in others maps and discussion of only those Telugu inscriptions that fall within the borders of contemporary Andhra Pradesh. Her maps plotting the geographical distributions of Telugu inscriptions during various pre-colonial time periods, for example, leave out or mention only peripherally all Telugu inscriptions found outside contemporary Andhra Pradesh, despite the fact that many have been found.

38. Narahari Gopalakrishna Chetty, 1872, *Sri Ranga Raja Charitramu (The Story of Ranga Raja)*. Kandukuri Viresalingam, 1991 (1880, serialized 1878), *Rajasekhara Charitramu (The Story of Rajasekhara)*, Hyderabad: Visaalaandhra Publishing House.

39. D. Anjaneyulu, 1976, *Kandukuri Viresalingam*, New Delhi: Publications Division, Ministry of Information and Broadcasting, Government of India, p. 89.

40. Jayanti Ramayya, 1896, *An Essay on Telugu Language and Literature*, Vizagapatam: S.S.M. Press.

41. Ibid., p. 18.

42. Ibid., p. 19.

43. The earliest known Telugu *Desa Charitramu* (History of the Country) is D. Venkataranga Setti's, published in 1890, followed by another published in 1916 by Gidugu Venkata Sitapati. In the preface to his 1893 edition of *Kavi Jivitamulu*, Guruzada Sri Ramamurti also claims to have been working on a *Desa Charitramu (History of the [Telugu?] Country)*, his work on this preventing him from completing the second edition of his *Lives of Poets* earlier than 1893, but there is no evidence that he ever published such a text. Sri Ramamurti actually offers this as an explanation for why Kandukuri Viresalingam was able to publish the first volume of his *Andhra Kavula Charitramu* in 1887, six years prior to the completion of his own full edition (Sri Ramamurti, 1893, 'Preface', *Kavi Jivitamulu*).

44. Chilukuri Veerabhadra Rao, 1910, *Andhrula Charitramu, Prathama Bhagamu: Purva Yugamu (History of the Andhras, Volume One: Ancient Period)* Cennapuri (Madras): Ananda Mudrayantrashalaya; 1912, *Andhrula Charitramu, Dvitiya Bhagamu: Madhya Yugamu (History of the Andhras, Volume Two: Medieval Period)*, Cennapuri (Madras): Jyotishmati Mudrayantrashalaya.

45. Velcheru Narayana Rao and David Shulman, 2002, 'Introduction', in Velcheru Narayana Rao and David Shulman (eds), *Classical Telugu Poetry: An Anthology*, New Delhi: Oxford University Press, pp. 1–74, especially pp. 62–6, and their 'After-Essay', in *A Poem at the Right Moment*, especially pp. 148–59.

Contributors

SAMEETAH AGHA is Associate Professor of History at Pratt Institute in Brooklyn.

CLARE ANDERSON is Associate Professor in the Department of Sociology, University of Warwick.

MARINA CARTER is an Honorary Fellow at the Centre for South Asian Studies at University of Edinburgh.

NICHOLAS B. DIRKS is Vice President for Arts and Sciences and Franz Boas Professor of Anthropology and Professor of History at Columbia University.

ELIZABETH KOLSKY is Assistant Professor of History at Villanova University.

ALEX MCKAY is a former research fellow at the School of Oriental and African Studies and The Wellcome Trust Centre for the History of Medicine at University College London.

JAMES H. MILLS is an Economic and Social Research Council Research Fellow and Senior Lecturer in the Department of History at Strathclyde University in Glasgow.

LISA MITCHELL is Assistant Professor in the Department of South Asia Studies at the University of Pennsylvania.

DOUGLAS M. PEERS is Dean of the Graduate Studies at York University in Canada.

MRIDU RAI is Associate Professor of History at Yale University.

SATADRU SEN teaches South Asian history at Queens College in the City University of New York.

PHILIP J. STERN is Assistant Professor of History at Duke University.